MEMOIRES DE LA SOCIETE BELGE D'ETUDES CELTIQUES

11

GODS OF THE WEST
A STUDY IN LATIN AND CELTIC RELIGION
Part I
INDIGES

Fabio P. BARBIERI

Bruxelles

1999

COMITE DIRECTEUR

Frédéric BLAIVE (Faculté Ouverte des Religions et des Humanismes Laïques, Charleroi)

Anne CAHEN-DELHAYE (Musées Royaux d'Art et d'Histoire, Bruxelles)

Juliette DOR (Université de Liège)

Pierre CORNIL (Faculté Ouverte des Religions et des Humanismes Laïques, Charleroi)

Jean BOURGEOIS (Rijksuniversiteit Gent)

Véronique HURT (Musée des Celtes, Libramont)

Jean LOICQ (Université de Liège)

Jacques-Henri MICHEL (Université Libre de Bruxelles/ Vrije Universiteit Brussel)

Claude MISERCQUE-PIRET (Haute Ecole de Bruxelles)

Nathalie STALMANS de CANNIERE (Fonds National de la Recherche Scientifique, Bruxelles)

Claude STERCKX (Université Libre de Bruxelles) directeur

Marc VANDEUR (Université Libre de Bruxelles) secrétaire de rédaction)

Sandra VERHULST (Academia Belgica, Rome)

Christophe VIELLE (Université Catholique de Louvain)

D   1999-5447-6   I.S.B.N.   2-87285-070-8.

MEMOIRES DE LA SOCIETE BELGE D'ETUDES CELTIQUES

1 1

GODS OF THE WEST
A STUDY IN LATIN AND CELTIC RELIGION
Part I
INDIGES

Fabio P. BARBIERI

Who is this that cometh out of the wilderness
like pillars of smoke, perfumed with myrrh and
frankincense, with all the powders of the mer-
chant ? Behold his bed, which is Solomon's :
threescore valiant men are about it, of the
valiant of Israel. They all hold swords, being
expert in war ; every man hath his sword upon
his thigh because of fear in the night. King
Solomon made himself a chariot out of the wood
of Lebanon... Who is this that looked forth as the
morning, fair as the Sun, clear as the Moon, and
terrible as an army with banners ?

from *Solomon's Song,* slightly adapted

The truth, I have always thought, is curious and
beautiful

Agatha Christie, *Appointment with Death*

For want of me the world's course will not fail ;
When all its work is done, the lie shall rot.
The truth is mighty, and it shall prevail
Whether you want it to prevail or not !

This study is dedicated to Richard F. Gombrich and to D.W.*

Bruxelles

CONTENTS

4

PREFACE

From the moment it was published in defiance of its dead author's wishes, the *Æneid* became the standard for Latin literature. Latin was taught out of it, and Dark Age authors such as Gildas and Gregory of Tours, who knew no other classical Latin author, quoted freely from it. Despite a brief and rather silly period of nineteenth-century disparagement, it has remai-ned so ever since ; the standard for all intellectual-minded writers, the greatest work of art to emerge from the ancient world, and one of the greatest poems of the world. Above all, Virgil's philosophical talents have been fruitful down the ages : every poet who successfully attempted large-scale religious epics - Dante, Tasso, Milton - found his chief inspiration in him, and indeed it is doubtful whether, had he not existed, their work would have been conceivable.

It is in this light that we must regard Virgil's own work. Its nature was intellectual and religious much more than patriotic. He did not, as is sometimes said, exalt the valour of Italian heroes. In fact, the hosts of Italy fare quite badly in the poem, being overcome in no more than three days of bitter warfare. Virgil wasn't Italian - he came from the border between the non-Italian Gaulish and Venetic peoples - and, properly told, his account of Æneas' invasion would sound like an Italian Army joke from World War Two.

The task he set himself, at any rate, has less to do with Italy as such than with the broad culture of the Hellenistic world in which he was born. He took on himself to build the past and future of Rome into the epic Homeric cycle. This was a task of enormous significance. Homeric epic was the heart of all Greek culture and religion. Beyond their literary merits, those often singularly brutal poems were an extended account of the origin of the Iron Age, the current age of the world, began with the War of Troy. The Iron Age means nothing else than the world as it is now ; and the Homeric poems tell of its beginning, its foundation. What Virgil was undertaking was no less than to rewrite Greek beliefs in the light of the new situation brought about by the rise of the Roman Empire, and most recently of its trans-formation into a monarchy under Virgil's patron, Octavian Augustus.

From Virgil's standpoint, the Homeric epics were flawed on two counts : they didn't mention Rome, and they contained no hope that the Iron Age, the last and worst, will ever be reversed. To him, the two things went together. Though the matter is controversial, I feel certain that he saw in Octavian Augustus Plato's philosopher King, in his most messianic light, come to Earth to revenge the degeneration of man and the world and steer them back to the Golden Age. Therefore, Rome's worldwide rule was to him a fact beyond politics, a religious fact. He must have regarded it as inconceivable that the most central part of Hellenic heritage should have nothing to say about it.

Had there been no hint of a Homeric origin for Rome, both the Homeric cycle and Rome would have been, intellectually speaking, in trouble. The new empire, which looked set fair to unify all Greek-speaking lands, was something entirely new and unexpected, that chal-

6

lenged every Homeric and Classical category. The effect might have been as much of a cultural revolution as the Germanic invasions were later : a matter of Western barbarians simply swarming over and cancelling the older Greek civilization, replacing it with something largely different.

However, Rome had always claimed a Greek identity, and Latin epics on her origins not only existed but claimed to be a forgotten part of the Homeric corpus. Two poets, Nævius and Ennius, had given them written form two hundred years earlier, at the dawn of written Latin ; they were endowed with the chrism of antiquity. This was important to someone like Virgil who stood, generally speaking, in the tradition of Plato. He was too reverent and serious-minded to make up epic myths out of whole cloth ; we will find that he wrote one vast digression (Euryalus and Nysus) just to account for a non-Hellenic oddity in the Latin legend. To Platonic tradition, antiquity was almost a guarantee of superiority, because "the men of ancient times... were better than we are", since "they lived more near to the Gods"[1]. Plato clung to this view consistently, following the traditional Hellenic idea that the Gods had progressively withdrawn from the world in past ages, until (as Hesiod says) only Justice and Shame are left to represent them among men, and these too are constantly on the verge of departing.

The past, then, is the repository of wisdom, because what it knew it knew from the Gods, and from those who had had the unconceivable privilege of walking with them. From this follows a conclusion that must seem, to our modern ideas, perverse, but that we must see as inevitable (given the premises) if we want to make any sense of Classical literature : that is, that a story with a merely human author was automatically a fiction, a frankly base kind of literary work that Plato and his successors consistently condemned ; but a story with no known origin was a story with its roots in divine truth.

The imperial periphery to which Virgil belonged viewed Greco-Roman culture as a whole, and felt the difference between Latium and Hellas less keenly than true-born Greeks and Latins would. He had no feelings for Latium as a country : the poem has little worthwhile description, and less still that is identifiable. When the Trojans meet the unknown river Tiber[2], the poet is less exercised by the Tiber as a place than by the abstract idea of reaching a new, unknown land. As far as detail goes, the exiles might as well be sailing up the Amazon ; there are, in fact, some glaring impossibilities. And, as I said, he is not too impressed with the Latin character either. Except for king Latinus alone, the Italics are on the wrong side, and the smaller army of Æneas *fries* them in three days. Significantly, Æneas' son Iulus more or less executes one Remulus Numanus on the battlefield for braggadocio and impiety, under the eye and with the loud approval of Apollo, god of truth and religious ritual[3]. Numanus affected to despise the Trojans' religious fervour as effeminate, preferring to it the life of a cattle-robbing bandit ; his reward for which was a well-shot arrow. Remu-

---

1   *Philebus* 16c.
2   Virgil, *Æneid* VII 25-36, VIII 86-101.
3   Virgil, *Æneid* IX 590-644.

lus Numanus stands for Italy. Virgil could not have made his name more national : it hints at Rome's first two kings, Romulus (whose brother Remus was) and Numa Pompilius. This, Virgil seems to say, is the Latin spirit without the leaven of Greek (Trojan) wisdom : vulgar, thieving, brutal, blasphemous, big-mouthed and self-satisfied. And not terribly impressive in battle either.

But the marriage of Latium and Hellas, now ! That is a different matter. The marriage of Æneas, the rightful heir of Troy, and Lavinia, sole heir of king Latinus, is the essential condition through which the stream of historical destiny, defined by God's *fata* or words of doom, must pass ; it will lead to Augustus' reign, the Golden Age and universal peace.

Virgil's success can be measured by the fact that Greek Quintus of Smyrna, reworking the end of the Homeric cycle four centuries later, took Æneas' journey to Latium as established fact. In Virgil's time, Dionysios of Halikarnassos had to defend it, in a tone that shows that his fellow educated Greeks had not the least belief in it.

Having established, then, how Virgil saw epic poetry, we must ask how he treated his material. The question would be easier to answer if we had his sources Nævius and Ennius ; but we do not. Immediately recongnized as a classic, his poem obliterated theirs. Nobody wanted to read crude, primitive Nævius and stumbling Ennius when they had classical Virgil to hand, just as nobody today is very interested in reading the chronicles of Holinshed when they have Shakespeare. Save for a few fragments quoted by commentators or grammarians, we have nothing left of them. Our main sources for these epic myths are Virgil's work and the extensive account by his contemporary, the Greek rhetorician Dionysios of Halikarnassos, included in his huge if rather pedestrian *Roman Antiquities*.

There is another source, the Roman history of Cato the Elder, itself lost but with enough surviving fragments to give an almost continuous narration ; it is roughly contemporaneous with Ennius and Nævius, and therefore seems, on the surface, very promising. You may then imagine my frustration when a collected edition of these fragments quickly showed me that Cato is, to say the least, a most unreliable witness ! He had the nerve to invent a quite artificial town *Laurolavinium*, joining together two different place-names, despite the fact that not only did Lavinium exist in Cato's own days and was known to be different from Laurentum, but also that the two places have absolutely opposite roles in the story. He is also the only authority to deny that Æneas' son, Ascanius/Iulus, was the ancestor of a line of priests ; he claims Iulus had no children. And these are by no means the only freaks in his narrative. In other words, Cato seems willing to treat the story in a cavalier, self-willed manner, making changes - and none too convincing changes at that - where and how he pleased.

Dionysios of Halikarnassos agrees with all the basic elements of Virgil's plot from Acesta onwards ; but he includes several interesting differences in detail. He rejects the Dido episode ; his Turnus goes to war *against* Latinus, *after* Æneas married Lavinia ; his Mezentius is the enemy not of Æneas but of his son Ascanius ; etc. These differences will receive their due share of attention, and help us ; but they do little to help assess Virgil's attitude to his sources. Without once giving a divergent account or name, Dionysios follows a clear narrative tradition of his own, generally taken to come from the learned Roman writer Varro. Also, unlike Virgil, he had time to finish his work, putting a gloss on it, ironing contradictions out ; for instance, he gives no mention at all to Cato's bizarre version, though he was familiar with the old brute's writings and quoted them respectfully in other places.

Only from Virgil himself can we draw any conclusions as to how Virgil treated his sources. He probably liked at least Ennius, if not perhaps Nævius, as a poet ; the commentator Servius averred that the extraordinarily beautiful image of VII 698-705, where the troops of king Messapus are likened to singing swans flying dazzling white against a backdrop of floating clouds - even by Virgil's standards, a splendid moment - was a compliment to the older author, who was proud of his Messapic (Apulian) origin.

But his view of Ennius and Nævius as historical sources is quite another matter. Virgil prayed to the Muses, not for poetic power, but to be able to relate facts that his predecessors had almost lost altogether :

> *Et meministis enim, diuae, et memorare potestis ;*
>
> *At nos uix tenuis famae perlabitur aura.*
>
> For you, Goddesses, you may both remember and tell ;
>
> But we hardly are left with the thin air of hearsay.

He appeals to divine memory because he feels that human memory has failed him.

This is not Greek imitation. Though the special appeal to the Muses is standard epic convention, no other epic poet declares such distrust of his sources as far as I'm aware. This is Virgil's reaction to his material : Nævius, Ennius, annalistic traditions such as Varro and Dionysios reported, all this really large mass of material amounts to in his view *tenuis famae aura*, the thin air of hearsay.

His reason to distrust the shape in which these ancient tales had reached him can have little to do with historical improbability in the modern sense. No age is utterly credulous ; but areas of skepticism vary according to the accepted ideologies of the day. Livy, the historian Titus Livius, was as skeptical about miracle stories as any modern, but believed in omens without question. We tend to overestimate those areas in which the ancients sound and feel much like us, because we have inherited some of their mannerisms ; the rationalistic element in Greek thought, therefore, tends to be overrated. Virgil believed in the primacy of immemorial tradition, and would have wanted to recover the essentials of those ancient events not only for the sake of knowledge but above all because Homeric epic had a special religious significance. It established the world as he knew it ; and he went back to Ennius and Nævius with a solemn and intensely-felt burden of ideas that included Greek traditions, Platonic philosophy, the world-changing events of Virgil's own lifetime, and his fervent partisanship of Augustus.

Seen from this Hellenistic and messianic prospect, Nævius and Ennius must surely have fallen short ; and fallen short, at that, of a world of ideas to which they themselves subscribed. Ennius was a Hellenist, and even Nævius (who wrote in the older Latin epic metre, otherwise almost unknown to us) accepted without hesitation the Greek interpretation of the legend ; it never occurred to any of them that Latin religion might not be a sub-case of Greek paganism, but a separate thing with its own ideology and value system. The ancient world did not think like that ; even the Egyptian gods, different as they were from anything recognizable among the Greeks, were nevertheless the object of robust and constant efforts to tie them up with them. That all the religions of the world could be understood in terms of each other, and that each god or object of cult could be either paralleled with a Greek god or hero or else fitted into the Greek pantheon, was an unchallenged article of faith. Virgil was therefore bound to find much amiss with Latin - purely Latin - epic tradition ; believing as he did that it came out of a Greek stem, any sign of an alien ideology was bound to seem to him not a local pecularity but a barbarous error.

No great artist has ever had so hard a time with his masterpiece as Virgil had with the *Æneid*. Ancient report makes him a fast worker, yet he worked on the poem for ten years and died leaving it unfinished. According to the best ancient biographies, long before his final illness he tried to make his friends Varius and Tucca promise to burn his unfinished manuscripts if anything happened to him. This was not the depressed babble of a dying man, but a decision reached well ahead, contemplating the possibility - even likelihood - that he might fail in his goals. He would have the poem perfect or not at all. His friends refused, and, seeing he could not shake them, his will ordered that nothing more of it should be released other than the extracts already published. It took a decree from Augustus to overturn this.

This forms a coherent picture. Virgil believed as a matter not of despair but of calm and reasoned decision that to publish a less than perfect account of the origins of Rome would be worse than useless. I doubt that artistic conscience alone can account for it. Virgil must have known that he was writing the greatest Latin verse ever made, in the service of a narrative sweep that had little comparison outside of "Homer" and Æschilus at their greatest. I believe his long, painful, and finally unresolved labour is due to the fact that, on many levels, he could not make his story fit. It claimed to belong to the Homeric canon ; it had to fit a Greek frame of reference ; it was the accepted, indeed honoured, account of the origin of a nation, Rome, which not only believed itself to be of Greek origin, but whose empire had become one with the Greek world. And yet those darn impossibilities, those Latin accretions that made so little Greek sense, kept cropping up. They could not help but. They were not details, they were the whole : an independent epic tradition that owed nothing to Homer.

When Nævius wrote his epic poem - a structure, we need not doubt, of respectable proportions -, he used, not an adopted Homeric metre, but a native Latin one ; and he wrote thousands of verses in it. That means that he had at his disposal a narrative verse-form which he felt could deal adequately with a vast and very important narrative subject. Otherwise he would, like all later Latin poets, have adapted Homeric verse. No doubt that he was wrong ; what we have left of his verses does little to convince us that this so-called

"Saturnian" metre was a match for it. But if he used such a verse rather that the prestigious Greek equivalent, that means that such a verse was there to be used. There was a native Latin epic poetic form. Nævius was not the first of a new tradition of epic poetry received, basically, from Greece, but the last of a lost line of *native* poets telling large-scale stories in a *native* epic form : the first, probably, to write his verse down. Now, we simply can't suppose that a Latin epic form existed and a Latin epic tradition did not. There were Latin epics before Hellenization.

We must go back to my original statement : the work Virgil had undertaken was not merely that of an artist. It was a religious work. The best modern term for it would be "prophet" : he tried to use his extraordinary poetic skills to *reconstruct the truth* that lay at the bottom of all the Homeric corpus, both Greek and Latin, to harmonize it all and bring it into the service of the new universal empire of man, from which he hoped for peace for the whole human race. When he prayed to the Muses, it was not just a convention : he really was praying for divine help in reconstructing "what really happened", using poetic insight, Greek religious categories, and a methodical mind. If he had lived his threescore and ten instead of dying at the wretchedly early age of fifty-one, he might have achieved his purpose ; but it is clear that, from a religious point of view, it did not matter how fine the unfinished work might be, if it did not bring into being that truth in which Virgil so deeply believed. It would indeed have been worse than useless. A prophet cannot promote heresy, even the most melodious heresy conceivable : melody isn't the point, truth is.

I am travelling in the opposite direction. Taking the Mantuan's work as a point of departure, I try to reconstruct the content and meaning of those earlier - and from Virgil's point of view fatally flawed - accounts of the origins of Rome. We shall reach areas which the great poet never suspected could ever help explain the story he was telling ; in particular, the fragmented tradition of the Celtic lands, so far from the spirit of Rome, yet so close in so many surprising ways. And yet, as we go on, we shall meet, again and again, with his immense questing mind and with his unforgettable verse ; and it will not be the least of the results of this study, if we gain even a little more understanding of this great genius.

This book is the record of a long, exciting adventure, started years ago in Victoria tube station ; when, reading a freshly-purchased translation of the *Æneid*, I was struck by the similarity between the visual images used by Virgil to describe the burning ships of Æneas in Sicily and the billows of smoke from the burning ships of the gods, described in an Irish legend.

I started work as soon as my ideas began to come together, and wrote as my research went on. As a result, though the first draft was much the easiest, a good deal of rewriting was needed to turn the record of many stumbling intuitions, blind alleys and sudden, stunning rays of light, into a coherent and comprehensible argument. I believed that what I have been uncovering is nothing less that the record of a prehistoric yet profound system of theology and philosophy, as it underlay the narratives of the earliest Latin sages and those of related peoples. I am no academic, and though I have tried to make my work honest and respectable by academic standards (as with proper indications of all sources, clear and copious footnotes, etc.), I would not insult any readers, academic or not, by pretending to be one. If specialists find all the explanation grating, I beg their pardon. The argument is aimed mainly at them, because I am confident that this work opens new perspectives in Latin pre-history and related areas ; and I hope it meets with their approval. For the general reader, I hope you enjoy it. The only thing it assumes is a knowledge of the *Æneid* ; for which I don't apologize. If this book drives you to read the great poem, you'll be the better for it. You are far more likely to enjoy that than this ; if you enjoy my work, it's because of the subject ; if you don't, it's because of my writing. Virgil is good enough for anyone.

CHAPTER I : THE IDENTITY OF THE HERO

I.1 The Trojan *Männerbund*

The *Æneid* - *P. Virgili Maronis Aeneidos libri XII* - is the the story of the long search of Æneas, royal heir of the foundered city of Troy, for a new land in which to establish the new nation that the gods promised him, of his finding of Italy, and of the wars he fought there before he could establish his kingdom. A devoted and conscious instrument of the gods' will, and especially of the will of Jupiter, Æneas, in the course of the poem, grows increasingly aware that what he is to establish is not only a single town, but something that has relevance for the whole future of mankind ; he is in fact the first forefather of the universal empire of Rome. God Himself, Jupiter, promises Æneas' mother,the goddess Venus,

His ego nec metas rerum, nec tempora pono ;

Imperium sine limite dedi...

To them I place no end in space, in time ;

To them I gave empire without end...[1]

As in the war of Troy is involved the whole future of Greece, so in the journey and war of Æneas is implicit all the great history of Rome, to which Virgil never saw an end.

The commonplace scholarly view is that the Latins borrowed Æneas from the vast complex of Homeric legend and built their own epic mythology around him in stages. I read studies in which the characters of Æneas in the *Æneid* and the Aineias of Greek[2] epic are treated as exactly alike, especially in their *pietas* or religious excellence. But in terms of who they are and what they do in the two stories, that cannot be right ; the Æneas of Latin legend - even of our great Hellenist Virgil, soaked as he was with Hellenic poetry - is by no means the parallel of the Hellenic figure. He shows fundamental differences, and shows them exactly in those features which are the core of the Trojan hero : his position in the story and his role as the preserver of the dynasty.

Aineias is the preserver of the dynasty, and because of that, also the preserver of the city. Troy's future in the *Iliad* cannot be separated from the fact that *his descendants* are going to rule over it, by the word of Zeus himself, interpreted by his brother Poseidon[3]. It's because he has a family, because he has children and a descent, that he will insure the fallen city's rebirth. His absolutely standard image in Greek art is that of the hero who carries away the old father on his shoulders, while the wife walks along at his side with his young heir's hand in hers : clearly a dynamic vision of the family, in all its generations, being preserved, especially if we remember the ever-young grandmother, the goddess who looks

---

[1]   Virgil, *Aen.* I 278-279.
[2]   I shall be spelling them differently for convenience.
[3]   Homer, *Il.* XX 307-308.

14

after them like Athena after Odysseus. Around this living dynasty a new Troy can be formed, with all classes of citizens, and with the sacred objects necessary to the existence of a Greek free state.

On the way to Italy, the Trojan expedition does not merely lose members ; it changes character. The dynasty (its ideological, emotional, political, and poetical core) all but fades from sight. Creusa is never heard of again. Anchises' fate is uncertain ; only vague fragments of Cato and Nævius seem to indicate that he reached Italy. Most extraordinarily, Aineias' son, Euryleon, clearly the heir, becomes Ascanius[4] Iulus, the king either without progeny[5] or whose progeny become priests[6], who did not wear the genuine royal title of Silvius[7].

As with the dynasty, so with the *polis*. Virgil relates that all the women and old men were left behind, and that it was three hundred young men who came to Latium[8]. Dionysios of Halikarnassos says neither how many people, nor what kind, stayed in Acesta, nor how many, and of what kind, reached Latium[9]. However he confirms Virgil's outline and two important details : that Æneas *left behind all those who were worn out with hardship or weary of the sea*, and that the *women set the ships on fire*. These are essential parts of the Virgilian rationale for leaving women and old men behind ; so we see that Dionysios does all but confirm that *all* the women and old men were left behind.

Therefore the company that reaches Latium has nothing in common with the party that left the ruins of Troy. That was a city on the move, a picture clear and dear to Greek minds from archaic times : men, women and children on ships, venturing on the open sea in search of a shore on which to build a permanent town, with a god's oracles leading them on. Æneas, however, takes to Latium only men in the vigour of age, with no women or old men at all. They build no city of their own, only a fortress, until after they have married Latin women and settled, not apart from their host nation like a Greek colony, but in the middle of

4   There is a problem about the traditional name of Ascanius for Æneas' son, which I shall not attempt to solve. In Homeric tradition, Æneas' son seems to have been named Euryleon, and Askanios is an independent and insignificant character, a minor Phrygian warlord, mentioned in *Il.* II 862 and XIII 792 (the latter in no complimentary guise : his only battle appearance shows him making like a rabbit !). How this extremely secondary character came to be affiliated to the heir of Troy I do not pretend to guess, although I take it that it was a local Asian process (Askanie and the Askanian lake are places in Asia Minor) rather than anything in Latium.

5   Servius, *In Aen.* I 267, 570 ; Hyginus, 260. However, these passages are in fact quoted from the highly unreliable Cato. Everybody else agrees that Ascanius had priestly descendants, and that the Iulian family was descended from them. Did Cato, whose feud with the Cornelii Scipiones is well known, also have it in for another ambitious senatorial clan, the Iulii ? Is this why he wished to deny their claim to be descended from the great ancestor ? There seems to be no other likely reason for his denial that Iulus had any descendants. This is important in assessing both the political atmosphere in his period and the antiquity and consistency of the Æneas-legend : if Cato could hit at his enemies by denying them places in it, that means it was important enough to use in politics, the stormy, forum-centred politics of the Republic. Every free Roman citizen must have understood the significance of his attack.

6   Dionysios of Halikarnassos, *Roman Antiquities* I 70 4.

7   Livy, I 3 7 : *Mansit Siluiis postea omnibus cognomen qui Albae regnauerunt.* Likewise Dionysios of Halikarnassos, I 70 3.

8   Virgil, *Æneid* V 715-717.

9   Dionysios of Halikarnassos, I 52 4, 55 3.

it, as part of Latinus' kingdom, most unlike the pattern of Greek colonization through the ages.

From the moment, therefore, when women, old men and anybody else who wished to stay, are left in Acesta, the expedition cannot really be called a city on the move ; it is nothing else than a *Männerbund*, a league of young men. It is to a band of womanless young men that the Latins are to give, not a wife[10], but wives. It is to a band of warriors that Latinus sends a warrior beast each, a horse, the gift that a priest of Jupiter could not ride[11]. It is to a troop of three hundred young men that he sends three hundred saddled and caparisoned horses, one each, as a gift[12].

What does this tell us ? It tells us clearly enough that the story we are dealing with has nothing Greek about it, neither protagonists, nor setting, nor plot. We should regard the hero who lands in Latium as a separate personage, ad not trouble too much with his identification with Aineias of Troy[13].

The identification did not arise by chance, however. Two famous wanderers of Hellenic legend had on occasion been associated with Latium as tribal ancestors in early documents : Odysseus[14] and Herakles. We may be sure that the Latins, whose contact with Greece went back a very long time indeed, had sifted through the ranks of Greek legend for centuries. If they settled on the comparatively secondary figure of the Homeric heir of Troy - a respected character indeed, but not an outstanding one - rather than on the legion of Hellenic travellers - Kadmos and Jason, Odysseus and Bellerophon, Herakles, Menelaos, even Theseus -, that is certainly because this personage, above all others, had characteristics that brought the Latin figure clearly to mind. Now, as compared with all those I listed, the special qualities of

---

[10]   That is, not just Lavinia alone. There is sufficient evidence to show that all the Trojans did in fact seek wives : Virgil, *Æneid* IX 600, X 79, XII 821 ; Dionysios of Halikarnassos, I 60 2, cf. also Virgil, *Æneid* X 280-281 where Turnus bids his men remember their homes *and wives*. G. DUMEZIL, *Mythe et épopée*, Paris, 1968-1973, I p.407 thinks that XII 835-836 refers to the mass wedding of Trojans and Latins, but that is not necessarily so. Jupiter promises Junon that the Trojan ethnic group will vanish into the Latin ; he does not say when or how this will happen.

[11]   The *flamen Dialis*, the Roman priest of Jupiter, was forbidden to ride horses (Pliny the Younger, *Historia naturalis* XXVIII 146 ; Plutarch, *Roman Questions* 40) ; so was the Dictator (Plutarch, *Life of Fabricius* IV), a magistrate who closely approximated God on Earth. He had a single colleague of inferior rank, whose function was to be Master of the Cavalry (*magister equitum*) : evidently the only office he could not fulfil himself.

[12]   Virgil, *Æneid* VII 274-275 : *Haec effatus, equos numero pater eligit omni ;*
             Stabant tercentum nitidi in praesepibus altis...
Solinus, II 14 gives the Trojans as "no more than six hundred", probably based on the fact that the "Laviniates" proper - the priests who performed the holy city's rituals - were six hundred in number (Dionysios of Halikarnassos, I 67 3). His authority is the commentator Cassius Hemina, who seems to have been a clever harmonizer : another story Solinus got from him was that Æneas received his Palladium from Diomedes. This has occurred to none of Dionysios' sources (I 68-69). The Palladium that Æneas took to Lavinium gave them headaches : Domitius Callistratus, a Roman-age historian, was forced to invent a set of two Palladia - only one of which was tolen by Odysseus - and Arctinus, the epic poet, went as far as to say that Odysseus had stolen a wooden copy ! Hemina's solution would have helped them greatly.

[13]   G. DUMEZIL, *cit.*, I p.337-422 (*Un dessein de Virgile*) investigated the Latin epic.

[14]   The virtually prehistoric wisdom-poet known as Hesiod, *Theogony* 1012-1016 mentions Circe and Odysseus as parents of Latinus and of one "Agrios", a name that many scholars understand as a Greek translation of *Siluius*, the dynastic name of the legendary Alban kings. This important document raises more questions than it answers, and I shall not deal with it here. Dionysios of Halikarnassos, I 73 5 gives other Greek sources that give Odysseus as tribal ancestor of the Latins, none of which, however, shows a Latin origin.

Aineias seem to be that he is the son of a great goddess, that the gods favour him particularly, and that he is fated to be founder of a future monarchy.

These features he certainly shares with the founder of Lavinium ; each of them is fundamental to the story of the *Æneid*. It is because he is the son of a great goddess that he gets, among other things, the favour of Jupiter and the miraculous weapons that will slaughter the armies of Italy. Without the favour of the gods, especially Jupiter and Vulcanus, the whole story would not be possible. And without the fact that he is destined to be the founder of a great dynasty, the story would not be worth the telling ; its point is that Æneas is in some way the father of all full-blooded Romans. That is the reason why they wanted to hear his story, even before the historical accident of a man of genius made the Julian dynasty, that claimed descent from his son, the lords of Rome.

The peculiarity of the choice is worth insisting on. Aineias was indeed the heir of Troy according to the will of Zeus ; but the only man called "King of Men", universal king, in the Homeric poems, is Agamemnon, leader of the Greek host. He incarnated universal sovereignty, and it seems natural that any ambitious barbarian dynasty wishing to claim at once the highest Greek blood and the right to universal kingship would lay claim to him, rather than to the subordinate and defeated figure of Æneas. If not him, another more likely figure would have been that of Herakles, a popular founder of dynasties (including the mighty kings of Sparta). If Aineias, and no other Greek hero, was selected, it can only have been for one reason : because he corresponded fairly closely to a native Latin heroic figure. The identification was so early and popular that the name of this Latin hero has not survived : but the story has been carried on, under a thin veneer of Greek legend, to become the greatest poem to come down to us from the ancient world.

I.2 Æneas and Romulus

Therefore we must look at Italic, not Greek, ideas. The legend of a league of wandering young men, homeless and looking for a place to settle, is only found in Greece once : in the foundation legend of Rhegium[15], modern Reggio Calabria, an Italian city. Now Massilia, a Greek colony in Celtic territory, had a foundation legend not Greek but Celtic in type, telling of a wandering Greek prince who married a local princess after a marriage contest, especially similar to one of the adventures of the Welsh hero Peredur. This shows that the Hellenes who settled abroad might in time absorb cultural traits of their host countries[16]. In Italy itself, on the other hand, this type of band of young men is well-known : it is a *uer sacrum*.

In Roman tradition, the *uer sacrum*, or consecrated spring, is a ritual of special solemnity carried out in times of distress, when a city has either grown too populous for its territory or is otherwise threatened by famine. Then all the produce of the country in that year is offered

---

[15]   Strabo, *Geography* VI 1 6. Unwittingly, Strabo, who is actually trying to supply a good Greek pedigree for the Roman concept of *uer sacrum*, confirms its Italian origin : the only parallel he is actually able to supply, out of the whole Greek world, is that of Rhegium.
[16]   The famous origin legend of Cyrene (Herodotus, IV 145ff) is almost certainly also of native origin, given Herodotus' notice that Battus is the native word for "king".

to the gods, and young men born then are declared consecrated : *sacri*[1 7]. Once they reach the threshold of adulthood, they are driven out of their motherland's territory. The legends claim this was a regular procedure, paying the gods a tithe of the harvest, which had to include human beings, the land's most precious produce[1 8]. It was equal to a mass human sacrifice and explicitly described as such ; the young men were from then on considered alien to their mother State, dead, as it were, to it[1 9].

This immediately brings to mind the most famous *uer sacrum* in tradition, that of Romulus, the founder of Rome. The legend of Romulus is the other pillar of Roman national mythology, and its turning point is a *uer sacrum* that leads to the foundation of Rome. Now, looking at the two stories, I find that they proceed along lines that are at all points equal and opposite ; at every important point in the plot, they involve exactly opposite ideas and concepts.

1° Both heroes preside over the union of three different nations : but the lists are different, with only the central Latin people in common. Romulus brings together Latins, Etruscans and Sabines of Cures ; Æneas brings together Latins, Trojans and Arcadians of Pallanteum[2 0]. Æneas, like Romulus, has an army of Etruscan allies, but there is never any question of his Etruscan army taking any other part than a temporary one. They are there to be revenged upon Mezentius ; after that, they'll go home. The treaty with Latinus never even mentions them[2 1].

2° Both of them come to the place of their settlement with only a body of marriageable young men in the flower of age, but no brides or families. They have left their people behind in a city already built : Æneas in Acesta, Romulus in Alba Longa. They have to find brides before the new settlement can turn into a city ; this will cause all the trouble.

3° Æneas comes with a body of three hundred warriors[2 2] in the flower of age ; Romulus builds his new state around a senate that will eventually number three hundred elders[2 3].

[1 7]   This word often designates the victims in a blood sacrifice.

[1 8]   A detailed description of this legendary rite is in Dionysios of Halikarnassos, I 16 23-24. Despite the fact that the *uer sacrum* was regarded as the tithe of the crop of all human beings, it was composed of young males alone : the girls stayed home.

[1 9]   I should add that I know of no historical instance of *uer sacrum*, and I suspect it may have been a myth rather than an actual institution. If it ever was anything more than a set of legends, however, it was the result of a city's distress, that made it impossible to feed its children. This may have helped to assimilate the Latin hero to Aineias, who fled a city in distress, though the Roman concept was something quite different from the Xerox duplication of a city that Greek ideas describe.

[2 0]   It's worth noticing that the two peoples that Æneas joins to the Latin state, Pallanteans and Trojans, are quite legendary, whereas those brought in by Romulus, Etruscans and Sabines, were real, contemporary (and hostile) neighbours of the Latins.

[2 1]   Virgil, *Æneid* XII 176-211. Dumézil was quite right in comparing the two events, but wrong in thinking the one was a "transposition" of the other, let alone in attributing the "transposition" to Virgil, whose faithful and reverent attitude to the legends he rewrote seems to me one of the more remarkable facts about the poem. The idea is rather that of theme and variations, with important ideological nuances and differences in the two legends.

[2 2]   The oscillation between Virgil's probable three hundred and Solinus certain six hundred (above) is interestingly similar to the oscillation between one hundred fifty and three hundred senators related for Romulus by some of Dionysios' sources (II 47 2). This also seems more acceptable than the usual number of two hundred, one hundred Latins and one hundred Sabines, given the lesser dignity of the shadowy Tatius (whose subjects the fifty or one hundred Sabines are) as compared to great Romulus, his colleague, whose

4° Æneas is an alien ; Romulus comes from fourteen generations of Alban kings and, unlike the earlier hero, has Latinus' royal blood in his veins.

5° In both cases, older settlers deny new ones wives, but the reasons are different. Nobody ever objects to the pedigree of the illustrious Trojan prince, whereas the low birth of the future Romans is the main sticking point in their case. Yet, as I just said, Æneas is not of the Latin royal family, while Romulus is the direct lineal heir of Latinus ! Whatever this might mean, these two startling internal contradictions seems to me to form a pattern : the complete alien, Æneas, is treated as high-born, and so are his subjects ; the subjects of a king of native blood, Romulus, are treated as base-born.

6° The story of early Rome's first war begins with a mass abduction of wives (the rape of the Sabines) that turns into a war and then resolves itself into a political union ; the story of Æneas opens with the regular offering of a father's daughter's hand in marriage and the proposal of a large-scale marriage and political union, which is then broken and ends with a war or a series of wars. There is no reconciliation between Trojans and Rutulians, as there is between Romans and Sabines.

7° Æneas takes a woman who had been virtually engaged to another, thus making himself a deadly enemy ; Romulus on the other hand takes good care that only unmarried and unengaged maidens would be snatched[24].

This takes us a step further. We can say with confidence that, not only is the legend of Æneas in Latium grounded in Italic, *voire* Latin ideas, but it also forms an exact opposite to that of Latium's other great hero, Romulus, for whom nobody, I hope, seriously postu-lates a Greek origin or any origin at all outside Latin culture. If the legend of Æneas is late and artificial (as scholars tend to assume), then it has been invented as an integrated whole as a direct counterpart of the legend of Romulus, which is indubitably Roman. We are dealing with a complex set of native Latin legends grounded in native Latin ideology, which only centuries of Hellenization could ever hope to annexate to the Homeric cycle.

---

subjects are the Latins. In Latin, "three hundred" usually means "an infinite number" (cf. for instance Catullus, XI 18, XII 10). Therefore, the traditional number of senators stood for infinity or totality : three hundred is a fullness. It follows that the stories of anoriginally smaller Senate enlarged by early kings must be read as myths, not constitutional history ; as long as it had any existence at all, the body that represented Roman government in its fullness must have had three hundred members, no more and no less.

[23] 1° I am tempted to seek a reverse parallel of the distinction between the legend's "original" one hundred senators and fifty or one hundred Sabines, which has a central part in the story of Numa, but I doubt anything of the kind may be found. Æneas' parallels are very specifically with Romulus, to whom the difference among the senators doesn't count, and not with Numa, to whom it does.

2° Rome also had a junior counterpart to the Senate : the three hundred *celeres* or swift men, chosen among the flower of Roman youth and entrusted with certain religious ceremonies. Their foundation legend also connected them with Romulus, whose bodyguard they were supposed to be. They never counted remotely as much as the Senate, but it may be that the six hundred "Laviniates" may have been counted in this way, that is three hundred elders and three hundred *iuniores*. The "Laviniates" and the set of Senate + *Celeres* were both artificial and religiously significant images of a city's people.

[24] Only Dionysios ever states this as true (II 30, esp. 4, where Romulus orders his young men to let the girls alone for one night and take them to him in the morning : an evident precautionary measure), but the facts of the matter bear him out. No versions of the Rape of the Sabines - neither Livy nor Plutarch's Life of Romulus nor Dionysios - ever speaks of disappointed suitors or cheated husbands : it is always a matter of fathers and brothers.

In and of itself, this should not suprise us very much : all the evidence confirms that Romulus and Æneas went together as the central figures of Latin sacred story. As early as Timæus, the learned philosopher who had been in Lavinium in the age of Plato, we hear of Æneas fated to rebuild Troy in Lavinium and of the twin brothers, his descendants, endowed with force : *rhome*, an evident pun on *Roma*[2 5]. This is our oldest reliable evidence, and it already associates the great twin with Æneas as son, grandson or descendant[2 6], and at any rate as the other peak of the Latin heroic age.

I.3 Bride-taking in Virgil and Dionysios

Æneas, unlike Aineias, has practically no family to speak of, but the family is very much a part of his legend. On the Latin side, the story hinges on an extended-family wrangle of what seems to me a thouroughly Italian stripe, centering on Amata's attemps to force a candi-date of her choice, the handsome young Turnus, as son-in-law, on her husband Latinus, king of Latium. Dionysios calls this woman not Amata "Beloved" but Amita "Paternal Aunt". This reading has been challenged[2 7], but it is right beyond doubt : Dionysios himself tells us, without any explicit confirmation from Virgil, that Tyrrhenos (Turnus) was her nephew[2 8], and it was she who wanted Turnus for their daughter Lavinia at all costs. He was a kinsman, virtually another son ; she had nothing but hate and fear for anything outside the family circle, and Virgil makes her hate Æneas inextinguishably before she is sure whether he is animal, vegetable or mineral. She only once actually lays eyes on him, and that glimpse is the death of her.

The mother of the family tries to seal the family within its own closed circle ; and this not just because she has a recognized and powerful position within it, as mother of the bride and aunt of the groom, but above all because of an unreasoning detestation of the "unfamiliar" world beyond. Apart from the question of Virgil's life experience[2 9], this gives me a sense of recognition, as with a spirit not yet lost in modern Italy. Families do tend to form large closed circles whose agenda tends to be set by a matriarch or a circle of older women. And I may be taking things too far, but I do find it interesting that this sort of social attitude is found more intensely, for good as for evil, the further south you travel in the peninsula ; it's

---

2 5   Source of the Alexandrian poet Lykophron, *Alexandra* 1231-1280. The Rome he speaks of (in 309 BC) is already a considerable power, ruling Samnium, Campania and even Etruria : the racial ancestors of the Etruscans are mentioned among the following of Æneas (they include a certain *nanos* or "dwarf" who most of the commentators identify with none other than Odysseus). Internal evidence shows that he had visited the holy city of Lavinium (as well as several other notable places in peninsular Italy) ; he mentions the temple of Minerva there, and a remarkable statue of the goddess is in fact one of the main archæological discoveries of the site.

2 6   Son of a daughter : for instance, Dionysios of Halikarnassos, I 73 2. The central importance of Romulus and Remus' relation with Æneas and nobody else is brought out by the fact that this version never mentions a father, except when he is said to be a God.

2 7   E. CARY, *The Roman Antiquities of Dionysius of Halikarnassos*, London, 1937-1950, I p.211n.2.

2 8   Dionysios of Halikarnassos, I 64 2.

2 9   The practice of psychoanalyzing a dead author is an abomination, but I cannot help feeling that the hysterical, intrusive, ignorant, power-thirsty mother-monster the poet paints so well in Amata does much to explain why Virgil (who left his Mantuan home early, never went back, and settled in that haven of disaffected Northerners, Naples) was a woman-hating homosexual.

the centre and south of the country (south and east of the Tiber) that was the pre-Roman home of the Italic tribes of which the Latins were one. There are recognizable reasons why southern Italian mothers tend to behave in a certain fashion, to do with their life experience, the tasks they take up within the family, and the expectations laid on them ; and I think it's possible that those attitudes and expectations may have changed less than we might expect in 2500 years.

Amata's obsession with the family is not an isolated fact, much less an invention of Virgil's. The Latin epic tradition seems focused on kinship links to a remarkable degree : Turnus has not only his kinship with Amata, but also a father, at least two sisters, and a brother-in-law, all of whom have some weight in defining the character. And as well as having a family of his own, Turnus is also a part of Latinus and Amata's family circle, to which Æneas is entirely strange. A version of the legend makes Latinus the half-brother of Pallas, son of Hercules, and a sort of step-grandson of Evander[30] : Evander's daughter was said to have been Pallas' mother, but a slave of Hercules to have given birth to his half-brother. Again and again, I feel the shadowy sense of recognition of a very Italian obsession with family links[31].

Into this network of relationships, Æneas comes as a designated Outsider, alien to the whole network. This finally buries any idea that the Latin Æneas owes any substantial aspect of his personality, bar the name, to the Hellenic Aineias ; for, while the Greek figure is the core of a dynamic vision of the enduring, preserved family, the Italian character represents something extraneous, indeed opposed, to the family. His blood is completely foreign, unlike that of the half-Sabellian Pallas son of Evander[32]. His only blood relationships are with his son and with his dead father ; but Turnus' father is living. This is fundamental to the story. That Æneas' father is dead matters enormously to him : it is his dead father who initiates him into the mysteries of the universe, death, rebirth, and his own destiny, when Æneas travels to the world of the dead in the Sixth Book of the epic. Likewise the fact that Æneas can take the leadership of the Etruscan armies and marry the daughter of King Latinus depends directly on the fact that he is alien-born on both sides, with no Sabellian blood in him.

In this light, Æneas' involvement with the *Männerbund* is interesting. Between the family circle and the *Männerbund* there seems to be a functional opposition. The *Männerbund* is outside not only the Latin family circle but any family circle at all. Its foundation is not in family relationships but in age-class ones : its members are distinguished by being all

---

[30]   Dionysios of Halikarnassos, I 43.

[31]   An amusing manifestation of this Italian peculiarity, even today, is found in the country's soft-porn literature, which takes an extraordinary interest, unmatched elsewhere, in young undressed ladies who claim to be the cousin, or the niece, of this or that celebrity ; a classic example being Alessandra Mussolini, now a Fascist member of Parliament, who was featured in the Italian edition of a famous softcore magazine on the strength of being - get this - both Mussolini's grand-daughter and Sophia Loren's niece !

[32]   Virgil, *Æneid* VI 510. This verse actually only says that Pallas, Evander's son, is not allowed to lead the assembled Etruscan host against Mezentius because he is not a full-blooded alien ; but it can have escaped nobody that the same condition also prevents him from being Lavinia's designated husband (VII 98).

young and, in the case of the *uer sacrum,* all born in the same year. And in the same way that they are completely outside the world of family links, so too they are completely outside the world of the settled tribal state and its monarchy. They are a state in themselves, a self-contained society dependent on no state or league of states, opposing to the territorial sovereignty of settled states or tribes their own model of wandering sovereignty based on the recognition of a free leader dependant on no external authority. The Trojans come to Latium, not as a fragment of any organized society, but as themselves an organized society. They have their own ranking king, Æneas, who deals with Latinus on an equal basis, and who, though he governs no territory whatever, is always and everywhere referred to as a king. Even when he comes to be the king of a territorial state, it is that of the Etruscans, an alien people who must have been the image of the Completely Extraneous to the Latins, whom they resembled in neither language, nor tradition, nor institutions, nor background.

To jump the gun a bit - other Celtic parallels will not be introduced till the next section - this seems very close to the Irish institution of the Fianna[33], an independent band of young warriors whose commander had the rank of king and who were perticularly connected with the High King of Tara[34]. The Fianna were similarly an opposing term to the settled societies in Ireland, and to the world of the family and blood-kinship, to which they opposed a world of elective affinities based on similarity of age (what we may call all boys together).

The main difference is that I know of no legend of Fianna-like bodies founding territorial kingdoms such as Rome ; but even that is less sharp than it seems. The founding of Rome depends on the fact that the young members of the *uer sacrum* are given, as their own competence, such lands as are unsettled, unconquered and wild, outside existing territorial lordships. Now this is exactly the part of Ireland allocated to the Fianna : the wild lands and the sea, "her cliffs and her estuaries, her mast and her 'sea-fruit', her salmon, her hunting and her venery", leaving to the territorial lords "her wealth and her treasure, her cattle and her fortresses". (It is to be noted that the *uer sacrum* of Æneas was composed of all those in the original expedition who still had heart for the sea and wild lands.) That this never develops into a mythology of the foundation of new territorial lordships is probably due to the circumscribed nature of Ireland, where there is hardly a question of settling new lands except in the remote past.

At the same time, the *Männerbund's* young men seem to be bridegrooms by nature[35]. It is not only Æneas who is fated to marry : Faunus, Latinus' prophetic father, says that the Trojans come to be sons-in-law, that is, to take brides[36] ; it is not Æneas alone that he is thinking of. And Dionysios' account gives them a strong, even orgiastic sexual connotation. Virgil does not say explicitly that all three hundred Trojans are to marry Latin women, but

---

[33]   A.D. REES - B. REES, *Celtic Heritage,* London, 1961, p.62-69.
[34]   Romulus, before founding his own city, had rescued his grandfather, King Numitor of Alba Longa, from the oppression of Amulius.
[35]   This connection with marriage is also characteristic of the Irish Fianna, of which it is said that no girl in Ireland was allowed to be married until she was offered the the Fianna : A.D. REES - B. REES, *cit.,* p.65.
[36]   Virgil, *Æneid* VII 98.

Dionysios does, and, to increase unlikelihood, he makes the weddings happen at the same time : not, as might be expected, because of a decision by Latinus or Æneas or both, a treaty, or any authority at all, but as the fruit of a sudden mass *epithymia* of both Trojans and Latins[37].

This word *epithymia*, Liddel and Scott gave as "desire, yearning, longing", and "in a bad sense "desire, lust". Whether or not Dionysios meant its sexual connotations to shine through (and I don't see how he could not), it is clearly the opposite of *boulē* "counsel" or "plan". So we have this bizarre picture of three hundred young men and three hundred prospective brides all rushing at once into marriage (with, presumably, the approval of all the girls' parents and guardians !), not by plan, but because they all feel the same *epithymia* to get married[38] !

I.3a Do poets exaggerate ?

No wonder the poet played down this aspect of the story. In Virgil, the idea that "the Trojans want to take away the Rutulians' *brides*", in the plural, comes across as an exaggeration shouted by a fighting-mad Rutulian warrior or an outraged goddess[39]. There is something important here to be noticed about Virgil's mind and methods. We expect a historian to be more rationalistic and less inclined towards legendary oddities than a poet, and therefore, if we gave it any thought, would certainly be surprised to find the strange episode of the mass *epithymia* stated explicitly by Dionysios, but never by Virgil. And yet it is his own account that justifies Dionysios'. It is the poet, who tried to play down the legend of mass marriage, who yet tells us categorically that the Trojans had left all all their women and old men behind, and their company was therefore made only of young men of marriageable age. His statement, independent of that of the historian, makes the historian's extraordinary account both explicable and almost inevitable.

This would not seem so evident had it been written by a lesser poet. The women's agonies, their weariness of travelling, their desire for an abiding city - a haunting idea that St. Paul took over and Christian writers never forgot - and the desperate farewell at the end of the book five are moments of such hingh and unforgetable emotion that our minds don't notice how basically incredible they are. Even Virgil cannot quite make the Greek legend fit the Latin ; if it is the women only who could not longer endure this wandering life, then why leave behind the old men as well[40] ? He does not tell us.

This shows we should be careful of what looks like poetic exaggeration. It was not Virgil's poetic exaggeration that attributed to all the Trojans the aim of marrying local girls,

---

[37]   Dionysios of Halikarnassos, I 60 2.

[38]   It is interesting that Lavinia's wedding is less disputed in Dionysios than it is in Virgil : the lady is safely married off to Æneas before ever "Tyrrhenus" gets into motion (I 64 2. He increases the iniquity of Turnus/Turrhenus by making him a deserter from the Latins to the Rutuli, a charge we should keep in mind), and there is no indication that she herself ever favoured the unsuccessful candidate as she does in Virgil.

[39]   Turnus hints at it in VI 579 ; Remulus Numanus states it for a fact in IX 600 ; Juno lists it as one of the Trojans' supposed sins in X 78-79, etc.

[40]   Virgil, *Æneid* V 715-716.

and take them from the Rutuli. Virgil, on the contrary, was trying not to commit himself to the legend, hinting at it enough to bring it unmistakably to minds that has heard it before; but not giving it as a statement of fact. He was clearly embarrassed.

Somewhat to our surprise, then, we find, that Virgil did not indulge his fancy, enlarge, embellish, did not in short act as people think poets act. Absolutely to the contrary : he seems keen to cut oddities down to size ; he shies before fabulous accounts. In fact, he is willing, if not to suppress them altogether[41], at least to mention them in such a way as to pass them for distortions or misunderstrandings.

This agrees with what we know of his views : Virgil was a learned Hellenist, as apt as any other Hellenist to be ashamed of fables and to feel the need to rationalize them. It will be useful to keep this im mind when we come across Turnus shooting lightning[42], sweating rivers of pitch[43], or challenged by Æneas to take any form he pleases[44], like an Italian Cúchulainn[45]. Shall we, each time, call it a poetic licence ?

I.4 Æneas and Celtic legend

Though given a Greek identity, the character of Æneas belongs to a type Hellas doesn't know. He is, in all its essential features, parallel to the Celtic Supreme God, Lug.

Lug does not exactly correspond to any known Indoeuropean type. The French historian Georges Dumézil discovered a complex scheme of thought common to all Indoeuropean cultures, whose most typical "fingerprint" idea, found in a staggering variety of connections, is what is called "the three functions", a complex of ideas that tends to divide the cosmos, mankind and the human soul into three "functions" which may roughly be summed up as

1° wisdom (magic and law), associated with the religious aristocracy (brahmins, druids and the like) ;

2° strength, associated with the aristocracy proper and with kings ;

3° wealth and fertility, associated with farmers, merchants, productive trades and women.

It would be wrong to reduce Dumézil's work to this discovery ; his analysis of Indoeuropean theology goes far beyond, explaining a vast number of Indoeuropean ideas. In a long and hugely productive life, he has been most succesful with Roman, Indian and Germanic mythologies, and the folklore of the Ossetes, a Caucasian tribe that is the only remnant of the great Scythian people of classical Antiquity. His Celtic research has been illuminating and has directly encouraged another great work of scholarship, that of the Welsh brothers Alwyn and Brinley Rees, whose *Celtic Heritage* I will quote frequently ; but his explanation of Lug in terms of the Indian god Varuṇa is in my view less than successful.

---

[41]   He did not suppress the multiple-marriage business, just avoiding saying it out loud : he mumbled it, as it were.

[42]   Virgil, *Æneid* IX 731-733.

[43]   Virgil, *Æneid* IX 813-814.

[44]   Virgil, *Æneid* XII 891-893.

[45]   The greatest hero of Irish legend, Cúchulainn could take monstrous shapes when at the height of his fighting fury.

2 4

Though compounded of recongnizable Indoeuropean features, Lug fits in poorly with any Dumézilian category ; he seems something of an original Celtic creation.

Now, it is surprising but true that language scholars believe the ancient Celts, so historically distant from Rome and all her works, to be extremely close to the Italics in language. Some have even spoken of a single Italo-Celtic group. Therefore, by the same token whereby Dumézil came originally to believe in a common Indoeuropean culture, it seems logical to believe in a peculiar closeness of Latins and Celts[46].

The legend that will most closely interest us occurs in the *Mabinogion,* a collection of Welsh stories compiled sometime in the Middle Ages. It is a well-known text, several versions of which may be found in any bookshop in Britain, whose first four chapters, the actual *Four Branches of the* Mabinogi, are a lively but not always easily understandable summary of important pagan British myths. How coherent these legends are, and whether their position in the text we have has any significance or is a mere jumble of material the compiler no longer understood, these questions have been hotly debated for more than a century. Although it is the Roman epic that concerns us most, this study will bring new material to bear on the issue (if Virgil may be said to be new !).

The Fourth Branch, called *Math ap Mathonwy,* contains the only important account of the Supreme God of the Celts under his own name (Welsh Lleu) to have survived outside Ireland ; a story of the god's birth, youth and arrival to adulthood. This is a summary of its second half.

Young Lleu, shaped and raised by the wise sorcerer Gwydion, has been denied weapons and name because of his mother's Arianrhod's curse, unless she should bestow them on him herself. By the same token he can have no wife of any race now living in the world. Gwydion, a form of the god Ogma or Ogmios, helps him to wring weapons and a name from her. Together with his uncle, the king-wizard Math vab Mathonwy, Gwydion gives life to a woman made of flowers, the fair Blodeuwedd, and to enable him to marry her, Math makes Lleu a land-owning feudal lord[47].

But Blodeuwedd is treacherous. She gives herself to a neighbouring lord, Gronw Pebyr, who becomes the enemy of Lleu for her sake[48]. Told by her how the young hero should be slain, he creates a blasphemous weapon : a spear on which he works only during the sacred period of Sunday Mass, when everybody else is praying. With this he traps Lleu and kills him. Gwydion then looks for Lleu until he finds him at the gates of Death in Maenawr Penardd[49], where a pig is feeding on his flesh. Resurrected by the sorcerer, Lleu challenges

[46]   I did not embark on these researches with that preconceived point in mind. It was the purely casual observation that both the *Æneid* and an Irish text, the *Lebor Gabála Érenn,* included a sequence of two similar episodes of burning ships, that marked its start.
[47]   The date of the *Mabinogion* is medieval and the compiler assumed a feudal and Christianized background.
[48]   We know no other reason why he should hate him.
[49]   Where Pryderi, a culture hero, had begun the battle against the gods that led to his death earlier in the same *Mabinogion* branch.

Gronw and slays him fairly : indeed, he gives him an advantage. Blodeuwedd is changed into an owl[50] and takes to hiding in the night and crying mournfully.

Readers familiar with the *Æneid* may have noticed similarities.

1° Both stories reach their climax with a clash between the hero (Lleu, Æneas), favoured by the gods (Math and Gwydion) or by Fate, and a dark counterpart (Turnus, Gronw) for the sake of a promised bride (Lavinia, Blodeuwedd).

2° The gods, or Fate, have made (Blodeuwedd) or purposed (Lavinia) the bride in question for the hero and for him alone, but she herself inclines to his enemy to the point of wishing for the hero's destruction[51].

3° There is no other reason for Turnus or Gronw to fight Æneas or Lleu, and without their claim over the bride (which is illegitimate) they would not be their enemies at all.

4° Special reference is made to the beauty of both Gronw *Pebyr* (a word translated as "the Splendid") and *pulcherrimus* Turnus.

5° Gronw and Turnus both start the war with a large number of personal followers, bound to them by ties of tribal loyalty, and are abandoned by them. In the case of Turnus the Rutuli are broken on the field, in the case of Gronw they betray him outright but the result is the same : the two pretenders find themselves alone in front of a betrayed, vindicative and invincible enemy.

6° When the end is approaching, both Turnus and Gronw try to plead or negotiate for their lives.

7° Turnus and Gronw were both lords by hereditary right in their own provinces before Lleu was made a lord by Math or Æneas came from beyond the sea.

8° Before they can win their bride, both Lleu and Æneas must be given

- a set of weapons,

- either a kingdom or a name.

These place the story within Dumézil's trifunctional system, with the bride belonging to the third function, weapons to the second, and kingdom and name deal in two different aspects of the first : sovereignty and magic[52].

---

[50] In more recent Welsh folklore, the owl hides from other birds because, either of clumsiness or of wickedness, it has upset a cauldron which was meant either to resurrect the king of birds or to drown an usurper (D. PARRY-JONES, *Welsh Legends and Fairy Lore*, London, 1953, p.154-155). The common themes between the older and the more recent legends of the owl are the resurrection of a dead great personage, the punishment of an usurper and the shame of the owl for having played the wrecker's part in either. The cauldron of rebirth might be connected with Lleu's rebirth after death and with the Birdless Lake of Avernus which, as we will see, is closely connected with another legendary Welsh cauldron : that of Cerridwen, from which Taliesin gains his second birth (see next chapter).

[51] In Virgil, this is unmistakable : Lavinia prays for Æneas' defeat and destruction (XI 477-485) and flagrantly shows her love for Turnus (XII 64-69).

[52] In fact, Dumézil did analyze both legends in trifunctional terms, though he failed to connect them : for Lug, *Remarques comparatives sur le dieu scandinave Heimdallr*, in EC, VIII, 1959, p.283n.1 ; for Æneas, *Mythe et épopée*, I p.337-422 in which he discusses the three functional *fata* that Æneas finds deciding his future in Latium.

9° Æneas receives his weapons from the hands of his mother Venus ; Lleu is actually armed, *cap-a-pe'*, by the hand of his mother Arianrhod. Both Venus ("Worship") and Arianrhod ("Silver-Wheel") are great goddesses of somewhat mysterious significance.

10° While still comparatively helpless and alone, Æneas and Lleu are taken under their wing by great and extremely wise elderly male personnages, Evander and Gwydion, who are instrumental in obtaining the necessary intruments of power for the young heroes, and who also take a more general role of teacher.

11° Gwydion is the first living being to see the new-born Lleu (and in fact causes him to be born) ; Evander and his people are the first living men that Æneas meets in Italy.

12° Lleu will succeed Math vab Mathonwy as king of Gwynedd ; Æneas will succeed Latinus as king of Latium.

13° The unpromising Lleu is identified with the supreme god of the Celts, Lug ; the unpromising Æneas is worshipped in Lavinium as Jupiter Indiges, Jupiter being of course the supreme god of the Latins.

14° And, in the light of 13°, is it not interesting that Lleu, after he dies at Gronw's hands, takes the form of an eagle, the peculiar bird of Jupiter ?

Some other similarities are more vague.

15° There is a theme of the "angry mother" running through both stories but the mother in question is Amata/Amita, Lavinia's mother, in the one case, and Arianrhod, Lleu's mother, in the other. However, both of them contrive to deny the hero what he wants and is due to him, for a while.

16° Æneas comes from the sea ; Lleu is actually shaped from the afterbirth (a salty, watery substance) produced by the birth of his twin Dylan Eil Ton, who took to the sea as soon as he was born ans became a sea being.

17° Evander is instrumental in helping Æneas gain the Etruscan kingship and he is present when Venus gives his weapons but he can do nothing to let the hero win Lavinia, who only her father Latinus can bestow ; Gwydion is instrumental in helping Lleu win a name and weapons and he is present when Arianrhod dresses him in his new suit of armour but (although he helps) the making of Blodeuwedd is Math's idea and it is Math's magic which seem to be the key factor. It is also the only one of the three tasks in which Arianrhod is not involved : and nor is Venus[53].

18° Given the other similarities, the accounts of Lavinia and Æneas' birth and origin differ *in similar ways* from those of Blodeuwedd and Lleu. Lavinia is the physical child of Latinus ; Blodeuwedd is created by Math's (and Gwydion's) magic. Æneas is the physical child of Anchises ; Lleu is given life by Gwydion's magic. The Latin heroes have natural

---

[53]   If the Latin Venus had anything in common with the Hellenic Aphrodite, the very first thing we should have expected her to do is to make Lavinia fall in love with her own son Æneas ! That she does nothing of the kind is proof enough that she cannot ; her powers must be in another sphere. If there is one Power in the *Æneid* that rules over love (or rather over the sudden, deadly fury of lust that consumes Turnus), it is Allecto, under the orders of Juno.

births, the Welsh heroes are created by magic. Both Welsh magic births use an unpromising but natural substance - afterbirth, flowers - connected with fertility and generation.

19° There is a general air of blasphemy about the enterprise of both Gronw and Turnus. Turnus is the brother-in-law of the blasphemer Remulus Numanus and the guest-friend and protector of the anti-god Mezentius, he himself insults Juno's priestess Calybe and blasphemously invents *fata* of his own, that no god had promised him[54]. Gronw builds his weapon only on the day of rest, Sunday, when everyone else is in church[55].

20° There is a specific air of blasphemy about the spears brandished by both Gronw and Turnus. The blasphemous spear with which Gronw kills Lleu is built during a year of Sundays, its building is therefore an act of flagrant, and in some way complete, disregard of the Lord, flouting the Church's entire sacred year, holiday after holiday to completion. The spear was the weapon of Lug, Lleu's Irish counterpart, so that even to brandish it against Lleu may well have been a blasphemy in itself. Turnus prays to his spear to kill Æneas, vaunting his conquest of the weapon without any reference to Jupiter, Mars or any other god of war or divine figure whatsoever, flouting the Latin pantheon in a singularly complete manner.

21° Both Gronw and Turnus hold a stone aloft as they are about to die : Gronw in order to ward off Lleu's spear - an advantage granted him by Lleu himself - and Turnus, it seems, in one final, failed attempt to crush his victorious enemy.

22° Lleu is killed by Gronw at first and Gwydion brings him back from death in Maenawr Benardd, a place in Wales, not in some distant Otherworld, but associated with death : the war between the culture hero Pryderi and Gwydion, a great god, began there and ended in Pryderi's death, the first death in the *Mabinogi* ; after this, Lleu returns and slays Gronw. Æneas enters the world of the dead in Avernus, a place in Campania, not in some distant Otherworld, but associated with death ; he returns from it with the help of an elderly initiator (not Evander) and later slays Turnus.

23° A number of female characters are seen, shortly before the hero's revenge on his enemy, fleeing before his face or the sight of the coming revenge. In Latium, Juno cannot bear to watch[56] and Juturna is twice seen fleeing, once from the noise of Æneas' coming[57] and again from Jupiter's Dira[58], from which she takes refuge in a river. In Wales, Blodeu-

[54]   Virgil, *Æneid* IX 136-138. The fact that Calybe is Allecto in disguise doesn't matter. Turnus believes her to be the priestess, elderly, consecrated and venerable, and still he insults her. As for the *fata* to which he lays claim (IX 136-138 : "To me as well | Are *fata* of my own, to destroy a wicked nation with irons | Once my bride is assaulted"), no god had pronounced such *fata* and indeed Lavinia had not even been promised. Turnus' expression *sunt et mea contra fata mihi* is in fact so ambiguous that it might even mean "And against (this) there are for me the things I have spoken" (*mea fata*), blasphemously placing his own pronouncements on the same level as the gods'.
[55]   Another text suggests that the sin of working on the Sabbath may have been keenly felt in medieval Wales : Gerald of Wales, *The Journey through Wales* I 2 describes a clearly pagan ceremony in the parish of St. Eluned (Brecknockshire), in which the people mimed various jobs. The Christian explanation was that they were atoning for the sin of working on a Sunday.
[56]   Virgil, *Æneid* XII 151.
[57]   Virgil, *Æneid* XII 448-449.
[58]   Virgil, *Æneid* XII 885-886.

wedd flees Lleu's approach together with fifty maidens who are all drowned in a river while she flies off transformed into an owl[59].

24° The owl into which Blodeuwedd was transformed is a bird that hides in trees, and the fact that he (she ?) is actually in hiding is a firm point in Welsh folk-lore[60]. After Æneas' death, Lavinia hid from Ascanius in the woods of Latium. The similarity is closer that it seems : as this study will show, Iulus is actually another self of Æneas and it is possible to see a triad Anchises-Æneas-Iulus. Now, the Lleu from which Blodeuwedd flees has had *three births* : the original one from Arianrhod, his magical one from Gwydion's box, and his return from the world of the dead through Gwydion's agency. It is this third and final rebirth of Lleu that Blodeuwedd flees, having married the second that is now dead ; not unlike the way Lavinia flees from the third generation of the Æneas family, having married the second who is now dead.

25° The fifty maidens who accompany Blodeuwedd are all drowned in a single river. Juturna, who like them flees headlong in a river from the sight of the vindictive hero, is the goddess of *all* the springs and watercourses of Latium. This seems to contain a curious double element of single and manifold identity, connected with feminity and rivers. Juturna is one goddess but rules many streams ; the fifty maidens are many persons but they are all bound up into one river[61].

26° Gronw and Turnus cannot escape their dooms because both are guilty of the death of a young man : Gronw of Lleu himself, Turnus of Pallas. Therefore their attempts to plead or negotiate for their lives avail them both nothing.

A third set of similarities is in the close and singular relationship of Lleu and Gwydion mirrored in unexpected and very characteristic ways by by that of Æneas and Evander. Gwydion is, I believe, the Welsh image of the god known on the continent as Ogmios and in Ireland as Ogma[62], whose features I shall use as part of the evidence.

---

59   It may be worth noting that the Latin epic has a total of three female flights. This may be systematic, adding up to a triad.

60   D. PARRY-JONES, *op.cit*, p.153-154.

61   The Rennes *Dindsenchas* tells that Boand, the wife of Nechtan mac Labraid, visited her husband's forbidden well that only he or his three cupbearers could visit without their eyes bursting. Being a woman of power, she defiantly went round the well three times. Each time, the well burst and wounded her, then it overflowed altogether. Boand fled pursued by its waters and when they met the sea she was drowned, giving her name to the river Boyne. Evidently, Celtic tradition found it easy to personify rivers as drowned women, even in the case of a great river like the Boyne and a great goddess like Boand, wife of Nechtan, lover of the Dagda and mother of the mighty young god Oengus. Juturna must be a correponding Latin figure and Blodeuwedd's fifty nameless maidens suddenly seem a lot more important than anyone ever thought (G. AGRATI - M.L. MAGINI, *Saghe e racconti dell'antica Irlanda*, Milan, 1993, p.720).

62   A piece of pottery found in the Roman excavations of Richborough seems to confirm that the name of Ogmios was known in mainland Britain as well as Ireland. From the purely geographical factors involved, I believe in the commonsense view that a god whose name was widely honoured both on the Celtic continent and in Ireland cannot have been unknown to that Britain to which, according to Cæsar's witness, Gaulish druids went to perfect their craft. Cf. J.P. BUSHE-FOX, *Third Report on the Excavations of the Roman Fort at Richborough*, Oxford, 1932 ; A. ROSS, *Pagan Celtic Britain*, London, 1967.

1° Ogma was, even by name, the inventor of the first known Celtic alphabet, the ogham ; Evander, says Dionysios[63], brought over the Latin letters.

2° Gwydion was the finest bard in the world[64] ; Evander was connected with the goddess of poetry, Carmenta, and taught the Latin music[65].

3° Gwydion displays the skills of a fine shoemaker ; Evander taught many crafts[66].

4° Gwydion was a wanderer and associated with the vault of heaven[67] ; Ogma was a wanderer and a type of the outsider ; Evander is a wanderer (he has come over from Greece) and a type of the outsider[68].

5° Gwydion and Lleu were particularly associated as a pair of Old and Young ; Æneas and Evander were allies and the old king's (grand)son Pallas, himself a type of the young man, remarks on his guests' youth as soon as he first sees them : two thousand years of readers must have wondered at this singular greeting, so thoroughly inappropriate to the Hellenic Aineias[69] !

In the face of all these parallels, it seems impossible to deny the connection between Latin hero and Celtic god. The rest of this study will expand on them and draw certain conclusions which, while warranted by the Latin evidence, may seem surprising. The fact that Latin culture has been investigated largely in the light of Hellenic civilization had led to certain Hellenistic points of view being taken more or less for granted. Never, for instance, at any time from Homer to the destruction of Greek paganism by Justinian, do we hear of Greek gods becoming incarnate. The division between mortals and gods is very strong indeed in the Greek mind, and therefore I doubt whether any scholar investigated or even considered the possibility that Latin heroes might be incarnate divinities. By the same token, there has been far too much emphasis on the Greek view that the Romans had few or no stories of gods, and therefore no mythology. Has anybody ever considered the possibility that we might in fact have the Latin mythology in our hands, and that it might be an epic mythology ?

Every important point in Æneas' career, in fact, can be paralleled by similar points in

---

[63]   Dionysios of Halikarnassos, I 33 4. Note the contrast with Plato's very Greek contempt for writing. Hellas considered it a step backwards and attributed it, even before Plato, to the epic villain Palamedes, enemy of the truly wise Odysseus. But Rome gave its legendary inventor heroic cult : this is much closer to the sacred status that Celts and Germans attributed to ogham and runes.
[64]   In *Math*, this skill helped him deceive Arianrhod and keep her attention and goodwill, to help Lleu in his quest.
[65]   Dionysios of Halikarnassos, I 31 1, 33 4. Virgil seems to make Carmenta his mother and not his wife (VIII 336) but the title of *mater* by which Evander describes her may well have been no more than the typical title of honour by which Romans frequently addressed their gods and goddesses. Virgil, in my view, is significantly ambiguous here, with that kind of ambiguity that shows that there was some embarassing content he whished to dissemble. In prehistoric Rome, Carmenta must have been an important deity, since an important city landmark, the Porta Carmentalis, was named after her. It lay directly under the imposing NW side of the Capitol. This is only a guess but Virgil may have been embarassed by the notion of a mortal hero married to a divinity.
[66]   Dionysios of Halikarnassos, I 33 4.
[67]   *Caer Gwydion* "Gwydion's Castle" means the Milky Way in Welsh.
[68]   Dionysios of Halikarnassos, I 31 2.
[69]   Virgil, *Æneid* VIII 112.

1° the coming of the gods to Ireland in the *Lebor Gabála Érenn*[70] and associated texts ;

2° the story of Lleu in *Math* ;

3° the story of Taliesin[71] ;

4° the story of Lug's revenge for his murdered father in the Irish romance *The Fate of the Children of Tuirenn*[72].

Most characteristics of the son of Venus will be easy to analyze, but one episode of his adventures, his journey into the world of the dead at the Birdless Lake, will give me occasion to range all over the Indoeuropean world in search of parallels, partial parallels, and explanations.

---

70   Ed. transl. R.A.S. MacALISTER (Dublin, 1938-1956).

71   Transl. P.K. FORD, *The* Mabinogi *and Other Welsh Texts*, Berkeley, 1977 (which also contains one of the many translations of *Math* available and a worthwhile commentary).

72   Ed. transl. R.J. O'Duffy (Dublin, 1901).

CHAPTER II : ÆNEAS AND TALIESIN

II.1 Taliesin and Lleu

Alwyn and Brinley Rees' superlative study of Celtic traditions has this to say about Taliesin

> While individual beings in some of these stories retain their identity through diverse incarnations, the child Taliesin... envisages himself as a ubiquitous presence which has witnessed the history of the world and will endure to the end. The blessed drops [that made him supremely wise] did no more than to make him aware that he was there when it all happened. The poem, like several others in the same strain preserved in the medieval Book of Taliesin, exalts him to a plane which trascends that of finite human beings :
>
> > I have been teacher to all Christendom,
> >
> > I shall be on the face of the Earth until Doom,
> >
> > And it is not known what my flesh is, whether flesh or fish.
>
> ... He claims to have seen the fall of Lucifer, the Flood, and the birth and crucifixion of Christ... He says that he was created by Gwydion [but also] that he was in the court of Dôn[1] before Gwydion was born... Some of the poems... are replete with utterances beginning 'I have been' and the things he has been include inanimate objects - stock, axe, chisel, coracle, sword, shield, harp-string, raindrop, foam -, animals such as bull, stallion, stag, dog, cock, salmon, snake, eagle, and a grain which grew on a hill... He was not made of father and mother but was created of nine things : fruits and various flowers, earth and water from the ninth wave... Taliesin is everything...[2]

It is hard not to see in this character a supreme and not human figure. The Reeses have not, in fact, mentioned a few important facts that virtually identify Taliesin with Jesus Christ : he claims to have been in Caer Gwydion (i.e. the Milky Way, the sky) with the Tetragrammaton, that is with YHWH, God himself[3], to have been with Him in Heaven when Lucifer fell, to have been on the Cross with the Son of God ; and to have been with Him when He contended with the Jews. The last two claims, riddling as they are, can only have one meaning : when Jesus "contended with the Jews" in the court of the Sanhedrin, and again in front of Pilate, he was totally alone. Even Peter had failed, skulking around a fire outside the palace where his Master was being tried for His life, and denying Him. And certainly there was nobody with Him on His Cross. We are talking about the most famous story in all Christianity : there is absolutely no possibility of misunderstanding. "Taliesin"

---

[1] A mysterious character, probably the mother of the gods, equivalent of Irish Danu and certainly the mother of Gwydion himself in the *Mabinogi*.

[2] A.D. REES - B. REES, *cit.*, p.230.

[3] According to P.K. FORD, *Ystoria Taliesin*, Cardiff, 1992, the passage might actually mean that Taliesin was one of the four letters of the Tetragrammaton : part of the divine substance himself ! But even if the reference is to the letters as letters rather than to the divine hypostasis, this is still very significant since we will discover that Jupiter Indiges can himself have the form of letters and words.

cannot have imagined a fictional, unscriptural character to stand by Our Lord when great Peter himself, the first of the popes, had deserted Him.

Who, then, is with you when you are alone ? Why, *who else but yourself !* Taliesin is claiming identity with the Second Person of the Trinity. I suggest that this hero of ancient Wales, the caste-figure of the class of bards[4], was in fact a figure or an avatar of the supreme god. And it is interesting that one of the Reeses' mass of details identifies him starkly with Lleu : while Taliesin lived in the court of Dôn, Gwydion's mother, before Gwydion was born, he also claims to have been made by Gwydion, and made not as a father or mother but from a substance that may not be either flesh or fish and is in fact compounded of sea-water, earth and certain kinds of fruits and flowers[5]. Now, the role of Gwydion is to "make" Lleu, not out of human substance and not as father or mother. Remembering that Lleu is Lug and Lug is the supreme God, it seems impossible that any lesser figure should benefit from his initiation.

Other details seem liable to similar interpretation : Taliesin was "three times in the prison of Arianrhod". Lleu was three times in Arianrhod's castle : once when he was in her womb before being born, once when Gwydion deceived her into giving Lleu a name, and once again when he deceived her into giving the boy his weapons.

Again, "there was not born in Adwy anyone who attacked me | Except Goronwy from Doleu Edrywy"[6]. Goronwy is the same name as Gronw, and in fact nobody except Gronw actually attacked Lleu. He was alone when he lay im ambush to kill him, and alone again in their final duel : his faithless retainers had abandoned him.

The riddle that he existed in the court of Dôn, the mother of gods, long before Gwydion, the god who "made" him, had even been born, is the same riddle asked in Hesiod's Theogony when Kronos, king of the gods, hears Earth and Heaven foretell that he shall be overthrown by one of his own children, through the *boulē* (the will, the counsel) "of Zeus the mighty", before he himself had given birth to Zeus. The counsel, the will, and the divine plan of a supreme god not yet born have already doomed his own father to defeat. What is the relation of the supreme god to time ? Is he born in it, is he beyond it ? The question, itself a riddle, is expressed in riddling terms.

II.2 The legend of the Birdless Lake

The legend says that Gwion Bach[7], the boy who was to become Taliesin, was one of the attendants of the wise and wicked witch Cerridwen during her year-long labour to produce

---

4   The poets whose job it was to sing the king's praises.

5   In *Math*, as we remember, Lleu is made by Gwydion out of salty, watery afterbirth, clearly connected with the ocean, while it is his destined bride Blodeuwedd who is made of flowers. Eliminating fruits, which may be reduced to the same category as flowers, this seems to divide two of the three categories mentioned in Taliesin's poem - water from the ninth wave (of the ocean), earth and fruits/flowers - between bride and groom, as though Taliesin claimed identity, at least in substance, with both Lleu and Blodeuwed. The "earth" element remains, for the present, unexplained.

6   Transl. P.K. FORD, *The* Mabinogi, p.186.

7   What follows is a summary of the legend of Taliesin given by the Elizabethan Welsh chronicler Elis Gruffydd, translated by P.K. FORD, *The* Mabinogi, *cit.*

an enchantment to make her unbelievably ugly son Morfrân "Great Raven, or Great Brân" the wisest man in the world. She boils together a secret number of herbs for one year and one day : when the time comes, the boiling will yeld three blessed drops containing all the world's wisdom, while the rest of it turns into a peculiarly virulent poison. When the drops finally come out, Gwion jostels Morfrân and gets them[8]. Cerridwen pursues him in various forms. She swallows him, only to fond herself pregnant with him. Eventually she drops the baby into the ocean, where he floats for forty years before reaching land to become the greatest sage of his day[9].

The legend of Gwion Bach is in two parts. The first takes place on the very local stage of Llyn Tegid, the lake that is the apanage of Cerridwen's husband, the nobleman Tegid. It is there that Cerridwen and her assistants live and, though the spell she is working is in some sense cosmic[10], the whole of the action is firmly rooted in a single place in a known region of Wales. It has to be : the boiling has to go on, continuously, relentlessly ; Cerridwen and her assistants have to stay there and pay attention. No wonder that, when the blessed drops finally appear, she is asleep !

The stage works itself out with the apparition of the blessed drops but there is a postscript. The remaining liquid has now turned into a poison so destructive that the cauldron cannot contain it : it splits its flanks and spreads across the countryside[11]. As Elis Gruffydd phrases it, this part of the spell seems to have been specially designed by Cerridwen's wickedness for the purpose of spoiling the country : while she is working to make sure that her hideous son is superior to all other men because of prophetic wisdom and bardism, she is also trying to make one and the same spell ruin men around him. But curiously, we hear no more of the poison.

The setting of the second stage is quite different : instead of firm and localized landscapes, we have enormous distances and indeterminate places. First over the Earth as she pursued him, then in her womb, and then forty years in the waters in which she has cast

---

[8]   The reason for his jostling him is never explained and parallels from Britanny suggest that this way was always the case : the boy who was to become the cosmic sage demanded, for no apparent reason, the apparently worthless tokens that were to make him the world's geatest sorcerer. It seems as though he was guided to them, or to the three blessed drops, by instinct.
[9]   There is a riveting and unexpected similarity between the legends of Taliesin and the important Indian tale of Kāvya Uśānas. Kāvya Uśānas, the guru of the demons, stole the world's wealth from the god of wealth himself, Kubera. In punishment for this, the great god, Śiva, swallowed him. Kāvya Uśānas survived within the almighty destroyer's body and underwent a paradoxical male birth from Śiva's penis (an object of enormous reverence in Indian religion). From this he acquired a new name, Śukra "the Seeed" : the Seed, if you please, of the honoured male member of the great god, the liṅga (Mahābhārata XII 290 Ganguli's version). The theft of the world's wealth here does duty for the theft of the world's wisdom in the Welsh legend, but the parallels are so close and numerous that they demand attention.
[10]   It will take the significant time of a year, a symbol of infinite time, and a day and will endow Morfrân with infinite wisdom.
[11]   A legend of a mighty wise woman brewing a terrible poison is preserved in the Rennes Dindsenchas. "Dreco daughter of Calcmael was a good poet and druid-woman. She brewed the poisonous and deadly drink that slew Fergus Lethderg and his twenty-four sons. The place where they died took the name of Nemthen 'Mighty Poison' ". It is interesting that one of Dreco's skills is specifically said to be poetry (G. AGRATI - M.L. MAGINI, op.cit., p.723).

him : at no point in Gwion Bach's career do we glimpse a single stable spot. In the end, he is cast in the ocean, the ultimate instance of cosmic formlessness.

Now there is a story that resembles strongly, but in a negative fashion, that of Taliesin : that of Idwal son of Owain Gwynedd. Owain was a great medieval Welsh sovereign whose many children are the protagonists of some famous fables[1 2]. The type of the lovely child untimely lost, Idwal was said to have been sent for protection and instruction to a handsome, learned, but vain bard-harper called Nefydd Hardd, who lived near St Curig Capel and the lake that now bears Idwal's name. This man, a distant relative of the prince, had an ugly and dull-witted son called Dunawt, whom he absurdly hoped to bring up to be as attractive and erudite as himself. The splendid boy only showed Dunawt's inadequancies, and father and son were consumed with jealousy. Nefydd eventually suggested to Dunawt to throw Idwal in the lake and murder him. The dullard did it but the prince came to suspect how his son had died. Unable to lawfully prove what had been done, he nevertheless punished the vain Nefydd, who had put such misplaced hopes in his progeny, by degrading him and all his descendants from noblemen to serfs. Since then, no bird will fly over Llyn Idwal[1 3].

There are many Taliesin-like elements.

1° Both stories are concerned with one particular type of traditional learning - bardism - and no other ;

2° wisdom is transmitted to the wrong boy ;

3° the failed candidate is notably ugly ;

4° nevertheless, the initator misplacedly plans a great future for this unfortunate off-spring[1 4] ;

5° when thwarted, the initiator decides to murder the successful candidate ;

6° his/her murderous plan succeds ;

7° the successful candidate is put into a body of water, whether lake or ocean, for the purpose of killing him or at least getting rid of him[1 5] ;

[1 2]   One was Madoc, he of the sea voyage.

[1 3]   I haven't be able to trace this legend beyond S. STYLES, *Welsh Walks and Legends*, London, 1979, p.58-61. I wrote to the author but he couldn't remember his source after so many years.

[1 4]   However, if Morfrân-Great Brân is, as I suspect, connected with Brân the protagonist of the *Mabinogi* of *Branwen Daughter of Llŷr*, then we have to remember that Brân and his whole family are the very type of the Dispossessed. Indeed, the similarity of the permanently dispossessed house of Nefydd with the house of a character named Great Brân is a not insignificant argument to identify the latter with the Great Dispossessed, Brân ap Llŷr Marini.

Some extraordinary Welsh legends, now lost, seemed to make of Great Brân son of Tegid - of all people ! - the type of the adulterous lover :R. BROMWICH, *Trioedd Ynys Prydein*[2], Cardiff, 1979, p.103. In fact, his whole dynasty seems linked with the idea of adultery : his sister Creirwy the Fair was an adultress and her lover Garwy's daughter was one of Arthur's lovers (R. BROMWICH, *op.cit.*, p.351, 354). The link between the ideas of dispossession and adultery is clear.

[1 5]   Elis Gruffydd's narration makes it clear that Cerridwen placed Taliesin in a coracle as a substitute for killing him ; which, having borne him for nine months, she couldn't bring herself to do. Her act was equivalent to the practice of exposing unwanted children. As we are on the track of similarities between Celtic and Latin legend, it is possible to feel here something not unlike the expulsion of the young men into the great Outside that is the essence of the *uer sacrum* ; this might offer a parallel between Æneas and Taliesin.

8° finally, though the murderer succeeds in his/her plan, nevertheless his/her ultimate purpose is completely and conclusively frustrated[16].

An interesting detail is that neither Idwal nor Dunawt can swim. This means that, up to the actual moment of immersion/drowning, they are equal in status vis-à-vis the lake ; either of them might have drowned. In the same way, Gwion and Morfrân are equal in status before the great cauldron : the three blessed drops might have struck either of them. Idwal's lake, therefore, is somehow correspondent, not only to the water in which Cerridwen places Gwion, but also to her cauldron. Indeed, if the lake had no connection with Idwal's gifts, there would be no point in drowning the boy, rather than kill him any other way, as a punishment for being so clever. We remember that Taliesin, once thrown in the water, floats, and we know that his bardic wisdom was perfect ; evidently Idwal's wasn't, despite his promise, and he was thrown in before he was ready. He had no certain knowledge. And neither had his father, who could not prove how his son had died : as Nefydd Hardd successfully kept his knowledge from Owain Gwynedd's son, so he kept the knowledge of his death from his father, who had to act without it. Lack of certain knowledge, and knowledge withheld by those who have it, are the hallmarks of this story[17]. And it is surely a related fact that the story never moves to the cosmic and indeterminate distances in which Cerridwen and Gwion, initiator and initiate, contend ; young Idwal simply drowns in his little lake, and stays there.

However, the story sheds no light on the question of Cerridwen's poison ; to explain it we must go to another area of the Indo-European world. The business of a lake which no birds will cross is thoroughly untypical of Welsh tradition[18], whose many lake legends are all of a quite different type, about ancient cities or kingdoms drowned because of wicked-ness. On the other hand, two famous classical legends involve similar bodies of water : our own subject of study, the *Æneid,* and the Greek story of Phæthon. We shall forget about the *Æneid* for a while and concentrate on the Greek legend, which may supply us with a few useful facts.

---

[16] So far as we know, this frustration was more complete for Nefydd than for Cerridwen. Though Morfrân lost his chance of wisdom, nevertheless he does not seem to have been permanently degraded from his aristocratic rank (his father, Cerridwen's husband Tegid, was a nobleman) like Nefydd's whole race.

[17] It is possible to see in it a reflection of the decline of native Welsh cultural institutions. We know that the legend of Taliesin, with its staggering claims about the bardic caste, was still widespread in Wales in the sixteenth and seventeenth centuries ; yet the reality did not conform to the theory : Welsh poetry was not particularly highly regarded after the fall of the native princes. Why, the Welsh must have wondered, was there such a decline ? Obviously, because of sin. The story of Idwal describes one such sin : jealousy and pride of family and caste lead one very gifted bard to squander his gifts on a treacherous murder ; hence, he is degraded to a bondsman. No doubt, Tudor and Stuart-age Wales cannot have been short of families who were of lowly status but claimed descent from bardic lineage.

[18] Though a Birdless Lake with many of the same characteristics was known in the neighbourhood of Leek, Staffordshire. Among the various legends connected with it are that a mermaid lay at its bottom waiting to drown unwary travellers, that it was bottomless, and that if its waters were let out, they would drown all the country round about. Except possibly for the murderous mermaid, this obvious Celtic survival in an area not far from Wales tells us little we might not have learned elsewhere ; but it does tell us that the Birdless Lake of Snowdonia comes directly from the British Celtic Antiquity (J. WESTWOOD, *Albion,* London, 1985, p.263).

Phæthon, like Idwal, is a beautiful boy untimely lost. Two great and learned poets, Apollonios of Rhodes in the *Argonautica* and Ovid in the *Metamorphoses,* give authoritative accounts of his legend : a mortal boy, but the son of the Sun, he demanded to be allowed to drive his father's chariot, lost control, and devastated the Earth until the lightning of Zeus slew him and smashed him down into - what do you think ? - a lake that no bird will cross. The reason why they won't is quite clear and not at all metaphysical : the boy's ever-burning body poisons the air[19], birds are caught in the poisonous vapours, flutter, and die.

Apollonios also says that the lake where his body still smoulders is the source of the mythical river Eridanos, which is in fact - as we find by the fantastic geography of the *Argonautica* - a branch of the cosmic river Ocean[20]. According to Apollonios, the Argonauts, cursed to wander by Zeus because they had treacherously murdered Apsyrtus, entered the Eridanos at its mouth, the Isle of Amber, and rowed upstreams all the way to its source, the Birdless Lake. There they saw Phæthon's sisters, daughters of the Sun[21], who stand around his lake in the shape of poplars ; their divine tears float downriver till they are collected at the Isle of Amber, which Apollonios calls holy.

The Birdless Lake of this legend is not a pleasant place : reekingly poisonous, hot with Phæthon's perpetual burning, and haunted by his sisters' banshee wails, it was one of the worst things the adventurers ever experienced. But the Eridanos is not the only cosmic river to flow from the Lake. Instead of going back, they enter another, that flows in the opposite direction. However, without realizing it, thay have put themselves in terrible danger : this new, unnamed river has two branches, one of which could lead them straight to the great outer Ocean and perdition, if their patroness Hera hadn't come from Olympus to warn them.

To us, it is not the story itself that matters so much as the legendary geography behind it. It can be used to explain the peculiarities and connections of the legends of Gwion Bach and Idwal.

Two rivers flow down from Phæthon's lake, and no less than three rivers flow from the Llyn Idwal area : the Seiont down to Caernarvon, the Ogwen to east of Bangor, another whose name I don't know to Betws-y-Coed and the Conwy. And while not as evil a place as the Greek Birdless Lake[22], the bitter mountain heights of Snowdonia, rocky, sterile and snow-covered in winter are no doubt as unpleasant a neighbourhood as you might find in Wales[23].

---

19   Apollonios of Rhodes, *Argonautica* IV 595-603.
20   In Virgil's book VI, we find the doubtless Hellenic idea that Eridanos was in fact one of the rivers that flowed through the world of the dead ; not, however, through the world of the unrighteous dead (like the infernal rivers that both Dante and Milton borrowed from him) but through the Blessed Fields where the righteous go. Whatever it is, it is certainly not a river of Earth, even if it was identified with Virgil's own river, the Po in northern Italy (*Æneid* VI 659).
21   Circe, Medea and Apsyrtus, the tragic relatives who play a large part in the epic, are also of the household of the Sun. In effect, the Argonauts have travelled to the ends of the Earth and the country and people of the Sun.
22   Which reminds us forcibly of a volcanic crater, and there are none in Britain.
23   The Birdless Lake near Leek was among evil-smelling peat bogs. See above p.35n.18.

7

But the parallels between Llyn Idwal and Cerridwen's cauldron invite us to consider possible connections between the latter and Phæton's lake. The reek and bird-killing poison of the latter remind me of the poison that came from Cerridwen's broken cauldron after the theft of the blessed drops[24] : a poison of infinite power, that, once the blessed drops had been secreted, would burst its vessel and spread across the land[25]. Now it is interesting that, although we no longer hear of the poison after this notice, the very next stage of the legend involves Cerridwen throwing Gwion Bach into the ocean to kill him. To be precise, Ellis Grufydd's sources were uncertain whether the witch has thrown him into a lake, a river or the sea ; but what is certain is that he eventually got to the sea, one way or another, since we are told that he floated on the surface of the waters for forty years.

It seems to me that the two stages I identified in the myth of Cerridwen and Gwion may be found, in something of an arrested state, in Greek legendary geography. The first stage is local and definite ; the Birdless Lake is clealy identified and described[26] : the second stage is vast and with little local description, ranging across the surface of the Earth and ending in the open sea. The Greeks see the prospect of ending up in the outer Ocean as a nightmare, and the poet breathes a sigh of relief (tough there are many trials still to be endured) when the ship is back in homely Mediterranean waters ; the Celts have no such fears, and Gwion/Taliesin floats quietly and unchallenged for his forty initiatic years, across the featureless surface of the universal sea.

Another element worth considering is Cerridwen's husband, Tegid Lord of Llyn Tegid (or Bala Lake). We know nothing whatsoever about him, and the only practical effect his mention has on the story is that Cerridwen is shown to be connected by marriage with Bala Lake. This is an element that seems to go nowhere, since the lake is never mentioned at any point in the story. The best we can make of it is that, if Cerridwen threw Gwion in a lake or in a river, the lake is likely to be Bala Lake itself, and the river the Dee, that flows from it. Yet, at the mention of a lake - and one with no less vigorous an outflow that the Dee, North Wales' mightiest river - our ears ought to prick up. However, the connection is on the face of it paradoxical : how can a freshwater lake and the flow of a clean, life-giving river, be connected with a sorcerous cauldron from which flows poison ?

Allow me a flight of fancy. The poison of Cerridwen's cauldron does not remain in the cauldron itself : it flows out, and naturally it flows downhill. It must find its final resting place in the sea. This image must remind us of the waters flowing - flooding - out of the lake, forming a river, going down to the sea ; the great salt sea, the final end of the journey alike of Taliesin and of the river that flows from Bala Lake, the Dee. Cerridwen's universal poison finds its final resting place in the universal ocean : well, have you ever drunk sea water ? It tastes like poison ; and, in large doses, it *is* poison. It will kill you. It's even

---

[24] There is no problem in Welsh legend about understanding a lake, however small, as a version of the Great Flood : the many Welsh lake legends always tell of great floods that drowned wicked or careless kingdoms (D. PARRY-JONES, *op.cit.*, chap.7).
[25] The land aound Phæton is described as blighted.
[26] Although in Greece it is quite legendary.

probable that the ancient Welsh had noticed that sea water, used in place of fresh water to irrigate fields or pastures, would, by over-salinating them, blight them as effectively as any Cerridwen's poison. I am convinced that the legend of Cerridwen's broken cauldron and its deadly contents must at some point have been an aitiological myth of "how the sea became salt".

This is un unprovable hypothesis ; the following conclusions, however, are based firmly on the evidence. There existed a Welsh legend of bardic initiation that included immersion in a lake and possibly some sort of ritual death, after which the initiate was somehow supposed to travel through the universe and either acquire or prove his wisdom. The fact that birds never fly over Llyn Idwal connect it with the poison of Cerridwen's cauldron, which is almost certainly connected with Llyn Tegid (Bala Lake) through a Greek legend that includes both elements, as well as a vision of a fair young boy of great promise (Phæton) who was slain and drowned in the lake by the lightning of Zeus, the all-wise god ; in Wales, we find the wise Cerridwen, after a chase in which she displays mastery over the universe[27], throwing fair young Taliesin[28] into the waters (lake, river or ocean) to kill him, and wise Nefydd Hardd throwing Idwal into the lake to kill him. But Taliesin, at least, was to return from this ritual death mightier, wiser and stronger than any man had ever been, to be seen, almost certainly, as an avatar of Lug, and to fight and put in his place the arrogant King of Britain, Maelgwn. We will find his career has many points in common with Æneas', and Maelgwn, despite the difference in moral value, with Latinus'[29].

II.3 Æneas, Anchises and Avernus

When I first noticed that Greeks, Welsh and Romans all knew a Birdless Lake, I tought it a mere oddity. But the the oddities began to multiply before my eyes, until no reasonable person could deny that something more than casual seemed to bind the stories together. Consider : we are at the very start of the properly Italian figure of Æneas' adventures. Here, but not before, he is for the first time Æneas the head of a *Männerbund* of three hundred youths rather than Aineias king of a city-state in motion ; here, if not before[30], we may be certain that the Hellenic figure has quite given way to the Italic.

---

[27]   As P.K. FORD, *Taliesin*, *loc.cit.*, rightly points out.

[28]   He gots the name when Elphin, opening the coracle in which the boy had come ashore, exclaimed on the beauty of his forehead : *tal iesin* "fair forehead".

[29]   The Hindu legend of Krishna and the serpent Kaliya has several points in common with the stories of Avernus, Idwal, Taliesin and Phæton : the Birdless Lake, poisonous and surrounded by blighted country ; the beautiful boy untimely lost, whose body is in the lake, mourned like Phæton by weeping girls ; and the fact that the boy is in the final analysis not lost at all, but rather, like Taliesin/Lug and Æneas/Jupiter Indiges, the supreme god of his mythology. Cf. W. DONIGER O'FLAHERTY, *Hindu Myths*, Harmondsworth, 1975, N°60. The monstrous snake that hides in the lake and (apparently) kills Krishna might possibly be compared with the murderous mermaid of the Staffordshire birdless lake cited above.

[30]   I want to underline, however, that if any identifiable suture between Greek and Latin legendry exists, it must be sought before Acesta. Whether identified with Acesta, with Troy, or whatever, the fact that Æneas' band is so recognizably a *uer sacrum* presupposes a city to send it out ; even if the city is in all likelihood fabulous. This may also explain the many legendary cities and fortresses beyond the sea from which some of the invaders of Irish legend reached Ireland.

At this point of all points, where he reaches Italy and, at the same time, his expedition has for the first time the form of a *uer sacrum* rather than of a whole nation with women, children and old men ; here and nowhere else, we see him entering the World of the Dead - i.e. dying - by way of a Birdless Lake. A wise but rather fearsome old woman, not at all unlike Cerridwen, is his initiator, and bears him out again after he "died". He meets his dead father. Now, Lug is often the orphaned son of a murdered father ; and so is Lancelot, a hero identified with Lug by the giant of Arthurian studies, R.S. Loomis, in a classic study[31]. In the *Fate of the children of Tuirenn*, Lug demands from the protagonists the wergild for his dead father Cian, which consists in weapons and talismans of unique power that will enable him to fight and win the great war against the demonic Fomoire. That is to say, Lug gets his weapons of victory as a result of the fact that his father is dead. The Cian of the *Fate of the Children of Tuirenn* knows exactly what he is doing, and manipulates his killers so that his son, following his prophetic will, may both avenge him on his killers and acquire an invincible set of weapons and talismans.

Book VI of the *Æneid* has a lot in common with this. The prophetic intellect of dead Anchises points his son and his son's descendants the path of universal victory. Anchises is not murdered[32], but his absence is a very notable presence troughout the *Æneid*. Until he meets him in the Otherworld, Æneas is much more orphaned than we would expect an adult to be. On the other hand, the Æneas who has spoken with Anchises is a formidable being ; he has taken back from the world of the dead a more than mortal insight into the nature of the universe, denied to Odysseus, and the beginnings of identity and purpose, later to be refined by wise Evander and by prophetic Vulcan's shield. It is not exaggerated to call book VI a Western *BhagavadGītā*, and, of all of Virgil's works, it is the one that influenced Dante most.

Is this powerful religious content in any way mirrored in the *Fate of the Children of Tuirenn* ? The product of a Christian age[33], the piece is largely a romance, and its story is somewhat suspect. The protagonists are called "the three gods of Dana", and in another version, *The Second Battle of Mag Tuired,* the "three gods of Dana" bestow the weapons and plans for the great war on Lug and his allies quite freely and without any mention of compulsion or revenge. It is not clear that the characters are the same ; they might be the gods of skill, Goibniu the smith[34], Creidne the precious-metals smith, and Luchta the car-

---

3 1   In his foreword and footnotes to *Lanzelet. A Medieval Poem by Ulrich von Zatzikhoven*. Krisna, the supreme god of the *Mahābhārata*, is also the son of a persecuted and murdered father, and his story is particularly reminiscent of certain versions of Lancelot's story.

3 2   I am not suggesting that Latium ever knew of a legend of the murder of Æneas'/Indiges' father. In fact, our documents argue against the possibility, because, if such a legend was known, would Virgil, that mighty dramatizer, have passed the occasion of presenting such a dramatic plot element, and perhaps tying up a revenge story with Æneas' Latin wars ?

3 3   "Although... there is mention of an early transcription going back to the eleventh century, the tale reached us in a comparatively late modern version, preserved in several quite recent manuscripts of which the most recent, Egerton 208, goes back to the ninetheenth century" say the Italian editors whose translation I have : M.L. MAGINI - G. AGRATI, *cit.*.

3 4   There is a possible connection between Goibniu the smith and tragedies in the house of Lug. Apart from the matter of "the three gods of Dana", which seem to link them with Cian's slayers, his Welsh

penter. In the *Wooing of Etain*, the title actually belongs to Lug, the Dagda and Ogma. The subject is riddled with difficulties, but one fact stands out : in both the *Fate of the Children of Tuirenn* and the *Second Battle of Mag Tuired* - but not in the *Wooing of Etain*, whose subject matter has nothing to do with it - Lug gets the instruments of victory over the Fomoire, enemies of the gods and of Ireland, from "the three gods of Dana". So far as we can judge, this is the central tale of the gods of pagan Ireland, and the role of the three gods of Dana seems to be decisive.

What is more, Lug is more like a supreme god in the *Fate of the Children of Tuirenn* than anywhere else in the whole of Irish literature. Before the saga's protagonists are so much as mentioned, he has an awesome opening scene in which he comes to the plain of Tara literally like the rising of the Sun[35], he imposes a wergild on them that covers the whole of Earth ; and his wisdom is such that he manages to win both the instruments of his victory and revenge for his father. Even though he is absent through most of the story, he dominates it from end to end, as the children of Tuirenn are driven sadly from sea to sea, from battle to battle, from raid to raid, by his unappeasable demands. I think there are grounds for believeing this story might have had a peculiar religious importance.

II.4 Sailing around Latium

After meeting his father, Æneas puts to sea to reach Latium ; and this is a matter for analysis in itself. There should be no need for a sea journey, since Lake Avernus is part of Latinus' kingdom : certainly a distant southern fief but belonging to Latinus' vassal Œbalus, Lord of Campania[36]. Likewise, Bala Lake (Llyn Tegid, the fief of Cerridwen's husband Tegid) is a distant border part of southern Gwynedd, and Taliesin entered the sea only to be swept to land, forty years later, in a weir on the river Conwy (on Gwynedd's north coast). There was no need to imagine a forty-year sea journey from Gwynedd to Gwynedd : it's not that big a country !

Taliesin and Æneas make landfall at the mouth of a major river : the Conwy, the Tiber.

They arrive at a very sacred time and in the middle of celebrations in which a large number of people take part. Taliesin is found on the eve of Samhain[37], the beginning of the Celtic year, in place of the great catch of fish with which, every year, Elphin used to feast all his friends ; Æneas meets his first Italians just as the great yearly sacrifice to Hercules is being celebrated by the whole assembled people of Evander. Although Elis Gruffydd gives no religious dimension to Elphin's yearly fish dinner, several facts amply prove that it was a supernatural kind of thing, both magical and mystical. It was found in that particular weir

---

counterpart Govannon is known as the slayer of Lleu's elder brother Dylan eil Ton in the *Mabinogi of Math ab Mathonwy*.

[35]   St. Patrick's *Confession* makes it certain that the pagan Irish he knew identified their supreme god with the Sun. He dedicates a longish passage towards the climatic conclusion to pointing out that the true God *made* the Sun. It seems therefore unchallengable that, in pagan Irish cult, Lug was identified with the Sun.

[36]   Virgil, *Æneid* VII 733-743.

[37]   P.K. FORD, *The* Mabinogi, p.165 : Taliesin is found at All Hallows' Eve (Hallowe'en), that is well know to correspond to the Celtic festival of the turn of the year.

every year at a sacred time, the fish being magically provided ; and the matter of a miraculous catch of fish could not help suggesting, to Christian readers[38] the many miraculous catches of the Gospels[39].

Both Taliesin and Æneas meet, and are made welcome by, the king's enemies, Evander and Elphin, which is to lead them to conflict with the king. Maelgwn rules over Gwynedd, and is overlord of all Britain. Though a darker figure than Latinus, he is, like him, a great national figure, a king by right, descended from several mighty ancestors, yet at the same time the founder of a new dinasty and new ethnic realities[40]. And there is a distinct possibility that Elphin might originally have represented an element ethnically distinct from the Welsh of Maelgwn : Elphin is Welsh for Alpine, the Goidelic leader of the Scottish settlements of Dalriada in the sixth or seventh century. If Elphin was originally seen as a foreigner[41], this would give us a further parallel with Evander, a Greek whose nationality is highly relevant to the dialectic of Insider and Outsider in the Æneid legend[42]. Both Maelgwn and Latinus find themselves having to fight the heroes, Taliesin, Æneas, not of their own will - Maelgwn knows nothing about Taliesin until the hero actually appears at his court - but because the heroes had befriended their enemies. It is an unequal clash, in which Taliesin is quite as crushingly victorious as Æneas ; in both cases, too, the hero spares the king and even establishes certain sacred aspects of his kingdom on a sound footing, despite the fact that the king has behaved badly towards himself and/or his hosts, Elphin, Evander. I think there is no doubt that the stories of Æneas' arrival in Latium and Taliesin's arrival in Gwynedd are closely related.

There is a geographical dimension to this that deserves close attention. To follow it, we must look at a discrepancy between Virgil and Dionysios. The poet made his heroic company land at the mouth of the Tiber, rather than, as the historian, near the site of the royal capital Laurentum. In so doing, he involved himself in such geographical nonsense as to make me wonder whether he had any idea of the country around Rome at all. The messengers of Æneas make straight for the king's court at Laurentum ; before they do this, they have already explored as far as the Numicius marshes, which are actually farther south than

[38] And all surviving Welsh myths of Lleu and Taliesin are strongly Christianized.
[39] The connection of fishing and the capture of supernatural wisdom is however probably older than Christianity. It is well attested in Ireland, where Finn mac Cumhaill gains the magical wisdom of a poet by sucking his thumb after scorching it while cooking a magical salmon (M.L. MAGINI - G. AGRATI, *op.cit.*, p.354). Salmon have always been the kings of fish in the British Isles, and it cannot be doubted that the nobleman's feast of fish that Elphin was to provide his friends would have been mainly salmon, fish of rank. Instead of which, he found Taliesin.
[40] Maelgwn gained the rule of all Wales in a challenge involving the waters of the ocean, and was the successor of Arthur, but in a greatly changed Britain. Tradition makes him in effect the first ruler of all Wales after the rise of the English kingdoms.
[41] I must however add that the existing legends of Elphin and his father Gwyddno Garanhir do nothing to suggest either a Goidelic origin or an ientification with the historical Alpin. The latter, however, is both unnecessary and not suggested by Latin parallel. Evander was not a real Greek historical or legendary character, but a Latin idea of a Greek settler ; the character was invented in Latium. By the same token, all that is necessary to make a parallel is to suppose that, at some point in the Welsh cultural past, the name Elphin should have been recognizable as that of a non-Welsh foreigner ; which it almost certainly was.
[42] For one thing, his son Pallas cannot claim the leadership of the Etruscans or the king-making hand of Lavinia because he is of mixed blood, half Sabellian.

4

Laurentum's traditional site. Meanwhile, the god of the Tiber bids Æneas sail up his river to meet Evander and be given a royal title and weapons. The great poetry in this episode cannot disguise the bare incredibility of the time element[43] : Æneas takes one and half days to get there by boat, from Ostia Antica to the Forum Boarium, less than a day's walk, and we are told that the Tiber stilled its current to make the ships go faster !

The end result is nothing else thant this : Æneas' effective landfall is not in the centre of the land, but on the Tiber ; the northernmost and greatest river of old Latium, its border with the dangerous Etruscan outlands. He emerges from the Birdless Lake in the Campanian southern marches of Latinus' kingdom, only to sail to its Tiberine northern marches.

Now, as we saw, Cerridwen threw the future Taliesin either into a lake, or into a river, or into the ocean. I do wish that Elis Gruffydd, the honest and consciencious Elizabethan chronicler who wrote down (much against his better judgement) the whole story, had seen fit to tell us which river, or lake, or sea, this was ; but we can guess. Cerridwen was based on Llyn Tegid ; well, look at a map. If it was either Llyn Tegid or its river, the Dee, the boy would have floated downstream in a large curve all around Gwynedd, to reach the sea near Chester. If she cast him directly into the ocan, the most likely spot must have been Barmouth Bay or Tremadog Bay.

The thing to be noticed is this : that whichever way Taliesin went, he would have floated in a half-circle around Gwynedd before he reached Conwy mouth ; and there, he did not meet Maelgwn, king of the land[44], but rather a character, Elphin, who was going to become that king's opponent. It takes a further journey to reach the royal centre. In a closely similar manner, Æneas sails from the Gulf of Naples to Rome, and thence to Agylla ; since the coastline from Naples to Rome is fairly straight, this is as close to a half-circle around Latium by water as circumstances allow. When he makes landfall, it is not the king or the king's men that he meets, but his enemy Evander. To reach King Latinus he must make two more journeys : one by sea, and one overland through thickets of enemy spears. Since Maelgwn's fortess is on Anglesey, whereas Taliesin lives with Elphin on the mainland, he too has to cross both land and sea to beard Maelgwn in his halls. When Æneas approaches the walls of Laurentum bearing fire in book XII, it is the first time he has been near the king ; likewise, Taliesin has never been near Maelgwn's castle until he comes in wrath to deliver his patron Elphin : a coming, in its way, as terrible as Æneas'.

This, then, is the situation.

The site of Taliesin's initiation, and the site of Æneas', are near the southern borders of their respective kingdoms ; their further water journeys bypass the royal centres of the land (Anglesey, Laurentum) to reach its other extremity, where they make final landfall on the shores of a great river, on a sacred occasion. We might add that both cases involve oddly unrealistic mixtures of deep-sea and river sailing, especially if we take Taliesin to have floated down the Dee. Anthough I have never been in county Merioneth, the upper Dee

---

43   Virgil, *Æneid* VIII 94-95.
44   Who lived not there but in Anglesey.

seems an unlikely place for sailing downstream ; and although the Tiber is a broad and comparatively even river, I cannot envisage Æneas' ships travelling up it as far as Agylla[45], let alone Tarchon's large fleet coming down it. As a matter of fact, unlikelihood seems to be the keynote of these journeys ; there is something deliberately not credible about them[46], for it seems impossible that their tellers, familiar as they were with the geography of Latium and Gwynedd, did not realize the sheer oddity of the routes they described.

II.4a Back to Anchises

Be that as it may, parallels between the initiation of the Welsh Cosmic Sage and that of the Latin National Father are definitely too many and too peculiar to disregard. We have to accept that the two stories are related, going back to a time before the two peoples settled their historical homes ; their imagination had simply seized on actual features of the landscape - Llyn Tegid and Llyn Idwal in Gwynedd, Avernus in Italy - as corresponding to the lake of their legend. The question springs to mind : how did the Latin account come to be so disfigured as to lack cauldrons, spells, or even deaths ?

I propose the following hypothesis, adding that it is hardly more than guesswork. Legends, we know, only live[47] if they are associated with a living cultural reality such as a temple, a festival, a social group. Explanation myths connected with some natural or geographical feature always turn out to be religiously or culturally significant. What isn't interesting isn't explained ; our ancestors had no myths for the origin of the donkey-cart or the working apron. The myth of Æneas and Avernus must therefore have been the myth for some ceremony or initiation. This would certainly have been milder than the myth itself, including a symbolic death and rebirth and some instruction into the lore of the profession or caste involved, given by one of its older and wiser members.

The best-known symbol of death and rebirth is of course the descent into, and re-ascent from, a cave ; which in turn, if a lake was the mythical instrument of death, had to be in the area of one. What we have, I would suggest, is not the original legend of the Golden Boy and the Birdless Lake, but rather a fabulous record of initiation rituals based on that legend. The young initiated went down into a cave to receive his instruction "from the dead". This would explain the Virgilian cave, which corresponds to nothing in any Welsh story ; the cave stood for death, which the Welsh stories presented explicitly.

The circumnavigation of the land and the elaborate and rythmical crossings of sea and land and sea are clearly part of a ritual whose precise content escapes me, though experts in Indian rites may find them significant. One important aspect is however worth discussing : the dead father's involvement.

---

[45]   Modern Cerveteri. The town itself is nowhere near the river.

[46]   Did the Mantuan ships, for instance, double southern Italy and sail up the Tiber to reach Agylla ? In that case they would have undertaken a greater journey than Æneas' own, and Virgil could have written a local patriotic epic about his own town. Or did the Mantuans come overland, crossing the Apennines ? That might have been even more of an epic. Unreality just glares at you every time you consider this group of episodes.

[47]   Unless set down in writing.

44

Initiation as such would not necessarily demand the presence of the father of the initiated : the initiator might as well be a priest or priestess or god. Anchises' presence doesn't correspond to anything in the Odyssey or other Greek journeys to the Otherworld, either. It must be specific to the ritual I am postulating. I suggest that this ritual placed the father in the position of a dead person with respect to his son. The fact that he actively instructed his son means that, in ordinary non-ritual reality, the parent in question was alive and healthy, *compos mentis* enough to transmit a body of sacred learning to his son. The father "died" ; the son went down to the "world of the dead" to be instructed by his "dead" parent ; he came back an initiate, a full adult with an identity of his own, removed from the control of his parents. This feels like the reverse of the *uer sacrum*, where it is the young men who ritually acquire the status of dead men[48].

This makes a lot of sense. Latin culture lay immense emphasis on paternal power and filial obedience. In theory, Roman parents had absolute power over children their whole life long. They were said to be allowed to sell them into slavery or execute them. It is quite possible that a ritual of initiation should exist that allowed an adult to function as an independent being, while satisfying the absurd claims of the ideology by making the all-powerful father as though dead to his son. If only the parent's death extinguishes his authority, then the ritual death would function as a practical release from it. Certainly no society could function in which any adult whose parents happened to be alive could be subjected constantly and at a moment's notice to any whim they might be pleased to entertain[49].

[48] Incidentally, I am certainly not saying that the Avernus initiation rituals survived in any form in Virgil's own days ; quite to the contrary, there is a tone of fable and misunderstanding in the whole sixth book that makes me think that any such activity had ceased so long before his time as to have become a myth itself. This is another aspect in which it parallels the *uer sacrum*, whose historicity, as I said, I likewise doubt.
[49] The Classical picture of early Roman views is simply too stern, and in my view any such picture of past societies will always be found to be at least exaggerated and probably legendary. No human society can live for a very long time with eternally long faces : if nothing else, the gift of humour is never quite absent from the human race.

CHAPTER III : THE COSMIC SON

III.1 Lug, Æneas, Jupiter Indiges and the Sun

So far we have established that Æneas has so many similarities with the Celtic figures of Lug/Lleu and Taliesin that it is impossible to dissociate them. Now Lug is, throughout the Celtic world, a god of many death-legends. Even in the Irish *Book of Conquests,* where the gods are quite pedantically assigned one death story each[1], his is the most widely mentioned, the one with most variants, and the most impressive. Lleu dies and is resurrected in the *Mabinogi* of *Math ap Mathonwy.* His son or incarnation Cúchulainn has one of the most baroque and beautiful death-scenes in heroic literature. Taliesin has no known death-scene, but his son Afaon had a famous one[2].

Despite the popularity of his death legend, Lug was, throughout the Celtic world, worshipped as the chief god, a living and everlasting cosmic power. This is not at all unlike the fact that Æneas, whose death in battle was well known, was nevertheless worshipped as a god in the holiest of places, the ritual centre of ancient Latium, Lavinium. But that is not all : the divine name under which he was worshipped was none other than that of Jupiter : Jupiter Indiges[3], the Latin supreme god.

An innocent observer would immediately conclude that this is the most important parallel yet found ; which is indeed my own opinion. But things are by no means so easy. Greece knew demi-gods, children of immortals, but not one hero who relates to a god as Kṛṣṇa does to Viṣṇu ; and Roman culture as we know is entirely under the shadow of Hellenism. If we are proposing to show that prehistoric Roman religion included ideas of divine incarnation, let alone that Æneas himself was an incarnate deity, the onus of proof lies on us : we are going against the whole stream of Classical thought.

The first point that springs to mind is the evident, though often doubted, identification of Romulus with Quirinus, third member of the divine triad of archaic Rome : Jupiter, Mars, Quirinus[4]. Classical culture had no trouble with this god, because his career, from his birth from a god and a mortal to his final apotheosis, is not unlike that of the great demigods of Greece : Herakles, Dionysos. We have already seen that the legend of Romulus is closely connected with that of Æneas, answering to it at every point, and certainly his final mysterious apotheosis (wich, like that of Romulus, has two contradictory accounts) corresponds to that of his forefather.

---

[1]   *Lebor Gabála Érenn* (henceforth LGE), poem LXI.

[2]   R. BROMWICH, *op.cit.,* triads 25 and 33. These are two of only three triads in this important collection that mention the son of Taliesin, so that we may be reasonably certain that his death-legend was the most important part of his legend. In one version of triad 25 he is said to have avenged his murder from beyond the grave, not unlike the Lleu of *Math,* who avenges himself on Gronw after his own death.

[3]   Livy, I 2 6. As we have already found some parallels between Lug, Æneas and the *Mahābhārata*'s god Kṛṣṇa, readers won't be surprised to be told that a whole book of the Indian epic (*MausalaParvan*) is dedicated to the death legend of this everlasting and eternally adored figure.

[4]   G. DUMEZIL, *Religion romaine, passim.*

Every source gives *Indiges* as the title of the divinized Æneas, but only one mentions the identification with Jupiter : Livy, the historian. Other texts treat *Indiges* alone, treating it as the god's name, though it is obviously an adjective, and is treated as such elsewhere[5]. One source speaks not of Jupiter Indiges but of Sol (the Sun) Indiges. No such confusion reigns about Romulus Quirinus. Why this confusion ? Were the Ancients ignorants about the hero ? No : many versions of his legend were known. Was the matter unimportant ? No : it could not be more important. Were the witnesses ignorant ? No : Livy, Dionysios and Virgil were among the most learned men of the age. Was the evidence hard to access ? No : Lavinium, with its six hundred priests, still existed. Dionysios visited it, as did Timæus before him, and was struck by its beatiful tree gardens.

No : if the Hellenized Romans of the age of Augustus did not agree on the divine identity of Æneas, it is because they genuinely could not understand the data. They had all they needed, but it made no sense to them. The theories Hellenistic Rome proposed for the word *indiges* prove that Hellenistic culture was quite incapable of explaining it. Terentius Varro of Reate, "the most learned man in Rome", in Virgil's time, gave an explanation, accepted by both Dionysios[6] and Ovid, that is one of the worst outrages ever perpetrated by timid, dogmatic intellectual prigs ("it is below the dignity of the gods to do this or that !") against long-suffering gods, not only removing Jupiter's great name, but translating the mysterious adjective, if you please, as autochtonous "born of the soil", as though the essential alienness of the hero were not the core of the legend ! This is Hellenism at its very worst, nervous before the supernatural and full of pat and inadequate explanations.

Clearly, the Hellenistic mind had run into something that could not fit its categories. Now Livy was Hellenistic with the best of them. If he committed himself to such a statement of fact in the great work of his life, then as fact we must take it : in Livy's own day, the six hundred Laviniate priests used to invoke Æneas by the greatest of names : that of God Himself. Livy, with his innate distaste for miracle stories, is absolutely not the kind of writer to toss that Name around for no reason. He did not believe that the gods manifested their power so directly[7]. His words, both troubled and solemn, show that he was terribly unhappy at such information

> He was buried (*situs*[8]) - whatever may be just (*ius*) and propitious (*fas*) to call him - on the shore of the river Numicius ; they call him *Jupiter Indiges*.

---

[5]   In the ritual of *deuotio*, in which a Roman commander consecrated himself and the enemy army to the gods as human sacrifices, the adjective is used in the plural *Indigetes* to describe a whole category of gods (*Di Indigetes*). Unfortunately, we know nothing about these gods. See Appendix III.

[6]   Dyonisios of Halikanassos, I 64 5.

[7]   On a couple of occasions we shall see him quite obscure a story so that it should not be clear that a miracle happened.

[8]   The word *situs* is a singular circumlocution, from the verb *sinere* "to place, to drop". Latin would normally use *humatus* or *sepultus*. While certainly part of the unusually solemn language Livy adopts here, it also has to do with Lavinium's religious meaning : after all his wanderings, the hero who sought Latium is now *situs* here for ever ; and yet, at the same time, he is the god of the whole universe. The expression *situs* removes the sense of finality and helplessness from death and of burial : someone who is "placed" or "left", does not have to be as passive as someone who is *sepultus*. He can be a spiritual reality, even a universal one, and yet be rooted in the one holy spot.

This is the language of a man caught between a rock and a hard place, convinced that it is neither *ius* nor *fas* to call a mortal, however great, by the name of Jupiter, and equally convinced that the locals do so and consider it both *ius* and *fas*.

What, then, of the expression *Sol Indiges* ? Is the hero identified with the Sun as well as Jupiter ? In a word : yes ; the two altars raised at Æneas' traditional landing place, mentioned by Dionysius as "Trojan work"[9], i.e. visibly very ancient, and oriented in the solar direction of East and West, are sufficient proof of the cult's solar character. The two things are not mutually exclusive, since it is by no means certain that the Sun as such was an autonomus deity or object of cult in Italy, rather than an attribute of one or more gods. I know of not one temple, priesthood, flaminate, altar or college dedicated to the day star as such. Arguments for a Latin cult of the Sun seems to depend on nothing more than a presumption that a Sun-god is an inevitable part of any mythology : surely a doubtful premise. There is something like desperation in the arguments, actually offered, that rely on Circe, a solar figure, no doubt, but an exclusively Greek one[10] whose location on a Latin headland was neither more nor less than a matter of lucky misapplication of legendary geography !

Among the Celts, solar aspects were shared between Lug and Ogma, both called "Sun-Faced", and Dagda, incarnation of Fire[11]. Of these it is Lug who appears most memorably like the star of day, in the above-mentioned *Fate of the Children of Tuirenn*. The identity not only between initiate mortal hero (who in fact dies) and supreme god, but also between supreme god and Sun-god, far from causing us problems, seems to be the strongest evidence so far for my identification of Æneas with Lug, and sheds a strong and totally unexpected light on the Latin Jupiter.

III.2 Ages

If we accept that Æneas' divine name Jupiter Indiges is no joke or mistake, but proof that the being worshipped on the banks of the Numicius was in fact an aspect of the Latin supreme god, one huge oddity springs to our eyes : he is young. A god who has fatherhood in his very name, whose name means nothing else than "the Father God", might not unreasonably be expected to figure as a fatherly middle-aged figure. That is how we think of him under the bearded Hellenistic guise of the god of the ambrosial locks ; broad, muscular, forceful, forty-to-fifty in human terms. And the youth of the Latin figure is not borrowed from the Greek hero either : Aineias, though of an age to fight sword in hand, was not a boy, but a married man with a son. His father was positively decrepit with age.

But the more we look at the evidence, the stronger the case becomes for the poetic intuition of Giuseppe Ungaretti[12], who saw Æneas as young and even ingenuous. Young Pallas

[9]   Dionysios of Halikarnassos, I 55 2.
[10]   Cf. Appendix I.
[11]   As shown by his names Aed Abrat "Fire of the Eye" and Ruadh Rofhessa "Red One of Great Knowledge".
[12]   A great modern Italian poet. Some of his words : "Perennial beauty... bound inexorably to perishing, to images, to earthly vicissitudes, to history... took in my mind the face of Æneas. Æneas is beauty, youth, naivety, always in search of a promised land..."

meets Æneas and his company by calling them *iuuenes* : a singularly inappropriate description of the patriarchs of Troy[1 3], and a seriously disrepectful thing to call them if they were in fact his elders. On the other hand, we have a good few reasons to suspect that he might be in fact describing what he sees, what was there in the earliest version of the legend.

1° Few things were as central to Roman thinking as the division between *seniores* and *iuniores* ; therefore we cannot, *a priori,* imagine that their national epic would ignore or pervert one of the bases of their society.

2° We saw at the very start that Æneas and his three or six hundred companions make up a *uer sacrum.* But the members of the *uer sacrum* are by definition youths at the threshold of manhood, all members of the same age class. And the *uer sacrum* - a *iunior* ritual death that Æneas and his three hundred companions embody - runs side by side with a *senior* ritual death, the one I proposed to see in the appearance of Anchises in Avernus.

3° Proceeding from this, we note that both the Welsh Lleu and the Irish Lug are presented as glorious youths in the episodes parallel to the legend of the *Æneid* : Lleu when he wins weapons, name, kingdom and wife, and Lug when he comes from across the sea with his glorious company (an age-class company of young males) to fight a great war[1 4]. Taliesin is a child, even ; and his pseudo-Christian identification is not with the Trinity or with the First or Third Persons[1 5], but with the Second Person, the Son. Two partial parallels, Phaeton and Kriṣṇa in the legend of the serpent Kaliya, are glorious golden youths.

4° If we accept the idea of a middle-aged Æneas, we tangle ourselves in all sorts of contradictions. Anchises tells Æneas that Lavinia shall bear him the only son of their union when he is not merely *senex* but *longaeuus* : not merely belonging to the category of the aged, but positively ancient[1 6]. Yet Virgil, in one of his telltale slips of the pen, makes Jupiter promise Venus (among many other things) that her son will rule Latium for no more than three years before becoming a god[1 7]. Therefore, according to the chronology, Æneas passed away no more than four years after his landing, at which he was, at the very least, hale and vigorous, and yet Virgil says *longaeuo* !

5° Structurally, Æneas is in a *junior* position, in the most literal sense of the word, as compared with Latinus, as he is to marry his daughter.

6° Latinus also "makes him a man" in another sense, by giving him land of his own. This places Æneas in something as a vassal position - although a *sui generis* vassal - and it is highly significant in term of the king's exclusive right of the land. The direct parallel with Math giving Lleu a fief and a bride confirms the point. Æneas' Etruscan kingship, found for him by Evander, is a transient and somewhat ghosty thing, with a typically Evandrian note

---

[1 3] Evander repeats the very same expression a few dozen lines later : Virgil, *Æneid* VIII 273.
[1 4] Especially in the *Fate of the Children of Tuirenn.*
[1 5] There is no suggestion of that beyond his ambiguous claim to have been "with" the Tetragrammaton.
[1 6] Virgil, *Æneid* VI 764.
[1 7] Virgil, *Æneid* I 265. Dionysios (I 64 3) says that Æneas' apotheosis took place no more than three years after Latinus' death in battle, which corresponds to the war of the *Æneid* ; therefore Dionysios confirms the *Æneid* I 265 chronology and contradicts the VI 764 one.

of impermanence ; Lavinium, on the other hand, is for all time. Yet the Etruscan kingship is also a gift from a *senior*, old Evander himself.

7° The war of the Æneid is structured as a double chain of vendette ; a hero kills another in revenge for the death of a third[18]. One of the two is distinctly an affair of *iuniores* : Turnus kills Pallas, who killed Halæsus, all of them very young men. Virgil underlines the fact that young Lausus, whose vendetta involves his majestic father Mezentius (certainly a *senior*), is not involved in this particular sequence of killings[19] ; but Æneas is. If a *senior* were at the end of the Halæsus-Pallas-Turnus chain of of *iuniores,* it would look odd and unbalanced ; but it is Æneas who is the end term of the chain. If Æneas had been conceived as a *senior*, it would surely have been his son Iulus, rather than himself, who put and end to Turnus' young life in the name of young slain Pallas ; and the epic would have a different end.

8° Lug is fostered away from Ireland by Tailtiu, who later follows him to the island and dies there[20] ; her close connexion with the great god is emphasized by the fact the the *oenach*[21] of his festival, Lugnasad, was celebrated in her holy place. It is probably relevant that the first clearly and undeniably Italian stage of Æneas' legend after the Birdless Lake is the death and burial of his "nurse" Caieta at Gaeta[22], named for her. Only young men have nurses living[23] !

9° The parallel with the conditon of *iunior* of the Irish and Welsh Lug/Lleu is strongest exactly in those things in which the Celtic figures appear as unformed, dependent, subject to acts of initiation and emancipation from older, more formed powers : in short, *iuniores.* Æneas must be given arms and wins a kingdom and a wife, like the just-formed future

---

[18]   Once again, this brings to mind some much later aspects of Italian - especially central and southern Italian - culture. Family feuds were an unfortunate and frequent occurrence down the centuries ; they contributed greatly to the spread of banditism throughout the Appennines and the South : when someone found himself on the losing side in a feud, or was forced to flee because of a murder, he often took to the hills and became a bandit, and the Mafia wars of recent times are only one of their developments (the Mafia itself being of course based, as a culture, on families). As late as the seventies - and, for all I know, even now - there were deep south towns where ongoing family feuds, which had little to do with Mafia activities as such, killed dozens of people. The element of personal and, more importantly, family hostility, in the war of the Æneid has a nasty, depressing kind of familiarity.

[19]   In *Æneid* X 433-438, he actually brings them quite close together, only to deny readers the spectavle of a clash. Following the slaughter of the previous verses, a heroic duel would have seemed very much on the cards, but Virgil delays the expected climax, to underline the fact that the two young men were not fated to die at each other's hand : "Soon are their fates awaiting, under a greater foe". Pallas was the destined prey of Turnus, Lausus of Æneas.

[20]   LGE VII 311.

[21]   "Sacred festival", but the word means more than that : it means "unity", and refers to the mystic reunion of a scattered world.

[22]   Gaeta lies outside the borders of *Latium uetus*, the traditional Latin heartland, whereas Tailtiu (modern Teltown) is at the core of Meath, the historical centre of Ireland. This fact has some consequences for the study of Roman origins. It is, of course, an accepted fact that the area which annalistic tradition regards as Volscan, including Gaeta, was only overrun in the fifth century BC, and was Ausonian (proto-Latin) before.

[23]   Dionysios mentions two women who died at various points on the Italian coastline and gave their names to the places where they died. This is *prima facie* suspicious, since all the women were supposed to have been left behind ; plus, neither of them plays any role in the story, and their names, Prochyta and Leukosia, are quite painfully Hellenic ; whereas Caieta is unmistakably Italic. She is also the only such figure to be mentioned by Virgil. Nevertheless this reduplication of the theme of Caieta's death and burial on a headland shows that it was deeply bound up with the Æneas legend.

supreme god must in *Math* ; and, like him, must receive them from a king (Math, Latinus), a wise initiator (Gwydion, Evander), and his mother (Arianrhod, Venus) ; all of them clearly *senior* characters in every way. In *Math,* these are *seniores* of Lleu even in the sense of being physically older, and it is for this reason that they are able to bestow on the unfortunate boy what he needs to be a man ; in the Æneid the age of both Evander and Latinus is stressed, and Venus, though ever-young, cannot but be *senior* to Æneas : she is his mother ! Likewise it is a mere boy, Gwion, who becomes Taliesin ; and the initiatic cauldron that makes him into a god is worked by a member of an older age class, Cerridwen. Cerridwen's rank as an elder is not something we infer. It is a structural part of the story : Cerridwen has a son, Great Brân, who is of Gwion's age[24].

Not only is Æneas young : he never stays to grow old. We have seen enough to know we must disregard the Hellenistic surface gloss and consider plot and situations ; once we stand back and consider his part in the legend, from beginning to end, a peculiar quality starts to become apparent. No other character in the legend bears so few characteristics of steady presence, duration, regularity : not Evander, the true *longaeuus* ; not great silver-haired Latinus ; not Lavinia, Silvius' brave and energetic dowager mother ; not even Ascanius of the fifty-year reign. The passing of Æneas through Latium has all the hallmarks of something swift, epiphanic, lightninglike. He does not even stay to see his son Silvius born. Amata's protests in VII 359-365 may well foreshadow this : she implies that it is the Trojans' very nature to come and go, not to stay, and paints a pathetic picture of deserted motherhood. If she were talking not of herself, but of her daughter - whom Æneas, in a very real sense, leaves alone with their child - these words would be prophetic.

III.3 Ascanius and his foster mother

But if Æneas is to be counted as a *iunior,* a lad in his twenties if not less, what does that make Ascanius, his supposed son, who is about ten in both the epic and Livy ? What indeed. There are perceptible problems with his family status, which separate him widely from his half-brother Silvius. The most important single feature of Silvius is that, despite the romantic and dangerous circumstances of his birth in the forests, he is the perfectly regular, justified link, expected at this point and necessary at this point, in the steady ordered sequence of Latinus' succession. We have already come across the dialectic of inside and outside, Latium and the legendary worlds beyond the sea, in the epic ; and he is of and for this world, a king sprung from kings and bearing arms, whereas Ascanius Iulus is an alien, a king with no Latin ancestors and no royal descendants. His descendants retire from the kingship to a high priesthood in holy Lavinium, a city built by the alien Trojans with no contributions from local Latins at all.

---

[24]   There is also a mention of a fellow-worker of Gwion's, a "blind old man" (sic !) who stirs ans tends the cauldron.

An interesting detail on Ascanius' background is found in the famous episode of Euryalus and Nisus[25]. These heroes' Greek names are reason enough to suspect that they did not belong to the original Latin legend ; elsewhere in the epic, true Greek names of their sort are only found on minor victim characters in Homer-style lists of warriors slain by the major heroes in the intervals of killing each other. The *Æneid*'s norm is that major characters purported to be Greek have either Latinized names such as Hercules (for Herakles) and Æneas, or, in one case, a very generic word like Evander (= "Good Man"), that anybody could have constructed. The rest are Latin. Also, despite its high emotion, the story of Euryalus and Nisus seems a bit pointless : it does nothing to advance the story , and when the bloody night is over both armies are just where they were when it began. Its homosexual context cannot, for that matter, be Latin ; the Latin view of homosexuality, found in that obstinate nationalist Juvenal, is not sympathetic, and I think it can be shown that Latin legend knew no homosexual loves. The *Æneid*'s only major homosexual passage is the story of Evander's youthful love for Anchises, which is clearly one of Virgil's inventions[26].

Let us add that the council of war before the boys' unlucky expedition is quite out of keeping with a *uer sacrum*, a company of young men of one age class ; for absolutely the only time in the whole epic, the Trojan voices we hear are those of old men, councillors with white beards, senatorial figures. It is probably true that Virgil himself did not understand the Trojan company as a *uer sacrum* ; but he mentions nothing like it elsewhere. It is Latinus and Turnus who are surrounded by friends of various ages and councillors ready to give advice. It is part of their role as kings, leaders of nations, sourrounded by relatives and courts ; Æneas has no court, no relatives, and no proper nation with him : only a military company of young warriors under his orders. He makes his decisions alone. Here, however, the camp of young men is suddenly transformed into a besieged citadel with old mothers, children, old warriors in council ; for a moment we are in Homer's Troy, not in Latium. I think that there can be little doubt that Virgil not only inserted this episode in the greater legend, but made it himself out of whole cloth.

Why ? Well, it must have a point for the larger story. Virgil took ten years to write as much as he did, and I can hardly imagine him adding a fancy embellishment purely for the sake of it ; it does not agree with the desperate seriousness with wich he approached his task. Indeed, if this great artist had a flaw, it was that he was markedly humourless[27]. So, to undestand what, beyond his picture of fair and courageous young lovers, it is doing in the greatest story Virgil knew of, we must look at it within the larger legend. And the only effect that Euryalus and Nysus' death has on the plot is this : Ascanius gains a foster mother. This is the promise he makes to Euryalus about his mother

> Thus shall she be my mother ; just the name

---

[25]   Virgil, *Æneid* IX 176-502.
[26]   Virgil, *Æneid* VIII 157-168. Other allusions to homosexual loves - such as X 324-327 - are merely part of Virgil's Homeric catalogues of dead heroes with Greek names, and he would be a brave man who tried to give them a pre-Virgilian origin.
[27]   Compare him to his great contemporary Horace.

> Creusa shall she lack...[28]

in case her son fails to return from his daring mission.

This promise is the obvious point. All the other rewards offered to the two young lovers are predicated upon their success ; if they make it through Latin lines, they will get such and such prizes. This, and this alone, is predicated upon their failure ; if they fail and die, then Iulus must adopt Euryalus' mother as his own. But if the episode is interpolated, from beginning to end, by Virgil, this means that this was the conclusion he wanted to lead it to : Iulus, extraordinarily, adopts on his own initiative a second mother who is never to be the wife of his father Æneas. And we notice that there are two bold and fair boys, but only one mother ; Virgil, I think, had to explain her, and created the beautiful episode of Euryalus and Nysus purely because he liked to think of fair and gallant homosexual boys.

Now it is interesting that Livy also had problems with Ascanius' mother. Her identity seems to have troubled him and his sources profoundly[29]. He speaks of Iulus' birth in tones of solemn doubt ; he is not sure that Creusa actually was his mother ; he wildly suggests there might have been twin Ascanii ; and, piling absurdity upon absurdity, he proposes that Ascanius foster mother was nobody else than... Lavinia ! The woman, if you please, whom both Virgil and Dionysios show hiding her pregnancy and her son Silvius from Ascanius, because, Dionysios explains, her son, rather than Ascanius' sons, is the true heir, and she has cause to fear Ascanius' jealousy[30] !

This leads to one useful conclusion : the problem of Ascanius' mother and foster mother was one of those points that troubled Hellenistic Latin antiquarians. We find Virgil inserting a massive and magnificent interpolation to explain, in the end, that he had a foster mother, and Livy botching up an extra Ascanius and making wild guesses as to who his foster mother was. It is interesting to find that Livy, difficult though he found this point, nevertheless is clear in his mind that Ascanius had a foster mother. Why should he ? Why should the Latin witnesses be so unanimous that Creusa never reached Latium, indeed that she might not have been Iulus' mother at all ?

This fog of evasion and concealed doubts is beginning to sound rather familiar. We have met it before. There was something unusual about Iulus' mother and foster mother, that agitated Hellenistic minds, pretty much as did the identification of Æneas with Jupiter.

As for why learned men such as Virgil and Livy went to such pains to explain the oddity, there is a most obvious reason : the ancestry of Iulus was quite a live issue in their time, when the head of the Roman state based his claim to power on his being the heir of Iulus' descendant Iulius Cæsar[31]. Both the Mantuan poet and the Paduan historian were

---

28   Virgil, *Æneid* IX 297-298.
29   Livy, I 3 2.
30   Dionysios of Halikarnassos, I 70 2-4.
31   on p. 14n.5, I gave reasons to suspect that Iulian claim to be descended from Iulus Æneas' son might have been a serious issue as early as the age of Cato the Elder. Cato is the only historian to deny it, and indeed he unifies the royal capital Laurentum and the holy city Lavinium ; the point of that being that if Lavinium is the same as Laurentum, then Æneas just moved into Latinus' capital instead of building a separate city, and Latin history had, literally, no place for the descendants of Iulus, who, in other versions,

very much of Octavian's party, his personal acquaintances and protégés ; his legal ancestry[32] was evidently a matter of some concern to them.

But if such troubled outgrowths sprouted in this place of the legend, there is every reason to believe that the original was enigmatic, troubling, and unacceptable to Augustan writers : and therefore every reason to believe it to be a genuine and probably important archaic survival. What troubled Virgil himself is, once we realize the trend of the episode, fairly clear : why should his story show Creusa - a well-established if secondary character in Greek epic - as lost, vanished, one way or another out of the story, only to add an unnecessary foster mother to the boy's family tree ? One can practically see his mind working : the foster mother is not only unnecessary, she is positively out of place in an all-male environment. Hence, there must be some peculiar reason why Ascanius recognized her as his foster mother ; and the reason must lie within the sort of behaviour you would expect of this all-male environment : in fact, of an army in the trenches. And what is more obvious in an army in the trenches, than young men die ? That's it ! She must have been the mother of some other young man who died (gloriously, it goes without saying) and whom Ascanius had taken, as a sort of compensation, into his own family circle[33].

I believe this is a probable and almost inevitable conclusion from the facts. The fact that Iulus acquires a foster-mother because of Euryalus' death is written in the epic ; and the fact that Euryalus was never meant to do anything but die, and that his death achieves nothing - his mission fails - except that, seems on the face of it quite obvious. That such a grandiose episode should end in nothing more than the adoption of a foster-mother, that all the blood and slaughter and high emotion and suicidal valour should achieve no more than this, is so curious as to beg for an explanation. Not only that : having gone to all that trouble to arrange the fostering, Virgil never speaks of it again. It even begins to seem odd that Virgil should have added such a marvelous tragic saga at this point, hiding the actual point of his narrative almost completely ; was he, by any chance, trying to take our eyes away from the question of Iulus' stepmother with the dazzling poetry of the fall of the lovers ? Was there something there that he didn't want his readers to think about too much ? This, too, is not unfamiliar to us ; it is not at all unlike his nervous and evasive behaviour in the matter of the sudden mass marriage of Trojans and Latin girls.

It is also; possible that the foster-mother character was already known to be, one way or another, without children ; and to take this speculation a bit further, it must have been a kind of childlessness that did not involve sterility. If Virgil's public had known this woman to be sterile, he would not has given her a son. We may suppose she was Ascanius' wet-nurse, as

---

were given Lavinium while the royal children of Silvius took Laurentum and Alba Longa. Cato used his historical writings as a political weapon, and I feel sure he was trying to deny the claims of Ænean descent of the Iulii of his time. If Iulian descent was a controversial issue as early as this, Livy and Virgil's nervousness is even more understandable : by their time, it was probably part of the cultural heritage of the Ænean legend.

[32]   He was only Cæsar's adopted son, but he was his legal heir, and therefore the legal head of the Iulian clan.

[33]   This is by no means far-fetched ; there is at least one famous episode in World War I of a motherless young soldier (C.S. Lewis) "adopting" the mother of a dead friend of his, Paddy Moore.

54

Caieta was Æneas' ; which would lead one to conclude that a wet-nurse character was in some way natural and indispensable to these figures.

If I am correct, this huge interpolation, inserted as it was to make sense of a difficulty in the original legends, shows to what lengths Virgil was prepared to go in order to avoid rewriting the story ; and gives the lie to all those interpretations, including Dumézil's, that understand the poet to have largely made made his story up. He did not ; he worked hard to understand and smooth out "apparent" contradictions between Greek and Latin traditions. That is surely why he worked so long at the epic and still left it unfinished.

III.4 The children of Lug

Interestingly, many figures of Lug present problems and ambiguities in matters of fatherhood and sonship.

The most famous son of Lug is Cúchulainn ; a slender and graceful boy, this horrifyingly powerful hero charges through his brief life with extraordinary dash and brilliance, doing his most renowned deed[34] at seventeen, by which time he is already married, and barely living into his twenties. There can be no doubt that he is an aspect of Lug, of whom he is occasionally said to be the avatar[35], but more often the son[36]. Not unlike Æneas, he has to win his bride by great deeds of arms.

A scene in the *Táin* brings father and son together. Cúchulainn has been fighting the hosts of all Ireland alone from Samhain (November 1st) to Imbolc (February 1st) ; he has also attracted the hostility of the Mórrígan[37], and they have hurt each other badly[38]. As he lies wounded, Lug comes to him in the guise of a handsome young warrior, and promises him three days of deep sleep and restoration. When he awakens, he is fully fit, and Lug promises him that the enemy host has now no power over his life.

A remarkable exchange takes place. Cúchulainn invites Lug to fight by his side and avenge the heroic children who defended Ulster while he slept. Lug refuses, saying that however great deeds anybody does, nobody can match Cúchulainn's glory. To feel the full flavour, try translating this scene into another mythology : imagine Zeus refusing to stand by the side of his son Herakles because "nobody can hope to match Herakles' glory" ! In fact Lug, who, in the stories of the Children of Tuirenn and of the Second Battle of Moytura, had shown a very aggressive, military face, is not, here, seen fighting at all ; although he promises his son to defend Ulster in his place, it is actually a brigade of heroic children who do and die through three terrible days. When the healed Cúchulainn, worried that nobody

---

[34]   His single-handed stand against the hosts of Ireland, told in the prose epic *Táin Bó Cuailnge*.
[35]   A.D. REES - B. REES, *op.cit*, p.59.
[36]   This aspect of preternatural, lightninglike dashing through life and rushing to die in glory is more evident in the case of Cúchulainn's own son, Conla, whose glory and heroic strength are greater even than his father's. He dies in the most tragic manner imaginable, fighting Cúchulainn himself in the moving saga *The Death of Aife's Only Son*. He is no more than seven years old ! The story also presents with terrible force the inevitability of revenge and doleful death in the kind of life of this particular aspect of Lug, which I will discuss later.
[37]   A goddess whose British version Morgaine le Fay is particularly hostile to Lancelot.
[38]   Nothing else had managed to hurt him before.

had opposed the hosts of Ireland while he was cured, questions his divine father, Lug, while reassuring him, only mentions the brigade of children[39]. He says nothing about himself. He has not been fighting. This means that nothing has dropped from the story here : whatever Lug may have done to defend Ulster, he never fought. Cúchulainn fights from one end of the Irish epic to the other ; Lug never does.

Both divine father and mortal son are young. The *Táin* makes much play with the boyish, beardless looks of the Lug-begotten horror of war that is Cúchulainn ; several blind and arrogant Irish champions go to their doom in foolish contempt of his graceful youth, or even refuse to fight until he has grown a beard, only to, dilly dilly dilly, go and be killed, with the squawking stupidity of geese in a farm, when he puts on a false beard of straw[40]. But when Lug and Cúchulainn meet, the hero addresses the god as "young warrior" : a "young warrior" who is the same as he appeared to his mother Deichtine daughter of Conchobar more than seventeen years before to tell her that he, Lug mac Ethniu, was the father of the son she was bearing[41].

This Lug is no fighter ; but he is a healer. He heals Cúchulainn faultlessly in only three days. Normally, in Irish paganism, such miraculous healings would be the province of the god Dian Cecht, but Lug is known as the God of All Skills, *Samildanach*. He is also a prophet : he knows that if he allows Cúchulainn three days of sleep, Ulster will not remain undefended. Perhaps, in some indefinite manner, he has directed the brigade of children ; he may even be a master of the fate of mortals.

His youth is outside the mortal Cúchulainn's reckoning of time. He was young when Cúchulainn addressed him as an equal[42] ; he was equally young when he begot him on Deichtine. And yet Cúchulann is in all likelihood an aspect of himself. The fighting, avenging, devastating face is in time, and dies ; the benevolent, healing, prophetic face is ever young, and immortal.

---

[39]   The idea of Lug taking on the shape of his son to fight in his place when the latter is excessively beleagured is found in Malory, where Lancelot does it, not for Galahad, but for Sir Kai (*La morte d'Arthur* VI 11-13, 18). Kai, who was a figure of fun in Malory's time, had originally been the greatest hero at the court of the Welsh Arthur ; he is still such in most early Welsh poetry, in *Kulhwch and Olwen,* and especially in the *Dream of Rhonabwy,* where he is so popular that Arthur's subjects crowd just to have a look at him. There is no evidence that he was ever considered as a son of Lug (Lleu, Lancelot), but plenty that he was regarded as a very great hero.

[40]   It's worth noting that self-inflicted ignorance born of vanity is the ruin of Cúchulainn's enemies exactly as those of Æneas. Warriors, no less than priests, need a form of wisdom. Two famous episodes of the *Iliad* make much the same point. Diomedes is allowed by his patroness Athena (goddess of practical wisdom) to recognize the gods on the battlefield (V 127-128), so that he knows enough to avoid terrible Apollo yet smite Aphrodite and Ares (the most sinister two powers in Greek mythology : to smite them, *Æneid* XI 276-2777 or not, must surely be a meritorious act !). Poor Patroklos, on the other hand, is fuddled by the same mist Athena has removed from Diomedes' eyes (XVI 789-790) and smashes right into Apollo, with much the same effect as running into a brick wall. It is no coincidence that the golden god's terrible blow affects, more than anything else, Patroklos' *senses,* making him whirl and reel, blinding him, and stunning him ; that is, he is conclusively deprived of the very perceptions and understanding which Athena's Diomedes had had raised to a preternatural sharpness.

[41]   J. GANTZ, *Early Irish Myths and Sagas,* Harmondsworth, 1981, p.130-133.

[42]   The only character whom the hero ever invites to fight by his side : he does not even invite his dear friend and foster father, the rightful king Fergus, to join him, although he does agree various parts of non-interference and non-aggression with him.

This, then, is why the militant Lug of public wars (*Second Battle of Moytura*) and private revenges (*Children of Tuirenn*) had an elaborate death story, and yet Lug lives forever. And it is worth remarking that the death story of Lug (and also that of Cúchulainn) arises entirely out of the cycle of the wars he has fought, and the revenges he has taken, in the course of his fighting life in Ireland ; death is not his fate in the sense of being independent of anything he might say or do, but the direct result of his activities. And nevertheless Cúchulainn and Lug may possibly be one and the same ; and Lug the Healer and Lug the Avenger certainly are.

Similar ideas also occur outside Ireland. Lancelot[43] is a sinner, and his illegitimate son Galahad is sinless ; Galahad wins the Grail and goes straight to Paradise, while Lancelot is trapped in a cycle of revenges that pit him against his best friends and his king, and will have, at best, to work out his ultimate salvation (if any) with much fighting and much asceticism. In the Christian context of the Arthurian legend as we have it, Galahad's early death is not an ill, much less a denial of his nature as the immortal Lug, away from mortality and death ; in fact, it is the best way a Christian poet can show him as removed from time and becoming. In medieval Europe, a swift passage to Paradise was the highest possible good. And given that the hero who found the Grail would remove the enchantments of Britain and heal the land, he may also be compared to the immortal Lug as healer.

In the Vulgate version of the quest of the Holy Grail, Galahad is, without any chance of error, a figure of Christ. Yet "Galahad" is one of the names given to Lancelot himself at baptism ; and, even more significantly, it is sin that makes him lose the right to it[44]. The hero of the romances only bears half of his original name. Surely a name, as such, cannot possibly be lost or won by being a sinner or the reverse ; surely this indicates a degradation in Lancelot's basic nature. Because of sin, we infer, the part of him that is great Galahad cannot be in him. The finder of the Grail will be a person other than himself[45].

Chrétien de Troyes' poem *The Kinght of the Cart* is our first account of Lancelot ; it is also the strangest, and must certainly come from a tradition different from that of most romances. This text knows nothing of fathers and sons ; Lancelot is one and one alone ; shockingly, he is both the adulterer - and there is nothing particularly delicate about his courting of Guinevere - and a flagrantly Christ-like figure, whose identity with the Second Person of the Trinity Chrétien exhibits in veiled yet clear and conscious terms[46].

But, after all, it is not really much more odd to find a Christian divinity in Lancelot than to find it in his "son". How many Christian writers present Christ in His Own person, on the stage, and in disguise yet ? The only one that comes to mind is C.S. Lewis' Aslan ; and Lewis was a keen reader of medieval romances, and accepted without question the explanation of Galahad as a figure of Christ introduced by design into the Arthurian corpus,

---

[43] Who is yet another image of Lug : cf. supra.
[44] *The Vulgate Lancelot* IV 176, V 114 (ed. Sommer).
[45] Surely such a conception of soul split between two selves cannot possibly be Christian ?
[46] Chrétien de Troyes, *The Knight of the Cart* 1842ss.

probably by some monastic author, in the later Middle Ages ; a theory popular among Arthurian scholars, but, to me, both unlikely and far from Celtic realities. To understand Lewis' use of Aslan in the Narnian stories, it is important to realize that the "artificial Galahad" theory was at the back of his mind as he wrote[47].

But, other than Lewis, who ever treated the Second Person in such a way ? Look from Milton and Dante to the silliest and most infantile hagiography ; you will never find the Messiah as other than himself. The identity of Galahad and Christ is one of those things that seem natural only because they have been part of our mental landscape for so long. I speak as a Christian and as a writer ; and I declare unconditionally that to write of Jesus Christ in any other character than either His historical or His eternal one is not an imaginative feat that comes easy. The two Natures, the two figures, so completely exhaust what we think, feel, and even want, about God, that nothing is left to be said.

The origin of Galahad's divine identity is no more Christian than that of his father ; in both cases, it pertains to the Celtic pagan heritage of the legend, in which Lug, the Young God, is both the Father and the Son. Why, otherwise, would Chrétien give the unchaste father the same Christ-like characteristics that generations of romancers have given the chaste son ? In fact, Chrétien's Lancelot is like Christ exactly in the things in which Lug - and Æneas - are like Christ ; that is, he is a saviour. In the *Knight of the Cart,* he is specifically the deliverer from the prisons of death, the kingdom of Gorre, from which "no traveller escapes". It is from the moment that the as yet unnamed knight enters its borders that Chrétien starts to make continuous and not over-subtle allusions to the New Testament and the apocryphal *Gospel of Nicodemus.* Their meaning is abundantly clear ; in his role of invader of Gorre and deliverer of its prisoners, Lancelot is like Christ. I hardly need point out that Galahad is also like Christ in that he is an expected saviour.

Chrétien's Lancelot, then, bears within himself, as a unit, the features which other romances apportion between father and son ; he is both Christ and the adulterer. More striking still, he is the Saviour for no other reason than that he is the Adulterer ! He goes down to Gorre to rescue Guinevere, because he loves her with that same adulterous love that we know from so many other romances[48], and which proves so disastrous elsewhere. This just proves the more the theory I have just proposed, that Lancelot and Galahad are one soul[49] in two selves. And I would like to point out that the nature and relationships of Lancelot, Galahad and Guinevere have been a crux for generations of scholars, a treacherous

[47]   Lewis was hostile, on unscholarly and sentimental grounds, to R.S. Loomis' investigations into the pagan roots of Arthurian romance. His reaction to Loomis' genius was the result of the occasional childish obstinacy that was the least amiable trait of this great man. The clash of Lewis and Loomis is one of those sights one would never wish to see : that of two great minds, of two great masters, in real and irreconciliable disagreement ; but great though my admiration for Lewis is, it was he who was in the wrong. He couldn't bear to have his pretty garden of romance and mystery trampled by the hobnailed boots of explanation.
[48]   This becomes more understandable once we remember some Indian religious ideas in which God is the victorious rival of the merely mortal husband. Cf. for instance the splendid religious poetry of the medieval Kannada saint Mahadevi, conveniently translated in English by A.K. RAMANUJAN, *Speaking of Shiva,* Harmondsworth, 1973, esp. pp. 88, 102, 114, 283, 328.
[49]   Or rather, one identity : I am not sure how far I can go using Christian categories like the soul in describing an essentially pagan concept.

breeder of feeble theories, unsound reconstructions and doubts. My solution builds upon one certainly sound theory, R.S. Loomis', takes into account the certainly Celtic and at least half-pagan origin of the legends, and explains their bewildering variations.

In so far as Lug is an avenger and a warrior, then, he is mortal[50]. In so far as he is benevolent and beneficent, he is a god and immortal[51]. Nor only that : the apparitions on Earth of this supreme being's face of anger tend to be brief, flashing, blazing meteors.

Except for the Christianized story of Lancelot and Galahad, the passage of the avenging Lug is always swift : the avenging enemies of Cúchulainn, of Lug himself, of Lleu, take care of it. When he does not actually die, as in the case of Taliesin and of his Breton counterpart N'oun-Doare'[52], he at least vanishes from the Earth in a clatter of hooves, and no man knows where he is gone.

III.5 Æneas and Iulus

The matter of Lug the Father and Lug the Son has a clear Latin parallel in the characters of Æneas and Iulus. We have seen Æneas come to Latium in a blaze of power and wrath, stay for three years and die in battle. He is mortal enough to be buried. The historian who informs us uses strange language, but it cannot be doubted that Livy means to say that Jupiter Indiges died in battle and was buried. Yet he is immediately given cult as a god ; and not just any god, but Jupiter and/or the Sun.

His son Iulus also died, but we are told nothing of the manner of his death[53], and his reign was long and peaceful. While his father's brief reign is a series of wars, Livy ascribes no wars to him. Dionysios allocates him only one ; and even that, as we will see, is in keeping with his pacific nature. He is no warrior. His main deed is the foundation of Alba Longa, in which he establishes the royal centre of Latium, while handing Lavinium over to six hundred priests and the *penates* or house-gods of Latium ; in other words, he separates the priestly centre from the royal capital. He is also concerned with the fertility of the fields, and, according to Dionysios, placed his capital at Alba Longa over the Lacus Albanus because that allowed him to open or close the lake's outflow at leisure according to whether the fertile fields of Latium, below, needed it[54]. Religion, civil organization, the fertility of the fields : every royal function, except war, is what Iulus is concerned with.

Iulus is merciful. Two completely different stories were told about the villain Mezentius. One was Virgil's : it showed him executed by a militant Æneas in the name of Jupiter, whom Mezentius had challenged :

> ... let the father of gods, and king of men

---

[50]   Or, in a Christianized version, a sinner.
[51]   Or, in a Christianized version, a saint quickly taken to Heaven.
[52]   F.M. LUZEL, *Celtic Folk-Tales from Armorica*, Llanerch, 1985.
[53]   Therefore he did not die in battle, like Æneas, nor cut to pieces by the senators, as Romulus was rumoured to (Dionysios of Halicarnassus, II 56 4-5 ; Livy, I 16 4 ; Plutarch, *Life of Romulus*), nor suffer any other spectacular and violent death.
[54]   Herodotus was told an exactly similar fable about the kings of Persia (III 117). However, the interpretation he gives of it is more tyrannical : the king can starve subject people of water at need.

See to me...[55]

and from whom he withheld his due, the gift of the spoils of battle, consecrating them instead to his own young son Lausus. The other is told by Dionysios : Mezentius[56] unreasonably demands all the wine of Latium for himself ; Ascanius then declares the wine sacred to Jupiter and marches out to war, in which the enemy is miraculously confounded till they are hardly seen to resist. Ascanius had shown a mild and friendly nature even before the war's start, making a sustained attempt to reconcile Mezentius by what Dionysios calls friendly and reasonable proposals, but failing because of the enemy's arrogance ; now, with victorious peace in his grasp, he conciliates defeated Mezentius, who, miraculously, becomes from then on the constant friend of the Latin nation[57].

In effect, war goes with Æneas wherever he walks ; and peace follows Ascanius whatever he does. With Æneas, peace turns into war[58] ; with Ascanius, war turns into peace, even the most unreasonable of enemies is reconciled. Even the blasphemous violence of Mezentius is no obstacle to pacification. When the Trojan women, maddened by Juno's emissary, are destroying the ships, it is the sight of him that stops them.

The Latin figuration is different from the Irish in that the heroic father and the peaceful son are both mortal and earthly ; the peaceful Lug, on the other hand, speaks to Cúchulainn as an immortal from another world.Lancelot and Galahad, however, are both mortal, and also succeed each other in the same order as Æneas and Iulus, the warrior preceding the peacemaker ; but we have seen this legend was subjected to strong Christian influence.

Indeed, it is practically impossible to separate Christian syncretism from the figure of Lancelot. In the *Knight of the Cart*, he is the Young Saviour who enters the Kingdom of Death (Gorre) by a peculiarly humiliating route in order to free its prisoners. He comes to Gorre in a disgraceful cart ; clearly the cart of death, one of the strongest visual images and most feared object in Breton folklore[59]. The element of disgrace cannot but be related to Our Lord's shameful death on the Cross, the death of a rebel slave. Even if the situation itself did not suggest Christian views so strongly, however, I know of no purely pagan account where Lug or anyone else harrowed the world of the dead and set its prisoner free ; this is a

---

55   Virgil, *Æneid* X 743-744.
56   Who had taken no part, in his version, in Turnus' struggle with Æneas.
57   It is worth noting that, even in the Hellenized versions of Virgil and Dionysios, father and son fought Mezentius directly in the name of Jupiter : they were, at the very least, the agents of Jupiter on Earth. This is not common in Classical Antiquity. Zeus/Jupiter might decree the fall of cities, even vengeance upon sinning sovereigns, but the jihad and the crusade are not often part of his province ; people rarely claimed to be going to war to defend his honour.
58   It is really remarkable how stubbornly the Latins of the *Æneid* pursue a campaign already lost.
59   A. LE BRAZ, *The Celtic Legend of the Beyond*, Llanerch, 1986, p.26-29. I believe it is accepted that Lancelot as a character belongs to the Arthurian legends of Brittany rather than those of Wales : cf. R. BROMWICH, *op.cit.*, p.414-416. And an important feature to remember about the culture of Brittany is that, unlike the Welsh homeland, and however many Welsh traits they may have retained, the Welshmen who colonized Armorica between the fourth and seventh century BC were all Christians, often led by monks or bishops. The Christian element in their legendry (and the Arthurian legend is peculiarly theirs) is not in the least surprising ; but it is a Christianity mythologized, out of time and place, very like that of Irish and Welsh lives of saints in which the saint in question is often more than hinted to be a reincarnation of Christ or of the Virgin Mary.

typically Christian idea. Celtic lore has plenty of heroes visiting the hereafter, and some stories of wives and husbands rescued from the world of the *síde* or from faerie-land by a devoted husband or wife, but no such generalized revolutionary act.

Yet the figures of Lancelot and Galahad can only be explained in the ligth of the Celtic supreme god. The only possible explanation is that this is the result of an early, heretical identification of Lug/Lancelot with the Second Person of the Trinity. We have already seen that such an identification seems more than likely in the case of Taliesin, and it seems more and more probable that it was a generalized phenomenon. There are vast areas of shadows in our knowledge of early British Christianity in which such a syncretism could have taken place ; the conversion of Ireland and Scotland is extremely poorly recorded, and even this side of the Roman border it is possible that Christianity may have been accepted earlier and more widely than most historians think. Already in the early third century, Origen and Tertullian claimed that the "wild British" had accepted Christ, even beyond the Roman wall ; Origen's language, indeed, appearing to signify that Christianity was the faith, not of a minority, but of the whole British nation beyond Rome. This is certainly wrong, and Origen probably misread Tertullian ; but Tertullian, whose pamphlet against the Jews goes back to as early as 200 AD, was confident, as of a proven and unchallengeable fact, that Christianity was widespread beyond the Roman border in Britain in his time[60].

This is by the way, and meant mainly to explain the peculiarities of Lancelot, especially the Lancelot of Chrétien de Troyes. But what all the various versions have in common is that the peacemaker is superior to the warrior not only in degree but in kind. In Ireland, the peaceful Lug is immortal and eternally young, whereas Cúchulainn dies very quickly. In the Christianized Arthurian legend, Galahad crosses quickly over to Paradise, while Lancelot is left here below to fight and sin. In Rome, Æneas reigns for only three years and does not even see the birth of his own son, whereas Ascanius Iulus reigns for decades and passes away when his sons are already adult. Perhaps the best way to describe the meaning of this is the Biblical passage

> For I the Lord thy God am a jealous God, visiting the iniquity of the fathers upon the children unto the third and fourth generation of them that hate Me ; and showing mercy unto the thousandth of them that love Me, and keep My commandments.

However great the terror of God may be, His goodness is infinitely greater.

III.6 Lug and Jupiter

These dualities arise in the world of human beings. It is when he intervenes in a material, physical, above-ground Ireland, that Lug fights and dies ; it is the ultra-human Lug, the Lug of the underworld *síde* and of otherworlds across the sea, that endures now, that is the

---

60   It is an amusing thought that the Arthurian cycle, today the favourite stomping grounds of neo-Celts, neo-Pagans and New-Age cultists of all kinds, may in fact turn out to be the only part of Celtic heritage to have its roots in a Christian past !

object of cult, the helpful and ever-young father of Cúchulainn[61]. Now, something exactly like that may be noticed in Roman religion and epic, if with a quite different slant.

We have seen the functional separation between Æneas and Ascanius ; but it corresponds to no internal dynamic known in the purely divine figure of Jupiter, in his grand and candid oneness. Readers of Dumézil's studies on Roman religion must have been struck by how, while his reading of the couple Romulus-Numa as a Varuṇa-Mitra pair is in the highest degree convincing, his attempt to retrive the same structure in the divine world have proved singularly feeble[62] : the Mitraic counterpart to Jupiter's towering "Varuṇa" being identified with a notably obscure and unimportant figure named Dius Fidius. While among the Indians and among the Germans the division of the First Function between an amicable figure and a punisher (Mitra and Varuṇa in India, Týr and Odhinn in Iceland) is in fact easily recognizable, no such thing is true, in Roman thought, of the divine level of the universe, or of the form of existence proper to such a being as Jupiter.

This statement, properly read, provides the key to the whole question. Jupiter really is a different entity from either Mitra or Varuṇa ; only among mortals do dualities arise. At no level of the Roman trifunctional triad of Jupiter, Mars, Quirinus, do we find any doubleness whatever ; even the third-function figure, most evidently double in India, is very noticeably single in Rome : indeed, he bears the notion of gathering into a unity in his very name, *Co-uiri-nus*, the Lord of men-together, *Co-uiri*. Yet as son as this god becomes incarnate in the other great hero of Rome, he is born as a twin. Only his twin is mortal, and, indeed, his death is caused by his aggressiveness, a fact surely connected with the sour fate of the militant avenging Lug.

It is probable for this reason that the myth-image that Dumézil called *le Borgne et le Manchot*, a couple composed of a one-eyed character who terrifies armies and a heroic character who loses one of his hands in a magnanimous false oath to save the society of which he is a member from an ultimate peril, is found among the gods (Odhinn and Týr) in Germanic religion, but among mortals (Horatius Cocles and Mutius Scævola) in Rome. The concepts underlying this image had to do with the first function and its attitude in the face of external danger and aggression ; neither character, properly speaking, fights, and they preserve their societies, the one with the magic terror of his one eye, and the other with the binding power of the oath, falsely applied, which is why he pays for it with the hand that

---

[61] I believe we are in the presence of the same kind of fact when we see, in a charming little *Mabinogion* story, Lludd sail across the sea to ask for his brother Llevelys' advice on how to cope with a series of disasters that have struck his realm of Britain. Lludd is Nodons, Irish Nuada, the type and ancestor of Celtic royalty, comparable with Latinus ; he is very much of this world. Llevelys, on the other hand, is Lug (the name only slightly varied) ; he lives in an Otherworld clumsily identified with France, reached by an oddly dangerous sea journey ; despite being Lludd's brother, they can only converse by way of magic trumpets ; and his prophetic healing wisdom allows the king to save his realm. This is benevolent face of the god ; and it is in another world across the sea, not in the human country of Britain, than he can be found.

[62] In many studies, such as *Mitra-Varuna* (Paris, 1940), *La religion romaine archaïque* (Paris, 1967 ; English version : *Archaic Roman religion*, Chicago, 1978), *Les dieux souverains des Indo-Européens* (Paris, 1977).

was his pledge. The very conflictual and divided background is incompatible with our picture of the Roman divine world[63].

Doubleness, division, is the feature of our finite world ; and doubleness and division bring about two things : either violence or healing. Lug, and the Jupiter who takes the forms of Æneas and Ascanius, can be both an avenger and a healer. He may come down in rage to smite some evil such as the Fomorian domination of Ireland or Turnus' and Mezentius' criminal power in Latium ; or he may come as a healer, helping his wounded son in Ireland or freeing the land of Logres from its enchantments in Arthurian legend. Even his blessing may not always be immediately clear : Taliesin's presence in Gwynedd is undubitably positive, but it may not have seemed so to King Maelgwn as he was being defeated, or to his bards as they were being humiliated. It all depends on the situation. The face that God turns towards us is the face with which we ourselves gaze at the world ; either to surpass doubleness and arrive at divine unity - to heal, to make whole - or else to take on ourselves the unchallenged fact of division - wich is necessarily violence, as it denies healing - and assume violence and eventual death.

Far from being (like our Christian God) the Eldest, creator who pre-exists His creation, this god is the Youngest. He comes last, or rather last of the first : Wales, Ireland and Rome agree. Lleu is the youngest of the Welsh gods, coming two generation after Math and one after Gwydion and Gilfaethwy. Lug comes to Ireland after the other gods have already come and conquered. Taliesin is a child ; Cúchulainn is seventeen at the time of the *Táin* ; even Lancelot is quite young, and his adultery with Guinevere puts him in what was in medieval convention an absolutely classic situation of *junior* against *senior*, the cuckolded husband being, like King Mark, always old, and the cuckolder, Tristram, always young[64]. And we have seen that there are many reasons to consider Æneas/Jupiter Indiges a quite young man.

What does this mean ? Adding up our evidence, we must conclude that the supreme god came to our world last of all things, when all other things had already been made or introduced. He comes to our world after the other gods have already acquired their roles and done part of their work. What does he do ? He does not have anything specific to bring : the world already has kings, warriors, craftsmen, even priests, before he ever gets there. In Irish legend, his one talent is that he has all talents ; while every other deity has a specific field of competence, he is the one that brings all these things together in himself.

An allied fact, surely, is that this superior, immortal figure, is a healer and a peace-maker. His very being as an immortal god is unity and reconciliation. Conversely, his very being as a mortal man is conflict between separate elements ; one way or another, mortal and immortal, he is the image of the way things relate to each other. He is the relationship between things, whether positive or negative. He is, if such a thing may be said of the greatest god, born, or even made ; when he appears in Welsh legend under his own name,

63   Cf. G. DUMEZIL, *Religion romaine*.
64   A.D. REES - B. REES, *op.cit.*, p.279-296.

he is actually made by Gwydion ; and he cannot be born or made until all the objects that are to find relationships, either of unity or of conflict, have already come to be in our world.

CHAPTER IV : THE COSMIC SON AND FORTUNA

IV.1 Jupiter and Fortuna in Præneste

The last chapter brought to our attention the character of Jupiter, not only as god of relationships, but also as son of a mother, or of a foster-mother. Therefore I will now examine one Latin cult in which Jupiter actually appears in the aspect of a child, and a boy, at that, under a mother figure as great and important as the Venus of the epic : the goddess Fortuna Primigenia.

Fortuna Primigenia was worshipped together with Jupiter and Juno, both represented as her children, in a majestic temple that dominated the little hill city of Præneste, and that was one of the greatest holy places of archaic Latium, visited by a constant stream of pilgrims. My discussion is based on the analysis by the archælogist Filippo Coarelli. To summarize his arguments[1] :

1° the enormous temple has two recognizable centres, the sanctuary proper, at the height of the line of ascent[2], and a covered well found a couple of levels below and to the right of the sanctuary, on the so-called "terrace of hemicycles" ;

2° this covered well corresponds to the place of worship whose origin myth is described in Cicero, *De diuinatione* II 41 85-86 ;

3° this legend says that a leading Prænestine was led by prophetic dreams to dig a well into solid rock - amid general derision - and, digging, found *sortes* written on slivers of oakwood, clearly of supernatural origin ; at the same time an olive tree, that grew at on the site of the central sanctuary, started dripping honey ; the local *haruspices,* fortune-telling priests, ordered a case to be built from its wood and the *sortes* to be preserved in it ; Coarelli identifies the well in question with the well of the "terrace of hemicycles" ; Cicero mentions that a statue of Fortuna breast-feeding a couple of new-born gods, baby Juno and baby Jupiter, was built next to it ;

4° archæologists have excavated the well itself, and found that the most ancient level of its inner stone-work includes a recess, apparently built into the fabric from the beginning, which Coarelli identifies with the spot where the *sortes* were found, according to the legend, and where the olive-wood case must have been historically kept ;

5° from several pieces of evidence, Coarelli reconstructs a divination ritual in which a male child, "led by Fortune", entered the well once a year to open the case and give *sortes* at random for one of the local priesthood to interpret ; a painting believed to depict this ritual shows the child emerging from the well to hand a rectangular object to a sacerdotal figure[3].

---

[1]   F. COARELLI, *I santuari del Lazio in età repubblicana*, Rome, 1987.
[2]   The temple is set on a hillside.
[3]   F. COARELLI, *op.cit.*, p.70-71 thinks the boy in the painting holds a single *sors*, but I think he has misunderstood the detail. The object the child holds is a perfect rectangle, but the *sors* explicitly shown in a coin (*id.*, p.76 fig.24.5) has the famous and typical "winged rectangle" form (*tabula ansata*) in which the Romans wrote important inscriptions (like the motto S.P.Q.R., or see also *id.*, p.176-177). If the *sortes,* that is the images of Sacred Word, were shaped as *tabulae ansatae,* then we can see why this shape was

66

Within the well itself a large marble woman's head was found, which must have belonged to the just-mentioned statue of Fortuna. Neither Cicero nor any other source say anything about this head in the well ; we may be fairly sure that it was no part of the original shape of the temple. In fact, it has clearly been assaulted with a hammer or sledge, and nose and mouth have been virtually flattened. This is typical of deliberate iconoclastic agression on holy images, as shown by the results of many a Cromwellian raid ; in any realistically sculptured head, the nose and the lips are always the first to go. It seems therefore certain that this particular statue of Fortuna mother of Jupiter has been deliberately beheaded, that the head has been deliberately vandalized, and that, once vandalized, it has deliberately been thrown into the well ; and that this must have been the act of Christians intent on deconsecrating the temple.

Points that I will discuss in the next few sections lead me to believe that this was not an act of random brutality against pagan religion, but rather an exorcism aimed specifically at the goddess of this shrine, attacking her in her own particular character. And from a modern investigator's viewpoint, the violence of these early Christians is almost a piece of luck, since it supplies an essential clue to the mystical meaning of the temple and the well, which we could only have suspected, but never reconstructed, if we had only had the unexplained Ciceronian account. The connection of a severed head and a spring of water or well could never have been discovered in the case of this cult without this clear physical piece of evidence, and it is a very significant connection, that opens up large areas of religious meaning.

IV.2 Heads and water sources

Coarelli analyzed the honey that poured from the olive tree in the Prænestine legend as a symbol of eternity. He is at least partly right. Honey does not go off, and it is one of the earliest and best-known methods of preserving meat and perishable foodstuffs. Though this does not cover all the meanings of honey, which cover intoxication and sweetness as well as eternity, it helps to explain its otherwise unexpected association with the olive tree in this legend ; the only feature that they have in common and that separates them from other agricultural products - hence, the only probable reason for them to be gathered together in a significant legendary image - is that both honey and olive oil make good food preservatives, used in Italy to this day.

But honey is also a frequent part or a remarkable mythological image, found across the Indo-European world, that associates a severed head or skull with a well or a source of water, and that occurred to me as soon as I heard of a marble head cut off and thrown into a well. Indo-European myths are full of bodiless heads in wells or springs. The latter are frequently connected with wisdom and/or healing, may pour honey or mead (fermented

---

popular in Rome. Also, I cannot believe that an important fortune-reading, such as the painting depicts, would take only a single *sors* to do ; and both the meaning of the word *sors* and the name of their finder point to them being used in numbers and according to complex patterns. The Prænestine fortune-telling technique must have hinged, like the Tarot, on the order of a number of pieces.

honey-and-water) rather than water, and often have some sort of primeval position in time. In Germanic paganism, the primeval sage Mimir, who initiated Odhinn god of wisdom, was a severed head who lived in what is described as a spring of roaring water[4]. The Welsh St. Winifred and St. Teilo both have sources named after them where their severed heads were supposed to have touched the ground ; pilgrims used to come to St. Teilo's well in search of healing, and had to drink water poured from a so-called St. Teilo's skull[5]. In Greece, the severed head of Orpheus, first and greatest of all poets, floated singing to the mouth of the river Meletes, a name surely connected with honey ; Meletes was also said to be the father of Homer[6]. There are many cases of this kind[7].

The content of this image is obvious. There is only one orifice in the head from which a spring of water may pour, as seen in the design of many ornamental fountains : the mouth. The water or mead must pour from the mouth of the head. The head has always been known to be the seat of the human intellect, and what normally flows from the mouth, apart from breath, is talk. Both the whole head, and the mouth in particular, are connected with this flow : it comes from the brain, but it pours through the mouth. And the fact that the head is severed means that the rest of the bodily faculties are not involved. This is a symbol purely of intellectual matters[8].

The water or honey that springs from the head - from the mouth - means nothing else than wisdom itself, as welcome and life-giving as a pure spring. Wisdom comes from the head of the wise, pouring from their mouths. Knowledge was transmitted by word of mouth, and anyone who loved knowledge would regard the tongues of learned men with the same affection some of us feel for libraries and the smell of old paper. Poetry is mead in Icelandic theory, and Hesiod says honey is on the tongue of a wise monarch.

This royal wisdom is, in Hesiod's view, directly connected with the prosperity of the land. This has two meanings. One is the purely practical advantage of wisdom : skill in wartime, peacekeeping in peacetime, sound policy at all times, make kingdoms prosperous and great. But Hesiod applied it not to this generalized purpose, but to the specific one of royal justice. And indeed the royal justice of the legends, such as Solomon's or Cormac mac Airt's was meant, not only to establish the proper end of a suit, but also to re-establish harmony between the suitors. In the small circumstances to which these ideas refer, among kingdoms most often no larger than a Swiss canton, peace among the subjects was not only a desirable thing, but the condition of the whole tribe's survival ; strife between subjects of

[4]   Snorri Sturluson, *Heimskrigla* 4, *Gylfaginning* 15 ; *Vǫluspa* 28. In Germanic myth, poetry, the purest form of learning, is always described as Odhinn's sacred mead of wisdom.
[5]   W.J. REES, *Lives of the Cambro-British Saints*, Llandovery, 1853 ; S. BARING-GOULD, *A Book of Folklore*, London, 1920 ; D. PARRY-JONES, *Welsh Legends*, London, 1953, p.123-127.
[6]   F. JACOBY, *Die Fragmente der griechischen Historiker*, , Berlin, 1923- , N°26.45.
[7]   A grisly instance may well be the severed skulls of dead enemies from which Celtic and Germanic warriors used to drink mead or beer.
[8]   An important Æneid scene (VII 71-80) gives the head of Lavinia an entirely different symbolic meaning. What flows from it is not honey, but fire. In that case, however, the part of the head the story emphasizes is the hair ; in all the cut head legends, it is the mouth, from which honey flows. Honey is not the same thing as fire, and must stand for something quite different.

any importance whatever could easily affect the whole society, involving it in civil war, with the more aggrieved or defeated party as often as not bringing in foreigners to settle scores. Stories of exiled princes coming back with foreign armies are very frequent, both in legend and in fact. Only wise man-management and honeyed language on the part of the sovereign could avoid such dangerous rifts.

The deeper meaning is in the power of memory, that is learning, to preserve things which are great of themselves and which risk being otherwise lost. Wisdom and memory are one and the same : the wise are those who know the great deed of the past, the names of gods and past kings, the names of countries, the exact rules of laws themselves ancient, and the names of the ancient sages who had introduced each law. These are old things, but they are also beautiful and beloved, and the learned man deserves praise in that he rescues for us the deed of old heroes and the wisdom of old sages. The whole of Ulster may once have depended on the heroism of one young man to be saved ; but Cúchulainn himself depended on the poets and sages of Ireland for his deeds to endure.

The two meanings were probably not separated in our ancestors' minds, or rather, they were two sides of the same medal : wisdom preserved, period. As sweet as honey, as intoxicating as mead, as everlasting as a perennial spring, wisdom preserved like honey what would otherwise rot and die. Therefore, incidentally, wisdom was good in itself, indeed the greatest good to be found among men ; all Indo-European societies exalted wise men.

This raises a good few echoes in the material connected with Præneste. We have a cut head in a well ; we have a stream of honey pouring from the olive tree ; we have a centre of pilgrimage where pilgrims came to be told their future[9], that is, in search of a wisdom that goes beyond the barrier of time.

In Cicero's legend, though, there is no head or skull of any kind. This seems to forbid us to believe that the Prænestine cult should have to do with the theme of the cut head ; the fact that the statue's head was in the holy well would be a mere coincidence. But as soon as the reader reaches this comforting idea, he cannot help but remember other aspects of Prænestine reality : the honey that streams from the olive as from as from a source ; a well to which pilgrims go for wisdom as Odhinn went to Mimir, as the Welsh used to go to St. Teilo's well to be healed. For the temple of Fortuna was a great centre of pilgrimage, and it was exactly to the well that all the pilgrims went to receive the benefit of the prophetic wisdom of the *sortes*.

We seem to have run into a paradox. Most elements of the cult seem to look back straight to the theme of the head and the water ; yet there is neither a head nor any water. This is no chance. Not only the well has no water, it was deliberately and always intended not to have any. It is impossible to believe it was ever meant to even simulate a real well ; its inadequate

---

[9]   I do wonder whether the still-existent Italian obsession with fortune-telling in all its forms, from astrology to tarots, may not be another cultural continuity such as I already suspect in many things from family matriarchate to pizza.

dimensions lay visible emphasis on the fact it is a false well from which no water ever could or will come. It even was covered by a *tholos*, a small chambering wall and roof, which made it rain-proof. No H_2O is allowed to get in, ever, under any conditions. And yet all evidence confirms that what we see in Præneste is a well and nothing else than a well, inevitably, ideologically bound up with water. What does this mean ?

Well, since we have seen that the water flow of the legend is really symbolical, there is no actual need for any actual water to be there at all, so long as the symbol system is clear and comprehensive. In this case, the emphasis on the lack of physical water in turn underlines the symbolic nature of the "well" of Fortuna Primigenia. In physical terms, only one thing ever did come out of that well regularly : but it was something very important, the box of olive-wood containing the oakwood slivers or *sortes,* each inscribed with a word or language symbol, from which a trained local priesthood claimed to predict the future. This was ever-flowing wisdom which drew pilgrims from all over Latium each year to avail themselves of it.

What we seem to have found is a form of imagination in which the presence of a mystical substance is shown exactly by the absence of its material counterpart. This absence is painstakingly underlined by a deliberately castrated image of the typical place in which the substance should be found ; if the mystical waters of wisdom are to be found in Præneste, the place where they spring is shown by the presence of a sacred well so built as to make it impossible to collect any amount of physical, unmystical H_2O, even to the extent of covering it with a waterproof *tholos*. The site itself was remarkable because it would be impossible to find water there, however far you dug : it was solid rock. The Prænestines of the legend, knowledgeable farmers, laughed when they saw Numerius Suffustius try to sink a well there of all places.

Into this well, Christian reformers throw a head. What head ? The head of the Mother Goddess, Fortuna. Therefore, whatever it is that may be found in this well bears the same relationship to Fortuna as the waters of wisdom bore to Mimir in Germanic myth. The severed head is a symbol of the intellect, and specifically of the articulate, speaking mind ; here, the intellect and mind of Fortuna.

This argument presupposes that Latium knew the theme of the head and the spring. Well, I know of no ancient Latin story about it ; but there is one medieval one, the legend of the Abbey of Three Fountains, famous in Rome to this day, that belongs to the mainstream of the theme. It says that when St. Paul, the archetypal wise man of Christian tradition[10], was beheaded, his head bounced three times, and at each of the spots a spring of clear water sprang up. Later, a celebrated monastery, the Abbey of Three Fountains, was built on the spot.

This is evidently the appropriation of the theme on behalf of the Church ; the hyperbole of having not one but three holy wells means that Christian wisdom was worth three times

---

[10]   As well as one of Rome's two patron saints.

any of its pagan adversaries. No other tradition knows of more than one spring per head, so to speak ; and that is not surprising, as the springs stand for everflowing wisdom, wisdom with no limit, like the springs of eternal rivers, always there for every petitioner, never failing ; wisdom, in short, that covers everything. That the legend should be attached to Paul is particularly important ; he was both the first and the greatest of the wise men of Christianity, and this shows that the theme, which joins ultimate wisdom and a position at the very beginning of time[1 1], was still understood. Rome has hundreds of martyrs, many of whom were beheaded, and many of whom were wise ; yet it was the founder of Christian theology, not anybody later or lesser, to whom the story was applied.

This compels us to believe that Latium understood the theme in all its implications and until very late. The Christians of late-Empire Rome knew it well enough to make it their own. As their correligionaries of Rome had appropriated the same theme, in full knowledge of what it meant, to proclaim the glory of one of the two great saints of the Eternal City, so the Christians of Præneste, only a few miles up the road, used it to deconsecrate the great pagan temple of wisdom. When they threw the severed head of Fortuna in her own well, they knew what they were doing.

There is a well-known parallel for this mystical short-circuiting of a pagan shrine. Coifi, hign priest of Woden in Northumbria, took the guise of Woden himself to turn that god's magic against him when Northumbria accepted Christianity. He rode wildly to the gates of Woden's temple on a stallion, as Odhinn (Woden) rides on his horse Sleipnir, and he threw a spear at the temple in the same way in which Odhinn throws his spear against the army whose defeat he has decided[1 2]. The severing of Fortuna's head must be a case of reverse-magic of the same kind, seizing a central aspect of the Goddess' cult to ritually deny her. For that matter, the Christian priest who advised Coifi about deconsecrating the temple was Paulinus, who came from Rome, and lived not long after the fall of the Prænestine temple.

IV.3 The theology of the *sortes*

The well of the Peænestine temple was therefore the spring from which Fortuna Primigenia's wisdom sprang, like sacred honey, for ever ; and the form it took was that of *sortes* made of oakwood, kept in an olive-wood case. What were the *sortes*, and how were they used ? The data we have forbid us to imagine a complex apparatus : an olive-wood case that a child could carry can have contained no more than a few hundred inscribed oakwood slivers at most, probably less ; the inscriptions cannot but have been very simple. They must have been a definite amount ; nobody, surely, would dare to add or take away *sortes* from the sacred box. This however does not mean that their application was simple : priests specializing in their interpretation lived in the temple, which suggest that some heavy

[1 1]   I am thinking in particular of Mimir, but also of Orpheus, who was not only the greatest, but also the first, of the great singers of Greek legend.
[1 2]   Bede, *Historia ecclesiastica gentis Anglorum* II 13.

elaboaration hung on this small set of objects[1 3]. Their combinations and permutations must have involved complex analysis, judging from the meaning of the word *sors* "what is sorted out, arranged in series" and from the name of their discoverer, Numerius "Son of Numbers"[1 4] or "Number-Man"[1 5].

However, we know that they stood for words rather than numbers. Now, the word for destiny in Latin, *fatum,* more commonly plural *fata,* means no more than "thing, things spoken". This means that the shape and destiny of things is *spoken* primevally. In the beginning was the Word. The Roman-Latin magistrate who approximated Jupiter on Earth was called *dictator,* an agent noun built, not on the roots of the verb *dicere* "to say" or *dicare* "to nominate, dedicate", which would have given **dictor* or **dicator,* but rather on *dicta.* *Dicta* is a neuter past paticiple of *dicere,* and it is plural ; that is, it means "things spoken", the exact equivalent of *fata,* which is another past participle (from the verb *fari*). In other words, the dictator, earthly image of Jupiter, is the agent of the "things spoken", the *fata* in action.

One sees immediately the relevance of these objects to the theme of the severed head and the spring of wisdom. What we have here is a set of words, the building blocks of a language. Can wisdom and languge be separated ? Certainly not in the complex of ideas enshrined in this myth, which lays particular emphasis on the role of the mouth and tongue, from which honey flows. Orpheus' head floats singing on a stream named Meletes for honey ; like all rivers in Greek mythology, Meletes is also a god, and he is to become the father of the greatest of latter-days poets, Homer. And both Orpheus and Homer are figures, not only of the art of language, but also of cosmic, religious, initiate wisdom - figures of the sage - in which the art of words cannot be separated from that of the truth. Odhinn, whom Mimir initiated, was the god of poetry as well as of wisdom, and one notice[1 6] says that he spoke only in verse. The wisdom which the severed-head-and-spring image embodies is a

---

[1 3]   The parallel of the Vestal Virgins in Rome shows that at least some Latin priesthoods had a very elaborate sacred science. The Vestals served only one temple and only one goddess, but they spent ten years being trained in their duties (Dionysios of Halicarnassus, II 67 2). Some modern professions take less time to learn !

[1 4]   *Numerus* is one of those words that have given etymologists trouble, it seems. G. DEVOTO, *Dizionario etimologico,* Rome, 1968, p.284, ascribes it to an Indo-European root **nem-* "to share out, to divide", but finds the derivation obscure. Given its association here with the *sortes,* expression of the divine will, and therefore with the complex notion of *numen* "the deity as will or assent", is it possible that the root **nem-* may have been conflated with the word *numen,* or an associate one, in the context of a sacred science of the *sortes* based on numbers and figures ?

[1 5]   There are a couple of other arguments for the existence, even at a very late period, of a complex Praenestine sacred science. The Christians who deconsecrated the temple by throwing the head in the well had a clear understanding of its theology. Where had they got it ? Not among Rome's educated Hellenists, where the temple had for centuries been an object of scorn. Cicero (*loc.cit.*) sneers that nobody of the better sort would think of consulting the *sortes* of Praeneste. Also, we know that there was a body of specifically Praenestine sacred literature (F. COARELLI, *op.cit.,* p.67 and n.63-65 : in n.64 he quotes as late a writer as Solinus) ; who used it ? The answer to both questions must be : a local priesthood. The deconsecration itself of the temple may have been directed and/or carried out by converted priests, as Coifi did in Northumbria ; the sacred writings may then have been burned.

[1 6]   Snorri Sturluson, *Heimskringla* I 6. This is not a wholly reliable document, as it tries to humanize the Germanic gods into mortal sovereigns of Augustus' period. The notice that the first of them, King Odhinn, "spoke only in verse", may have been no more than an attempt to explain away his title of god of poetry.

wisdom that, however unimaginable its scope, however eternal its flow, is not inexpressible : quite to the contrary, it take the form of the highest expressive pitch of human language, the form of poetry.

Coarelli analyzes the temple of Præneste as built around two sacred areas : 1° the well, built into an intermediate level called "the terrace of hemicycles", and 2° the circular sanctuary of Fortuna, built at the top of the whole temple structure. Despite the importance of the well, it is the sanctuary that is the absolute core of the temple, and it is dedicated to Fortuna as such, associated with no other god ; whereas the well was directly under a statue showing Fortuna as a mother, cradling the children Jupiter and Juno. The sanctuary is said to have been built on the site of the honey-pouring olive tree ; therefore it must be the tree, among the elements of the legend, that is connected with Fortuna alone ; and, conversely, any aspect of the cult or of the legend that have to do with the well must be connected with her maternity and her son, because the well is where the *sortes* were found.

We may draw another conclusion. An olive tree is something alive and growing, from which honey flows apparently without rule or restraint, like the roaring waters of Mimir's well. The *sortes* are made of a different substance, and it is certainly no coincidence that the substance in question is oakwood, the wood of Jupitrer's tree. They are dead and cut, not living and growing like the olive : Numerius dug them already carved. By comparison with a living and streaming tree, they represent something limited, with no potentiality of growth, defined, incised, codified ; but capable, unlike the olive - a single object - of many combinations and permutations.

The olive tree is used to make an olivewood box to contain the oakwood *sortes* ; and, in this olivewood container, they are placed in the well, and not in the sanctuary. If, therefore, the wood of her tree is used to make a container for the *sortes* and placed, not in her own individual sacred site - the sanctuary - but in that where the goddess is seen as the mother of Jupiter, she who contains him, who bears him in her body ; this has to mean that the *sortes* are as intimately connected with the essence of Jupiter as the olive tree is with that of Fortuna, and bear the same relationship to him as the olive tree bears to her.

The difference also signals that the being, the substance, of the supreme god, is different from that of Fortuna, in spite of their basic solidarity. It is possible to doubt whether she has anything to do with his conception, although there is no doubt that she is the one who bears him - she bears him in her body as her olive-wood bears his oak-wood inside itself. The name of Fortuna Primigenia - associated only by degeneration to luck, chance, randomness - indicates a kind of universal motherhood ; but motherhood in the sense of bearing, not necessarily in the sense of conceiving. It comes from the root of the verb *ferre,* which interestingly, can mean both "to bear" (children) and "to bear *away"* - the function of time as completer, fulfiller, destroyer even : *omnia fert aetas, animum quoque,* age *fert* all things, even a man's self. Fortuna is the goddess who *fert,* gives birth both to beginnings and to ends - to the whole of everything that is in time, from origin to dissolution.

Fortuna without her pregnancy seems to represent an unfated, unlimited, undefined, chaotic form of being, charged with potentiality but deprived of reality. It is alive, as alive as the olive ; but for her to be the bearer of reality, it must be cut, squared, reduced to defined proportions. We are to understand that fate itself only exists in a world of codifications and limitations, a world of proportions. Nothing could show more visually the distance between chaos and design than the difference between an olive - the most crazy, irregular, knobbly tree in Italy - and a wooden box carpentered according to the rule of the art.

Furthermore, the *sortes* are written objects, words or parts of speech. Words therefore amount to definitions in the etymological sens of the word : *de* + *fineo* "I place an ending (*finis*) that separates from (*de*) anything else" ; they are, and can only be, individual single things with no potential to be other than themselves. That is why the well of the *sortes* was bound up with the head of Fortuna and the theme of heads and springs : if what is born there is the divine Word, or Words, whose totality is the totality of definite being, then such a birth is also the expression of divine wisdom : the sense and understanding of existence, expressed in a coherent linguistic system.

The *sortes* predict the future. This strengthens my views on the meaning of Fortuna's name and the verb *ferre* ; what Fortuna bears is not merely the beginning in time of a universe which is thereafter to evolve autonomously, but rather the whole of time. Indeed, beginnings as such are the province of Janus, a relatively smaller divine figure, not of Jupiter or of His Mother. Jupiter's birth, then, is the same as a primeval, indeed an out-of-time act of speaking ; the person who bears him, bears him as the complex of interrelating facts and things that constitute reality[17].

We remember that we have already reached a similar conclusion, on different grounds, at the end of section III.6. God appears as the complex of interrelations, positive and negative, that rule reality. We should notice the fact that those *sortes* with which the nature of Jupiter is bound up contain in themselves all events : those which, in terms of human experience, exist (the present and the past) as well as those that do not yet have existence (the future) ; in Jupiter, past, present, future, they all just *are*. This god is the god of Things as They Are. The shaping norms and rules, laws and regularities, facts and relationships of the world, are not his creation, but his core ; they are born of his mother, and he is, not the maker of them, but the image of their existence.

On the level of divine reality, there is no need to separate the indivisibility and unalterability of words from the indivisibility and unalterability of the objects they designate. There can be no such thing as wisdom without knowable - defined - objects. This idea of Jupiter explains why he was so close to two minor gods, Terminus and Juventas ; Terminus is the god of endings, of borders, of limitations, and Juventas, as her name says, is a figure of youth[18]. Jupiter is intimately bound with the notion of limitation, and is in cosmic terms

---

[17] I must thank Professor R. Gombrich for pointing out that the conception of God as cosmic language (*SabdaBrahman*) is a fundamental and primordial idea of Hinduism, that goes back all the way to Vedic times.
[18] This is not to contradict Dumézil's bold and beautiful speculations on these two figures, but to integrate them. Dumézil proposed a historical origin for Terminus and Juventas, pointing out parallels in

74

young, as compared with his mother, Fortuna, the chaotic mother/matter (*mater/materia*) of the universe. Form is young, is new, as compared with absolute and formless being ; in conceptual terms, it comes later.

The speech that speaks the universe is the ultimate wisdom, and the words of that wisdom are Jupiter, son of Fortuna. The Goddess Who Bears, *Fortuna, Primigenia* or First-Born, mother and bearer of all things, gives birth to a divine definition that is at once word and existence, the object in the material world and its definition in the divine mind. And the sum of these words is Jupiter, the God Who Is Born.

IV.4 The Latin theory of destiny

The most important rite of the Præneste temple was the yearly opening of the olive-wood case and the extraction of the *sortes,* which, as I said, was performed by a boy-child "impelled by Fortuna". The extraction of the *sortes* from the olive-wood of the mother goddess must be understood as a ritual birth : the boy emerging from the well with the *sortes* is miming the role of Jupiter rising from the womb of Fortuna. In the shadow of the statue of the mother goddess and her children, this cannot be separated from the peculiar position of the god of gods in this temple, where he is only a child[19], subject to his mother as he is subject to no other entity in the world[20]. Remember Virgil's own Jupiter accepting *en bon enfant* the request of his mother to save her sacred ships from fire, even though he found it nonsensical ! Few things were as firmly embedded in Roman ideology as the inferior status of children to parents.

At the end of section II.4, I explained the legend of Æneas' meeting with his dead father in Avernus as a mythologized memory of a prehistoric ritual in which a *iunior* became free of his father's control by a religious fiction which made a living parent dead in law to his adult son ; and, incidentally, initiated the young man into the mysteries of his future. If Æneas was the archetype of the ritual, then the young man in question was also a member of a *uer sacrum,* a league of young men who had in turn the status of dead men to their fathers, as they were seen as a mass human sacrifice ; it seems that the legal fiction may have cut both ways. But, in another respect, Jupiter Indiges' adventures in Avernus are a prime instance of the dependence of the child on the parent : it is his meeting with Anchises in Avernus that closes his period of blind wandering and defines the course of his destiny.

Certainly, of all the episodes in the epic, this meeting with the father is one of the most surely Latin. Nothing about it suggests Homeric imitation. The one person Odysseus does not meet in the world of the dead is Laertes, and his fate is told him, not even by his mother (whom he does meet), but by Teiresias, a specialist in divination both sides of the grave. Neither his mother, nor any of the old friends and enemies he meets, can tell the Greek

Vedic and Germanic theologies ; I wish to show how, given the existing idea, the Latin theologians explained it in terms of their local religion.

[19] The presence of Juno by his side raises a few problems, but we should note that the fact that it is a boy and not a girl who extracts the *sortes* from the olive wood case shows that the *sortes* were connected with the male boy-god (Jupiter) and not with the female girl-goddess (Juno).

[20] Virgil, *Æneid* IX 94-97.

wanderer anything they did not know while alive ; indeed, they have to ask him for information about their own offspring. Anchises, on the other hand, does not limit himself to foretelling his son's course : he shows him the entire future of the race, descendant by descendant in order. The father has all his children *in potentia* before him ; not even merely his immediate son, but all who have his blood in their veins, to the end of time.

What I have observed about the relationship between Fortuna and Jupiter seems to have universal application. The Romans felt that to give life, as such, meant to give life in its every moment from birth to death ; which must be the reason for the immensely high position of parents[2 1] in Roman legend and law. The life of the child was innately dependent on that of the parent, the parent ruled the fate of the child.

It is easy to see that a philosophy in which "to give life" means "to give all of life" must lead to a psychologically-based determinism. If all the moments of your life are part of your being from the start - and they are, since that, and not just the start, is what your parents give you - then your future is made not of possibilities, not even of potentialities, but of inborn and true certainties that wait in you to become facts, from the time of your birth to the completion of your life.

Worshipping the physical parent on such grounds, therefore, implies fatalism ; not a fatalism based on correspondences between Man/Microcosm and Creation/Macrocosm (as in our astrology with its Greek and Chaldæan origins) so much as on a meditation on the nature of individual existence, seen as a unit in which all moments and all aspects of a mortal's life from conception to death amount to so many manifestations on one nature.

These things explain the vicious assault on the head of Fortuna's statue. The cult of Præneste was particularly incompatible with the new faith. The founder of Christianity had told his disciples to deny father and mother ; Præneste exalted physical parenthood. The Prænestine Mother of God opposed the Blessed Virgin in every way, but especially in being, not mortal, but equal and in some sense superior to her son : it is not a coincidence that the same Gospel in which the Blessed Virgin is more highly and authoritatively praised[2 2] is also the one in which she is most comphensively rejected, even in her purely physical role of mother[2 3]. Even worse is the reversal of the notion of Word of God ; and worst of all, for a religion that always opposed determinism, is the fundamental determinism implicit in the Prænestine cult, a far more profound one even than St. Augustine's *bête noire*, astrology. For a religion to which sin may be chosen or rejected by every man, and to which "no nature is wicked in itself, and the word *evil* denotes nothing else than the deprivation of good"[2 4], to say that our sins and crimes are manifestations of our nature and destiny is worse than senseless, it is a genuine encouragement of evil. And to say that these

---

[2 1]   Particularly the father, but, in the story of Coriolanus, the mother as well.
[2 2]   Luke I 28-38, 42-43.
[2 3]   Luke VIII 19-21.
[2 4]   St. Augustine, *The City of God* XI 21 22.

fata, with their burden of evils and sins, are implicit in the nature of God, is blasphemy : God is light, and in Him is no darkness at all[2 5].

Those familiar with the Greek mind will also notice important differences between Greek and Latin attitudes. Just as Roman fatalism came from the personality and Greek fatalism from the stars, so too Greek heroes are constantly dominated, for good or for evil, by the gods, beings outside their own reach and will. Achilles does not keep from killing Agamemnon or Priam because of his own personality ; that would have demanded blood for Briseis and Patroklos. He stops because the gods make him[2 6]. Throughout Greek writing there recurs the formula that the gods made such and such a fellow do this or that. With the Romans it is very nearly the reverse : the gods, when they appear, only make clear to a man or woman what he or she already bore not only in the soul but in the will, more or less disguised. Allecto does not need to use such undignified means as Athena when she pulls Achilles back from Agamemnon by his hair !

If Greek thought knows any theory of history, it is nothing else than a steady decline away from the divine reality of the beginning ; that was perhaps the most basic issue in Plato's philosophy[2 7]. While Æneas travels to the underworld to be initiated into a wisdom that will allow him to create a new world, the only positive thing that Odysseus takes from his own journey among the shades is the privilege of meeting the heroes and heroines of former ages, an experience that affects him deeply. "The men of ancient times were better than we are " and "lived nearer to the gods"[2 8], and he meets with them as the climax of a journey that has already led him beyond the world of men, that has taken him to fight the children of gods and to become the lover of a goddess ; and he himself is already a "man of old", "better and nearer to the gods" than we who hear of his adventures. Men are getting ever further from the gods, and the last gods left on Earth - Righteousness and Shame - are one day to depart from it. This Greek fascination with change as decline from a divine original rest would be quite alien to the Prænestine theology, in which the manifestation of divine wisdom is as much in time as beyond it.

A curious feature of Greek epic myth has some relevance to Æneas' journey : man is distant from the gods - and from man's own divine predecessors of the Golden Age - not only in time, but in space. In archaic Greek cosmology, distance in space seems to match distance in time : the farther out heroes travel, the farther from the mean realities of their age they get. The Golden Age exists still, at this moment in time, the time of the Iron Age in our world, in the Blessed Islands at the end of the Earth, where Kronos still rules untroubled by Zeus. The borders of the world seem to be kept by the children of the Sun ; beyond the homes of Circe, Æetes, and Helios, there is... what ? Olympus ? We don't know. But the

---

[2 5]   1John I 5.

[2 6]   Homer, *Iliad* I 188-200, XXIV.

[2 7]   Sir K. Popper's famous criticism of Plato, *The Open Society and its Enemies,* chap. 3-10, depends on an interpretation based almost totally on Plato's theory of cosmic change and rest. It must never be forgotten that all Plato's theories on society and human personality depended on a clear cosmological theory of creation and decline.

[2 8]   Philebus, 16c.

only thing that Odysseus meets beyond the island of Circe is the Realm of the Dead. From then on, he is not going forwards, but back, returning to his very modest little fiefdom and his middle-aged wife.

But Æneas does not journey from the inside outwards ; he journeys from the outside inwards. He takes divine reality and divine purpose to the mundane land of Latium ; not in worlds of distant wonders, inaccessible to the travellers of a latter world, but in the little slice of land between the mountains, the sea, and the Etruscan territories, home to the very singers who sang his deeds. It is important to realize that, in the earliest version of the story we can reach, Latium was home, the land of the here-and-now, whereas Greece was a distant and semi-fabulous land, the sort of place that legendary foreign heroes come from. Æneas came from Outside, and brought divine power and a divine plan to the Inside, to the Latin home.

This is a part of the original myth, and it underlines the whole story content of book VI ; therefore, however transfigured by Hellenistic ideas, the basic content of book VI must be Latin. We have found a Latin and certainly non-Hellenic significance for every major feature of it, from the geographical location in the Birdless Lake to the cast of characters beginning with Æneas' father, to the prophecies uttered, to the ritual involved. It is Latin ; and it is a crucial stage in the epic, taking us through a vision of the history of the world not as a decline, but as an actualization, the transformation of potentiality into reality.

However, we might also say that the loss of potentiality itself is, in its own way, a kind of degenerative process. The kind of being that Anchises was if he contained within himself the potentiality and/or the fate of such vast things as Æneas, Romulus the God, and the noblest heroes of Rome - and let's not add Cæsar the God, and Octavian Augustus the Saviour - must have been simply inconceivable to such beings as haunt these lesser days. We must call him a god, if the word has any meaning at all.

Nevertheless, the blank cosmic despair inherent in the Homeric world-view is quite alien to Roman ideas. We are used to consider "fatalism" and "pessimism" as synonymous, but in Rome we have a positive, indeed aggressive fatalism, that may be traced as far back in the history of Latium as native records get. Sir K.R. Popper's attack on Plato's historicism will be familiar to many, but not everybody may be aware that an equally brilliant man, C.S. Lewis, has written an essay on the same subject, that, while clearly influenced by Popper's great book, makes a useful and important distinction directly relevant to this study[29]. Lewis points out that it is Roman epic, not Greek, that is radically historicistic, that it is Roman epic that is certain that "history has a meaning" and that that meaning was spelled R-O-M-A. Rome (as Dumézil puts it) was the highest reality accessible to mortal senses. And as Lewis reminds us, Virgil did not invent his historicistic theory ; he found it ready made in his epic Latin predecessors, Ennius and Nævius. Lewis is indubitably correct : the subject of the *Æneid,* "such was the labour of the birth of Rome", is also the subject of Nævian and

---

[29]   C.S. LEWIS, *Fern-Seed and Elephants*, London, 1975, p.49 ("Historicism").

Ennian epic, whose ground plan is simply a contemplation of the rise of Rome, from Æneas' journey to her final triumph in the Punic Wars. Two centuries before Virgil, the Romans were already convinced that Rome was a creation of divine purposes, and that its history was the realization of divine plans.

For this reason Virgil turns the generally pessimistic cast of the Platonic mind around. Plato may or may not, as Popper suggests, have seen himself as the Philosopher King come to reverse the decline of the world, but Virgil's predecessors certainly saw Rome as sacred and predestined to some special fate. This made it easy for him to believe that the Golden Age was now bound, in solid fact, to come back : the climax of Roman history - the enthronement of the Julian dynasty, descended fron the national father Æneas - surely preluded to some special providence.

IV.5 Unsolved problems of the theology of fatherhood and sonship

Some characteristic problems in the idea of fatherhood and sonship within Jupiter and Lug remain unsolved.From the point of view of the Prænestine cult, Jupiter is One, and his manifestations are manifold ; it seems that his mystical content includes a functional opposition between the utter unity of his essential nature and the utter multifariousness of his activity. This distinction goes far to explain his division in two persons : have we, or have we not, agreed, the benevolent immortal person is the face of the healing unity - in the end, the face of the inner harmony between all things - and the angry, mortal, avenging face is the face he shows to those who oppose healing and unity ? The doubleness of God is not hard to explain. Nor, indeed, is the distinction between mortal and immortal identity ; for the distinction runs just there, between limit and limitlessness, end and endlessness, death and immortality. Latins and Celts did not know the Cross ; between death and immortality, as far as they saw, there was nothing but simple opposition.

What is not so easy to see is why the two aspects should be conceived of as father and son ; nor, indeed, why there should be no agreement between the couples in question. Cúchulainn, mortal and avenging, is the son of Lug, immortal and healing ; but Æneas is the father of peaceful Ascanius. Taliesin is the father of vindictive Avaon ; but Lancelot is the father of holy Galahad. Indeed, when we come to Lancelot, we come to something quite self-contradictory ; while in one version of his legend he is the fighting father of good Galahad, embroiled in a hopeless weave of revenges because of his adulterous love for Guinevere, in another he turns up as the rescuer of beleaguered Sir Kai, which is clearly to do with the image of the healing Lug helping his avenging son. But then this is in keeping with the eternally surprising double meaning of Lug, both Cúchulainn's healer and himself the avenger of the second battle of Moytura.

The matter is further complicated by the presence of a third, undeniably paternal figure - Æneas' Anchises, Lug's Cian - whose death shapes the life of his mighty son. In both traditions, the only real act of of this otherwise very shadowy father is his creative death ;

that is what brings about the rise of the son (who is both father and son himself) to colossal power. His presence is as though the presence of a death.

I fail to see how such a figure of paternity will square with the double identity of father and son within the hero-god. I can make only one suggestion : that is, that Lug and Jupiter may have been seen as in some way their own causes, self-generated, and endowed with a kind of mutual fatherhood, where one aspect is the cause of the other. Certainly, however, the arrival of Lug and of Jupiter Indiges is the arrival of the Cosmic Youth, who has a relation of sonship with older realities, who is himself a son ; but who is also, in several respects, a father to things that will follow him[30].

IV.6 Unsolved problems of the theology of motherhood and sonship

More questions arise in the area of the relationship of such a supreme God with "the other half of the sky". We have retrieved an important Latin cult whose core was the relationship of Jupiter with a mother goddess, but which features no father god at all ; and we add that one of the most important account of Lug - the *Mabinogi* of *Math vab Mathonwy*, already very familiar to us - gives him a mother, but no father ; his birth is mysterious[31]. Not only is this very like what we know of the Prænestine cult, but there are striking parallels.

1° The object connected with Jupiter in Præneste is a set of oakwood slivers which, *by order of the local wise men* (*who do not trouble to explain their reasons for this*), have been closed in a *square olivewood box,* which I have analyzed as *a mystical image of pregnancy.*

2° Lleu is born from his mother Arianrhod whitout any shape or identity ; *Gwydion, the local wise man* (*who does not trouble to explain his action*), encloses the mysterious object in a *square box,* over which he keep watch until Lleu is born, having undergone *a magical pregnancy in the box.*

The two stages of his birth, paralleled with the two stages of the emergence of the *sortes,* bring to mind the theme of the foster-mother, which so troubled Livy and Virgil. I have shown that a foster-mother character was an essential part of the Æneas-Ascanius, father-son complex ; both Æneas and Ascanius have a foster-mother, and the foster-mother of Lug in Ireland, Tailtiu, is very important to his cult, while his mother Ethniu, to the best of my knowledge, received no cult at all.

The cosmogonic myth that underlies the Prænestine foundation legend associates Fortuna with the olivewood box and Jupiter with the oakwood *sortes* : you might, in fact, say that Fortuna bears Jupiter in a box. Now, when Gwydion encloses the substance of the future Lleu in a box, Lleu has already had his first birth, and is mother is Arianrhod. The parallel dictates that Fortuna should be seen as the foster-mother, not as the mother. Her

---

[30] Æneas is the *pater* of Rome, we are told again and again ; that is why his story is important to Virgil.

[31] Lug has other birth stories, even apart from the matter of Cúchulainn's triple birth or the rebirth of Gwion Bach as Taliesin. Ireland attributes him both a father (Cian) and a mother (Eithniu) ; curiously, Lug is most often reffered to as mac Eithniu rather than mac Cein, even in the *Fate of the Children of Tuirenn,* where Cian plays a rather more important role than Eithniu.

name implies bearing, not necessarily generating, and her Præneste statue showed her breast-feeding him ; now, if we have to separate the roles of mother and foster-mother - which is bound to include that of wet-nurse - then certainly the Prænestine Fortuna was not Jupiter's mother, but his foster-mother. The Prænestine myth does not make his mother's identity clear, unless indeed she is the mountain in whose flanks the *sortes* were found.

We know from *Math vab Mathonwy* that Lleu's original mother, Arianrhod, regarded him with something like detestation, because he reminded her of when great Math tested her for virginity and found her wanting. This agrees with Lug's mother Eithniu detesting him ; though, interestingly, the reason for her dislike is very different. Ethniu is of the race of demons (Fomoire) ; her son ends up killing her kinsmen ; she mourns their deaths, and would rather, it seems, have seen him die rather than them. It seems possible that the rejection as such was the fundamental datum, and that different stories were made up to account for it.

But even this is uncertain. Lancelot, also son of a murdered father, has a mother and a foster-mother (the Lady of the Lake), but Roger Sherman Loomis, the same man who made the epoch-making discovery of the identity of Lancelot and Lug, showed that it is his foster-mother, and not his mother, who seems comparable to Arianrhod, with her high birth and an odd, unexplained sense of outrage[32]. There is no indication that Venus, the true mother of Æneas, felt disdain or hostility towards him ; but, like Arianrhod, it was she who had to give her son his weapons[33]. Some aspects of Arianrhod's hostility to Lleu are paralleled in the Latin legend by the actions of Amata/Amita and Juno : of these two, Amata is not related to Æneas in any way[34] and Juno is certainly neither the mother nor the foster-mother of Jupiter. She is his sister ; this is proved by the Præneste cult, in which she and Jupiter were both breast-fed by Fortuna, an image which owes nothing to Hellenism, and may well be the reason why she was identified with Hera, sister and wife of the Greek supreme being.

There is in fact a systematic ambiguity in type and function between mother and foster-mother, that brings closely to mind the ambiguities of Lug as father and Lug as son, Lancelot and Galahad, Æneas and Iulus. Præneste and other Latin sanctuaries worshipped two Fortunæ, and this has to be connected with the problem of mother and foster-mother. This is the state of my research as I write ; and, as the topic of this book is Æneas rather than Fortuna, I feel justified in leaving it at that.

---

[32]   R.S. LOOMIS, *Lanzelet*, p.165n.18(4).

[33]   The identification of Æneas/Indiges' divine mother (who is certainly the Latin deity Venus, to whom Lavinium was sacred) with Aphrodite is clumsy and uninspired, the least attractive result of the Greek interpretation of Latin divinities. The goddess of Latin epic is clearly a mother figure, whose shoes the Greek goddess of lust fills very badly indeed ; the Julian dynasty, living in a period in which Latin theology was practically forgotten, nevertheless was brought by the mere factual content of the legend to stress Venus/Aphrodite as a mother.

[34]   That is indeed why she hates him.

CHAPTER V : FIRE FROM HEAVEN

V.1 Introductory : burning the boats

After our trip to Præneste, we return to Virgil and the shores of Latium, where the hero and his three hundred young comrades have landed ; and we take a look at the craft that took them there.

Italy's Æneas-legends have a remarkable number of episodes concerned with fire, and more specifically with boats set on fire by women. Dionysios' useful pedantry saved us a few ; some of them pre-date any Latin story we have, proving that the image of women setting fire to ships was present even in that earliest and most confused Greek accounts[1]. Hellanikos, a very early historian[2], has Aineias reach Italy in the company of, believe it or not, Odysseus - Troy's worst enemy ! - and a Trojan woman called Rhome[3], who, weary with wandering, sets fire to the ships. One of Aristotle's encyclo-pedic works spoke of some nameless Achæans blown off course by a storm and dropped in "Latinion", where some Trojan women prisoners burnt their ships in the night ; a story so fuddled we would think it much older than Hellanikos', did we not know for a fact that this man came full a century before Aristotle.

This suggests that the theme was not well known among the educated Hellenes ; that it amounted to a set of notices that some of them might have heard, and some not. That Aristotle, the master of learning, is so little familiar with it, proves absolutely that even the most learned men in Greece knew little of it, despite the fact that writing had become common and information flowed freely within Greek world. In fact, it strongly suggests that the legend of burning boats was not a common Greek matter at all, that few Greeks would have heard of them, that they did not belong to the Greek world.

There is more. Aristotle's attitude, even more than his detail, is revealing. He is clearly not interested, and hardly bothers to give a name to these "Achæans". But Homeric epic lore was always a matter of central importance to Greek savants - and indeed to Greeks of all kinds - who used to discuss each morsel of the central tradition, tear it to pieces, challenge and counter-challenge it with quite liturgical seriousness. Aristotle's note, with the typical

---

[1]   Dionysios of Halicarnassus, I 72 2-4.
[2]   Dating back to the fifth century BC. This not only proves that the idea of Trojan women burning ships was associated with Rome from the very beginning, but also that the state of Rome was important enough for its foundation legend to get the attention of a mainland Greek historian of Perikles' age. Rome, therefore, was already a serious player on the Italian stage by 450 BC or thereabouts, in complete defiance of the picture given by annalistic legend, which shows her fooling around with her immediate neighbours, and doing nothing that could possibly trouble the counsels, or interest the writings, of someone like Hellanikos, who wrote on subjects like Athenian history and the chronology of the priestesses of Hera at Argos. Curiously enough, Dionysios' phrasing suggests that it was in this chronology that the story of Aineias, Odysseus and "Rhome" was found.
[3]   Greek for "strength", and clearly a pun on Rome.

82

flavour of something just tacked on for the sake of completeness, is at a hundred and eighty degrees from that. He is clearly relating an oddity of small concern.

Altough no written evidence from Latium can confirm or deny anything of so early a date, I feel confident, from the tone of these accounts, that they were ill-recorded sailors' news of a thing that they had heard, perhaps not from reliable sources and perhaps not at first hand, about the traditions of a distant country - Hesperia, the Western Land - and that their origin was not Greek at all, but native. The whole group has an evanescent air that places it very far indeed from the intensely-felt Homeric material ; but every tradition of burning ships and/or Trojan women was associated with Italy, and frequently with Latium and Aineias/Æneas. It was the native Italians, not the Greek colonists, who claimed Æneas for their ancestor, an Ægean origin for themselves, and said that a burning of ships had stranded their fathers so far from Greece.

The next generation of stories is far more reliable. They are undeniably Latin in origin and come from an intelligent traveller like Timæus and from learned Italians like Cato the Elder, Nævius and Ennius ; but they have the defect of being fragmented beyond recovery, and, in the case of Cato, very unreliable. It is not until we come to Virgil, Livy and Dionysios, that we get full and elabortae descriptions. Virgil and Dionysios[4] each know of two major burning episodes, parts of complete cycles that take the heroes from Troy to Latium and to the founding of the Latin holy city, Lavinium.

The Trojan expedition's boats have a notable habit of being set on fire. In the fifth book, Juno, taking advantage of the exhaustion of the expedition's women after years of travel, send Iris[5] to Sicily to suggest they torch the beached boats. At first shy of the suggestion, the women are suddenly seized with madness when Iris, previously disguised as one of them, resumed her original shape ; only to suddenly realize what they 've done, and flee in despair, when Iulus and Æneas appear on the scene[6].

This episode simply simmers with disguised deities. Iris, Juno's messenger, disguises herself as the aged wide Beroe, and it is her self-revelation in her true colours (literally) as the divine rainbow that sets the women aflame with rage ; then, when the hulks are already burning, Iulus and Æneas, who both seem to have been somewhere else at the crucial moment, turn up suddenly, to the women's immense dismay. As they flee from the sight of the hero, the flames subside at his bequest under the god's rain, sent almost toolate.

The second burning is even more full of the supernatural[7]. Iris inspires Æneas' enemy Turnus to assault the Trojan camp while Æneas is away. Looking for some harm to do to his well-defended handfull of enemies, he seizes on the idea of burning their bea-ched fleet ; the ships, however, are made of sacred pine, grown on the slopes of the Mother of Gods' holy mountain, and lent to Æneas to sail him to his destiny, but definitely not to be turned by

---

4   Dionysios of Halicarnassus, I 52 4, 59 4.
5   Who, in the Latin epic, is always at her service.
6   Virgil, *Æneid* V 604-699.
7   Virgil, *Æneid* IX 69-125.

some jumped-up Rutulian thug ! In an astonishing scene, by consent of God Himself - Jupiter in a superficially Hellenizing, Homeric guise - the ships are changed to mighty living creatures, goddesses of the sea ; and a voice thunders out a riddling threat against Turnus[8].

Our authors give very different accounts of the two burning episodes, especially the second. But they agree on no less than six different points.

1° There are two, and no more than two, burning episodes ; one of the two burning in Dionysios, and both both of them in Virgil, involve the Trojan ships.

2° Both episodes, as well as all the minor traditions, are directly connected with Trojan landfalls ;

3° The first of the two happens half-way through the journey, the other at its end.

4° The first of the two is carried out by the women of Æneas' expedition, weary with wandering ; the result is that women and old men are left behind, and the company is transformed into an age-class company of marriageable young men.

5° The second is carried out by no human agency, and is a direct if riddling prophecy of the war that Æneas is to fight against Turnus, and the victory he is to gain.

6° The first burning results in the founding of a fully-fledged city, while the second happens only at the beginning of the vicissitudes which are to result in the foundation of Lavinium, Alba Longa, end eventually Rome ; the first has the force of immediately achieved fact, the second only of the beginning of fact.

V.2 The figure in the carpet

These These episodes find an important Celtic parallel in the document which, of all Celtic documents, is the closest in spirit to Rome's elaborate pseudo-histories : the Irish *Lebor Gabála Éireann* or "Book of the Conquests of Ireland", a systematic and rather plodding compilation of pseudo-historical lore tracing Irish 'history" from the beginning. The episode that concerns us is the coming of the gods, the Tuatha Dé Danann[9], to Ireland, counted as the fourth of five invasions. The gods come in magic boats, and in two separate waves : the first is led by Nuada Silverhand and includes a whole nation of men, women and children ; the second consists of Lug, either alone[10] or followed by a glorious company of young men (young gods ?)[11]. Each of these arrivals is marked by a boat-burning : the first as soon as the people of the gods, men and women, but withou Lug, first land in Ireland[12] ;

---

[8]   Virgil contradicts himself on one occasion, making Juno assert that Venus, the mother of Æneas, was the one who made this miracle (*Æneid* X 83).

[9]   *Tuatha Dé Danann* means "People of the goddess Danu". Danu must be the mother goddess, though not much is known about her. The word *tuath* means a legally constitued independant kingdom with a king at its head ; the Tuatha Dé Danann, though otherworldly, were instinctively understood in the light of Irish law and policy. For that matter, their conquest of Ireland was taken to be a factual historical event, and to conquer Ireland they had to be a kingdom of the same kind as any other.

[10]   In the *Lebor Gabála* version.

[11]   In the *Fate of the Children of Tuireann.*

[12]   LGE V 267, 269, VII 306.

the second when the same gods burn the boats of the newly arrived Lug. The reason for this is not clear, but there is some sense of hostility to the young hero-god[1 3].

The structural parallels between these episodes and those of the Æneid are extensive and fundamental. Consider :

1° there are two successive burnings, and no more than two, and they are in the same order in both pseudo-histories ;

2° the people of the gods, men, women and children, come to Ireland after a great sea journey[1 4] and burn their boats ; they, and nobody else, are responsible for burning them ;

3° after the boats are burnt, the Tuatha Dé Danann establish a fully functional state in Ireland ; they are themselves a people with all the skills and specialities needed for a state to exist ; after the boats are burnt, Æneas leves the body of the expedition in Sicily, where they establish, not a fortress, but a full-fledged new city, leaving there, not only the women and the old men, but also anybody who so wishes, a whole *populus* in fact, with no desire for glory[1 5] ;

4° Lug then comes to Ireland, where the gods have already established a kingdom, either alone or with a company of young males ; the kingdom of Latinus, son, grandson and great-grandson of gods[1 6], was already established in Latium when Æneas came there with a company of young males ;

5° whoever was responsible for burning Lug's boats, it wasn't Lug, and there is a strong hint that it was an hostile act from the other gods ; this is different from the first burning, in which the gods themselves, after landing, burned their own boats ; Lug did not ; Æneas was responsible for neither of the burnings, and both of them, especially the second, are, in Virgil's version, hostile or rebellious acts coming ultimately from Juno ; but the first was carried out by the women of the *populus* who actually settled in the island of Sicily[1 7] ; in

---

1 3 LGE VII 358 (they are burned to keep him from fighting Nuada, the then king of the gods) and VII 59 (they are burned to keep him from running away, which is patently ridiculous).

1 4 They actually come down on a mountain of Conmaicne Rein, in the inland part of Leitrim and nowhere near the sea. Ireland, however, is as much an island culturally as it is geographically. The great mass of the ocean, cutting into the land through thousands of inlets and loughs, must be seen as its unchanging background ; the Irish have always been very clear about this. Therefore, any foreigner come from Outside to Ireland must be said to have crossed the sea ; all other four invasions of Ireland are said to have landed on the island's beaches ; and most versions of the Tuatha's coming say they came in boats, however magical.

1 5 Virgil, *Æneid* V 737-761. Is it a coincidence that Virgil (V 750) uses the word *populus,* almost exactly the translation of Irish *tuath,* to describe the inhabitants of Æneas' Sicilian "New Troy" ? I don't believe so : both words have a legal content, indicating the full functional and participating citizenship of a free state (*Senatus Populusque Romanus* "the legitimate ruling institutions and citizenship of Rome"). The Tuatha Dé Danann were a nation, not even itself exclusively divine, since a *Lebor Gabála* passage explains that the workers among them were not gods ; their recognizable characteristic, therefore, was not divine identity, but national cohesion.

1 6 He was the son of Faunus, son of the god Picus, son of the god Saturn ; and his mother was either Fauna or Fatua ("the Fate-Speaker", an oracular goddess, as was Faunus) or Marica ; all of them immortals. Latinus was, in short, of divine blood from both sides.

1 7 It may not be a coincidence that Ireland is also an island. They may have been some sort of pre-historic shift in the telling, in which the *tuath* of the gods landed, not in some other island, but in what, to its inhabitants, was the "island" *par excellence,* whereas in Latium they were left elsewhere, to serve as a sort of reserve for further invasion legends, like the shadowy figure of Fergus Lethderg and indeed the ancestors of the last three invasions in the *Lebor Gabála Éireann.* Fergus Lethderg's people never came to Ireland at all, just like the Trojan *populus* in Sicily never came to Latium. But these conjectures are unprofitable, at least at the present stage of our knowledge ; it is better not to expect perfect agreement.

other words, the first burning is connected with the settling of the Trojans, not in Latium but in Sicily, as a people of men and women, not unlike the settlement of male and female Tuatha Dé Danann in Ireland, but without Lug ; the second burning, on the other hand, is directed against Æneas and his splendid company of young warriors, just as the second burning in Ireland is directed against Lug (who, in the *Fate of the Children of Tuireann,* leads a splendid company of young warriors) ;

6° the coming of Lug to Ireland "frightened the horses" in some sense, upset a previously existing, if unfair, balance, and caused a war of liberation ; in the *Fate of the Children of Tuireann,* Nuada Silverhand has little pleasure in his presence because he seems resolute to bring about war with the oppressive Fomoire ; in the *Lebor Gabála,* he shows just up as war with the pretender Bres had his sinister Fomoire associates looms ; this is surely to be connected with the fact that his boat-burning is a hostile act against him ; likewise, the coming of Æneas to Latium upsets the previous balance, in which Turnus, not himself a king, had made himself indispenseble to King Latinus and all but usurped the royal power, associating with the sinister exile Mezentius ; for this reason, there is war till Latinus is liberated from such an overpowering courtier ; the connection of the second burning with hostility to Æneas is not unclear or hypothetical, Turnus strats it himself ;

7° the folk left behind in Acesta are specifically characterized as a *populus* with no desire for glory, who elect to stay behind while Acesta goes to Latium with three hundred young men to fight a great war ; in the *Fate of the Children of Tuireann,* Lug is not welcome to Nuada Silverhand's kingdom, because they have no desire to go to war against the Fomoire, in fact no desire for glory.

The mythological concepts involved are unique, starting with the very idea that the gods have, in a historical but remote past, actually come to live in the country concerned, Latium or Ireland, and reigned and fought wars in it. Both nations saw the gods as coming to their land from the ocean in boats, an interesting idea in itself, visibly out of place in Latium, whose history should if anything have instilled race-memories of invaders coming over the mountains ; but in fact just as strange among the Irish, an insular but not a seafaring people. There is no reason why they should not though of themselves as autochthonous ; but, in any case, the Latin parallel makes it certain that the idea far predates the Celtic settlement of the island[18]. For that matter, why boats ?

Equally unusual is the idea, found both in the *Æneid* and in the *Lebor Gabála Éireann,* that the gods or other settlers (such as the Children of Míl, fathers of the present Irish race) have to "seek" for Latium or Ireland ; and not only unique but incomprehensible except as part of a particular and well-understood theology, is the concept that the journey or journeys end with two boat-burnings of opposite and complementary kinds. The first boat-burning involve the people of the gods, understood as a national entity, whether you call it kingdom, state or tribes ; they burn their vessels by their own decision, and the women are predo-

[18]   It tickles the imagination to try and conceive how a landlocked La Tène Celt from Burgundy of Bohemia, far from the very knowledge of any actual sea, would have described the gods' ocean journey !

minant in the decision-making process. The second involves the supreme god, who was not a part of the first settlement, who arrives in the form of a young male warrior, either alone or together with a band of young men of his own age, and who is not made welcome : the burning is a hostile act bound in some way with the great war he has come to fight.

On the other hand, there is one vast structural difference that forbids us to suggest borrowings in either direction : the Irish gods come in two successive waves, impressing themselves upon the same reality and forming, eventually, one people ; the Trojans travel in one company, splitting up along the way and the people left behind in Sicilian New Troy leave no impression upon Latin reality, where Æneas and his people merge with a quite separate people. No, the Celts did not borrow this idea from the Italics, nor the Italics from them. The cultural ancestors of both people elaborated their original legend before they became divided in Central Europe, but after they had become a recognizable separate Celto-Italic group within the Indo-European complex.

(There is even a more unexpected conclusion to be drawn from this : it cannot be coincidence that these two myths occur in the middle of two elaborate pseudo-histories of the two nations from remote antiquity down to the writer's present day, the huge Roman complex presented by Dionysios and the even huger *Lebor Gabála Éireann*, which, in spite of vast variations, have a canonic chronology and a recognizably "learned" air. The Latin and Celtic propensity for creating pseudo-histories, evident not only in the texts we are studying but also in Geoffrey of Monmouth's compilation and in the improbably vast historical/genealogical material that underlies Welsh documents such as the Triads, must be pushed very far back in time indeed : much farther that the introduction of alphabetinc writing to either Latium or the Celtic countries ; as far back as their prehistoric common origin. Celt and Latins always, from the very beginning, thought in terms of long historical periods.)

The Rees brothers devote a whole chapter of *Celtic Heritage* to showing that the Celtic and especially Irish myths of sea-journeys in search of Ireland are images of "coming into existence", entering the reality of this Earth from an unknown Outside, and at the same time forming it when it was still formless and empty[1 9]. This dovetails the Latin theory of destiny as I described it earlier : we only have to understand the mysterious Outside from which the gods come to form Ireland or Latium as a visible, material counterpart of the idea of potentiality I described, and Latium's history is its realization. The process of destiny, we have already seen, is described in Jupiter Indiges' inwards journey from the distant Outside, through the cosmic ocean, to Latium : the world of realization, of becoming real.

This explains why the people of the gods arrive to Ireland, whereas the people of Troy are left behind in an intermediate island : in both case, this represents an imperfect stage of the process of coming into existence, whereas the arrival of Lug or Jupiter Indiges is the final and completing term of the sequence. In Ireland, the sequence is completed by two

---

[1 9]   A.D. REES - B. REES, *op.cit.,* p.95-117.

successive landings on the island ; in Latium, by two successive stages of the same expedition ; what matters is that the sequence is completed. The two boat-burnings must represent t fundamental successive stages in this process of coming into existence.

V.3 The ministers of fire

The first burning in the *Lebor Gabála Éireann* had the spectacular peculiarity of producing so much smoke that it darkened the sky for three days. The text more or less wonders whether the gods had set fire to their boats or whether they had come riding wild storm-clouds. There is an overarching vision of great black clouds, large to the point of blotting the sky altogether.

We are reminded of that the first burning episode in the *Æneid* climaxes with wild storm-clouds completely blotting the sky[20]. There is an unbroken, almost cinematographic sequence : the lovely, deceptive rainbow, sent by Juno to cause disaster, rises above the first wisps of smoke ; the clouds thicken ; Iulus, far away on horseback, sees them across the horizon ; he rides desperately, followed by the whole Trojan crowd and by his father ; his appearance marks a temporary reprieve, as the women are scattered by the terrible realization of what they have done. The effect is almost a ray of light in a dark place. But it's not enough. The verse rages across the page :

> Still this put not to rest the restless strength
>
> Of fire and flame ; within, under wet beams
>
> The tow's alive, and vomits out dull smoke,
>
> Slow vapour through the hulls...[21]

Then, as human efforts fail to deal with the disaster, Æneas raises his hands to heaven and calls on Jupiter, god of clouds and rain : and Jupiter *Pluuius* answers Jupiter *Indiges* :

> Hardly has he spoken, when the rains were pouring
>
> From a dark sky ; the clouds burst, and the earth,
>
> Hard lands and fields, was shaken all by thunder,
>
> And trembled. Scirocco-whipped, from the æther whole
>
> The rain ruined down, black as pitch and turbid ;
>
> The hulls flood, the now half-burnt oak beams
>
> Are dampened ; all vapours, quenched ; and all crafts,
>
> Save four, are saved from the plague[22].

---

[20] This coincidence between arrival of the gods to Earth and darkening of the sky is interesting. Latin legend has another rather similar episode : when Mars came down from Heaven to beget Romulus on Rhea Silvia, the Sun vanished and the sky was darkened (Dionysios of Halicarnassus, I 77 2). It seems Latins and Celts had a picture of gods coming to Earth and causing light to vanish from the sky. Dionysios irritably notes that most writers on Roman history insist on quoting this altogether unreasonable and fabulous account, most repugnant to his Hellenistic intellectual prudery ; this shows that it was a well-established tradition.

[21] Virgil, *Æneid* V 680-683 : *Sed non incirco flammae atque incendia uires*
Indomitas posuere : udo sub robore uiuit
Stuppa uomens tardum fumum lentusque carinas
Est uapor...

[22] Virgil, *Æneid* V 693-699 : *Vix haec edoderat, cum effusis imbribus atra*

This passage relies on a series of visual images bringing together smoke and clouds, water of the sea and water of the sky (rain), fire of the earth and fire of the sky (thunder). The rainbow, an object connected with all these things, appears not above the clouds as it should, but rather above the first wisps of smoke from the ships' fire. This immediately forms a sort of visual continuity, or confusion if you will, between smoke and clouds.

The second boat-burning, that of Turnus, associates fire, ship-wood, smoke, ocean and rainbow with still more strength. Turnus' assault on the Trojan boats bears some resemblance to a well-known Homeric scene, Hector taking fire to the Achæan ships[2 3]. But this can surely be no more than Virgil noting with pleasure (and perhaps some relief) that there was a Homeric episode - and not one of the less fine - that he could use. Any idea he may have imitated Homer's content completely breaks down when one considers what actually happens. Driven by a vision of Iris, Turnus dares try to set the Trojans ships on fire ; they, however, have been cut from a sacred tree garden (*lucus*) consecrated to the Mother of Gods, who pleads to her son Jupiter to be allowed to save them from the fire ; a light like a false dawn appears in the east ; and while the boats turn into water-spirits, an invisible voice speaks riddling words of doom against Turnus.

The scene is redolent with the Latin idea of the *lucus*: the ships are holy because they were made with wood from the *lucus* of the Mother[2 4]. *Lucus* is usually translated as "sacred wood", and the Romans thought of them as such, but Dionysios' description of the *lucus* of Jupiter Indiges at Lavinium[2 5] and the remains of the temple of Juno in Gabii[2 6] prove that a *lucus* was a garden with trees laid out in regular rows. This was a very Latin fact ; though Greece did have sacred woods, they were nowhere as important[2 7]. A *lucus* was a most sacred place, closely associated with the god of the temple, and to cut it down was an atrocious blasphemy. The god's voice was often heard there, settling disputes and announcing destinies, just as the prophetic voice declares in riddling terms the destiny of Turnus.

What is more, the sea-goddess ships are almost ludicrously distant from Homeric religion, style and method[2 8]. Not even Argo, and not by a million miles any single one out

---

Tempesta sine more furit tonitrusque tremescunt
Ardua terrarum et campi ; ruit aethere toto
Turbidus imber aqua densisque nigerrimus austris
Implenturque super puppes, semiusta madescunt
Robora, restinctus donec uapor omnis, et omnes,
Quattuor amissis, seruatae a peste carinae.

2 3   Homer, *Iliad* VIII 172-184, 335-349, 487-541.

2 4   Virgil, *Æneid* IX 86. The Mother of Gods is pleading to Jupiter to save "her" ships ; after saying that they were cut from a *silua* - an ordinary wood with no particular mystical meaning - belonging to her, she corrects herself within a line : no, it wasn't just a *silua*, it was a *lucus*. Ans is it too much to suggest that it is because of this correction that an unwilling Jupiter allows her to perform the miracle ?

2 5   Dionysios of Halicarnassus, I 64 5.

2 6   F. COARELLI, *op.cit.*, p.14-21.

2 7   Dionysios' remarks about the *lucus* of Lavinium show that he found it something alien, unexpected, and quite surpisingly beautiful. He singles out the beauty of the trees themselves ; I wish he had said what kind of trees they were ! But it is clearly not a kind of thing he found familiar ; he sounds like nothing so much as a Western visitor describing a Japanese Zen garden.

2 8   Even disregarding the miracle, however, this was military a senseless act ; you want to leave an invader a way to flee, not to pen him in, and make him desperate. Turnus' stated war aim was to drive the Trojans in the sea, and yet he tries to destroy the most convenant way to drive them ! The Latins, long used

of a thousand ships at Troy, ever had remotely somuch personality. Not only these ships turned into persons ; they are the true protectors of Æneas, warning him from a distance when there is need of him, and giving his new and ordinary fleet some badly needed extra speed[29]. It is through their power that Æneas returns to Latium in time with an army to fight his war ; they are evidently to do with opening ways (especially sea ways) from Outside to the Latin homeland. The warning they give connects them in some way with the prestigious virgin Vestals[30], keepers of the eternal flame of the Roman state, who ritually deliver the same warning to the King of Rome.

I see the role of the ships/Nymphs as that of the odorous smoke[31] issuing from the wood through the agency of fire, and coming originally from the water that those same plants had drank. The part of wood that fire transforms to smoke must be seen as the more volatile, aerial part ; what is left is ashes, a notorious sterile and dead substance. Primitive logic must suggest that, if plants made of wood were alive, and if what is left when they are done burning is the most dead of dead substances, then what is released in the air must be the life of plants ; without it, they die. It knows that water comes from clouds ; and when plants meet their ultimate end in fire, they release smoke : a substance very like the clouds of the sky, especially the stormier black ones. Experience will show that much of smoke is in fact steam, that is water, or other kinds of liquid. The ships, at that, are burnt near the shore of the ocean, the father of waters. This is why the ship-Nymphs are compared, if not even identified, with the virgin Vestals priestesses of fire ; the smoke of the fire carries mortal offerings to heaven, and these goddesses must be the helpers of the fire in its task as the Vestal help and tend it on Earth. For the same reason, I would suggest, it is their power that takes Æneas back to Latium in time for the war : the smoke of the sacrificial fire takes the gods to Earth, to their own sacrifice.

Thunder, finally, which is and always has been the peculiar attribute of Jupiter in Latium, forms another connection between atmospheric waters and fire, coming as it does from the ultimate Outside, the sky, unapprocheable by any man, in the middle of fierce rain and dark clouds, and striking and setting fire at will. In it, the mysterious and terrible power that unifies fire, water and air is most frighteningly manifest.

V.4 Fire, smoke and the gods

The association of smoke and the descent of the gods is compelling. Greece, for instance, knew well that the gods came to the site of a sacrifice along the trail of odorous smoke.

---

to war, were no doubt aware of this when the story was compiled. Hector's assault was not as senseless, since the enemy had been camped for years and the ships were not so much its means to flee as to communication line with its base, bringing supplies and reinforcements.

[29] Virgil, *Æneid* X 228-245, and especially 246-247 where
Dixerat et dextra discedens impulit altam
Haud ignara modi puppim. Fugit illa per undas,
Ocior et iaculo et ventos aequante sagitta...
they don't just speak to him in dreams, but give him powerful physical, corporeal help.

[30] G. DUMEZIL, *op.cit.*, I p.391-392, quoting festus, an ancient commentator of Virgil.

[31] A type of steam, hence of water.

An Orphic myth makes Zeus follow the smell of roasting meat down to the place where the Titans are carving up and cooking the body of his son Dionysos[3 2]. The Orphics were a dissident pacifist sect within the body of Greek religion, and this story is surely written in protest against the Greek practice of blood sacrifice ; therefore its testimony is precious, being built as a protest against a precise set of sacerdotal ideas. The Titans are presented almost in the same light as the Christian devils, originators of evil in the world : but please notice how the story agrees with Hesiod's "official version"[3 3] in every important aspect.

1° That aspect of sacrifice which has to do with carving and dividing up originates with members of the Titanic race : in Hesiod, the Titan Prometheus makes the shares by cutting up the sacrificial victims ; in the Orphic myth, the Titans are cutting Dionysos in pieces.

2° This takes place after the war of the Titans, when Zeus is already the unchallenged king.

3° It brings Zeus' rage over those members of the Titan race that devised it.

4° The downfall of the Titans, or of the Titan Prometheus, involves the future ruin of mortals, who are their, or his, descendants or creations[3 4].

We therefore recognize that its criticism of Greek blood sacrifice is theological, starts from the premises of Hellenic religion, is informed and effective ; so when it presents Zeus, the awesome god whose very nod makes Heaven tremble, coming down from Olympus along the trail of smoke, we have to accept that this was not a mocking idea of the writer, but a statement, however distorted, of ordinary Greek sacerdotal theory.

It is not Indo-European peoples alone who envisage fire smoke as the trail from Heaven to Earth.

Two famous related stories, the Great Flood of Mesopotamia[3 5] and that of the Bible[3 6], both involve a fascinating association of smoke, clouds, ocean, rainbow and the manifestation of God or gods at a sacrifice. The Mesopotamian Noah, Ut-Na-pishtim, gives a colossal sacrifice to the gods after being saved from the flood, in front of its still unreceded water ; they smell the odorous smoke, come down from Heaven along the trail of smoke and swarm around the sacrifice. Noah sacrifices to his God after being saved from the Flood and in front of the still unreceded waters ; God "smells a sweet savour", and the rainbow appears in the sky.

Of course, the Bible gives no such immediate meaning to either smoke or clouds or rainbow ; to say that an absolute, ever-present, totally free God could be impelled to do anything, would be ludicrous :

---

3 2   K. KERENYI, *The Gods of Greece,* New York, 1951, text to N° 287-283, 840, 842-844, and notes.

3 3   Hesiod, *Theogony* 535-616.

3 4   Nothing is more certain than that the Orphics believed that the the evils of mortality were due to the descent of mortals from the Titans ; an Orphic hymn (Hymn 37) says it in so many words.

3 5   *The Epic of Gilgamesh,* Harmondsworth, 1981, p.111-113.

3 6   *Genesis* VIII 20-IX 5.

> If I be hungry, I will not tell thee ; for the whole world is mine, and all that is therein.
>
> Thinkest thou that I will eat bulls' flesh and drink the blood of goats ?[37]

He does not need to follow the trail of odorous smoke to any place ; He is there already.

On the other hand, both stories strongly associate the re-emergence of the world from the universal waters with the first regulation of sacrifice. The Mesopotamian epic shows the gods, advised by Ishtar, partitioning the sacrifice among themselves, and this is the central action in the process of re-creation of the world from the universal flood[38]. Noah's God also proceeds to dictate the law of sacrifice, but in a different way. In His case there was no question of partitioning sacrifice : one sacrificer (man) was to offer one sacrifice (food) to one God. What His regulating act establishes is the proper rank and relationship of God (Creator, Ordinator, Lawgiver), man (sacrificer, made in the image of God, entitled to slay and eat any beast but only according to certain specific laws, and under no condition to be slain or sacrificed himself) and beast (food and sacrificial matter)[39].

This amounts to a statement of basic moral law. In Jewish thought, the laws of sacrifice cannot be separated from the moral laws od existence guaranteed by the God of Zion. The Mesopotamian epic, on the other hand, is more or less deprived of moral content, insisting only on the duty of mortals to offer regular sacrifices to the gods ; this, we infer, is enough to keep the horror of the flood from Earth. This mechanical non-moral idea of sacrifice cannot, in turn, be separated from the entirely negative picture of man's position in the universe in Babylonian religion : men were born out of the blood of Kingu, Marduk's enemy, when Marduk executed him, and bear the burden of his guilt[40] ; Marduk, immediately after being invested with supreme power by all the gods assembled, declares that man's work must be "faithful service" ; Ea, god of wisdom, declares man's "servitude" as soon as man is made ; and the Annunaki gods praise Marduk for having freed them and remitted their labour, from which we infer that man was created to do the work of the gods in their place and leave them free to enjoy themselves[41].

Both accounts, however, have sacrifice as their central element. It is around the ceremony of sacrifice that the proper relationship of man with the universe, whatever it may be, is established and shown. In Æschylus' *Prometheus Bound*, the protagonist claims that he has not only devised the shares of sacrifice, as Hesiod's story goes, and given mortal men the gift of fire (the chief element in sacrifice), but also that he has been the one who divided honours among the gods of Olympus, and given mortals every one of their skills from craftmanship to divination ! This is how far the concept of "sharing out" can be

---

[37]   *Psalms* LI(L) 12-13.
[38]   *Gilgamesh*, p.112-113.
[39]   *Genesis* VIII 21-IX 17, esp. IX 2-6.
[40]   *Poems of Heaven and Hell from Ancient Mesopotamia*, Harmondsworth, 1971, p.98.
[41]   I am not saying that the Babylonian civilization was immoral. The documents quoted in J. HASTINGS *ed., Encyclopedia of Religion and Ethics*, Edinburgh, 1908-1926, V c.445-446 form a quite acceptable set of moral demands. But their notion of divine happiness is astonishingly, and almost deliberately, ignoble : Ut-Napishtim, given to live the life of the gods, finds nothing better to do with his time than lie on his back and drink wine ! And his time is endless and immortal. Can anybody conceive of a more exquisite and infinite tedium, of anything more closely approaching Hell ?

pushed, and still keep its visible roots in the division of the elements of sacrifice : the figure of wisdom[42] who designs the shares of sacrifice can also claim to have given the gods their rank, and mortals their tasks.

It is around the ceremony of sacrifice that the proper relationship of man with the universe, whatever it may be, is established and shown ; and this is quite independent from any difference in philosophy. At least around the basin of the Mediterranean, it seems to be universal. The difference, and indeed contradictions, between Greek, Jewish, Mesopotamian and Celto-Latin conceptions of mankind, divinity and the universe, would give us enough to discuss for many books : but on the nature and meaning of sacrifice, all their myths converge, and show a common core of concepts.

The notion of "sharing out" in sacrifice has also a cosmic aspect. We must notice that in every one of these myths the sacrifice, or the burning, takes place on the shore between land and ocean, and under an open sky ; at border, as it were, of the three regions of the universe. Indeed, in the Middle Eastern myths this border is established, after the rage of the flood, at the same time as the sacrifice : the sacrifice is offered at the same time as the border between land, sea and sky is drawn once and for all (the God of Noah promises no more flood). Both of the Æneid's burnings take place on the Mediterranean sea-shore, under an open sky which is an important visual element in both cases : in the first, it is first crossed by Iris and then covered by Jupiter's clouds, in the second, it is crossed by Iris again, and then lit up by the Mother of Gods' light as the transformed ships soar away.

As compared with the Middle Eastern stories, the Latin one has an extra element : not only "border" between cosmic regions; but also between human territories. Turnus' burning takes place near the Tiber, the northern border of the Italic lands, marking out the dangerous Outside of Etruria from which Æneas is soon to bring an army. There is no directly comparable element in the Irish text, but the Fomoire, who take the place of Turnus and his allies, have an habit of turning into recognizable enemeies in Irish legendry : some textes make them come from Lochlann (Scandinavia), overseas home of Ireland's Viking invaders ; other suggest a connection with the Fir Bolg, the third invaders of Ireland, defeated by Nuada's invasion, who are certainly a kind of humanity.

What is more, the elements which are emphasized are those which in some sense cross over from one region to another : smoke, which rises from the wood produced by the earth (or from the earth itself, in volcanos like Vesuvius) to heaven ; clouds who send rain (and lightning, the fire of heaven) on both earth and sea ; the rainbow, a visible if deceptive[43] link between the regions of the universe ; thunder, that crosses from heaven to earth or to the sea ; and, finally, another kind of crosser of alien regions : ships, made of wood which belongs naturally to the earth, yet capable to bring men back alive from the inimical, the

---

[42]   *Prometheus* means "the One Who Thought First".
[43]   Is the distance and intangibility of the rainbow the reason why Iris' apparitions in the Æneid are always deceptive, leading characters to ruinous actions ?

"unpastured" as Homer calls it, region of the sea, where men could not otherwise go. This, surely, is why the image of boats is so important in both Irish[44] and Latin legends.

Though all this, under all this as one might say, there seeps a fourth component, a "border" component that seems to be the catalyst of change and motion from one region of the universe to another : fire, which Virgil's visual imagination, aided perhaps from hints in his predecessors, saw creeping under the surface of the wooden hulls like a plague. Fire makes smoke, and smoke - the proper kind of smoke - brings Gods, or the gods, to the Earth of mortal men. This means primarily the smoke of altar fires, during the celebration of sacrifice ; but the religious imaginations turns it also to the clouds of heaven, from which a particularly fierce kind of fire can thunder down on Earth. Fire is a basic part of sacrifice, and its presence - altough less stressed than that of its opposite element, water - is clear from the fact that its by-product, smoke, is seen rising through the air.

V.5   The failure of Latinus' sacrifice

The similarity between Middle Eastern and Celtic/Latin legend is evident : the Middle Eastern legends are strongly centred upon sacrifice, and the Hellenic idea of sacrifice - the Hellenes being Indo-Europeans - is clearly paralleled to that shown in the Middle Eastern myths. I think it is safe to assume as a working hypothesis that, beneath the intricacies of unexplained legend, the *Æneid* and the *Lebor Gabála Éireann* also are bound up with sacrifice myths.

Another parallel between the two complexes, in fact, lies exactly in the position of some of them in sacred history (or pseudo-history) of sacrifice. We are not told that the sacrifice of Noah, or any of the others we are studying, was the first ever offered by mortals : in fact, both the Bible and the Æneid include clear descriptions of earlier ceremonies : the sacrifice of Cain and Abel in Genesis[45] and that of Latinus before Æneas reaches Latium[46]. Both of these are described in such a way as to make it certain that they were not exceptional, but regular events : there is no indication that Cain or Abel are doing anything novel in offering the Lord the firstfruits of their work ; and Latinus' house-sacrifice, far from sounding exceptional in any way, shows all the tokens of regularity : the king does it under his own roof, in his own house, with his heir Lavinia by him.

But there are indications that something is very wrong about both those earlier sacrifices. Cain's offering goes astray, provoking his murderous anger against the more succesful Abel, and Latinus' sacrifice is visited by a terrible omen of war and the ruin of his house :

> And then, as he lit altar fires with chaste firebrands
>
> And sweet young Lavinia stood, a virgin, by him,
>
> He saw her - dear Heaven ! - run fire from the hair of her head,
>
> Crown royal, magnificent jewel aflame ;

---

44   And, of course, Mesopotamian and Jewish ! What else is the Ark if not one very big boat ?
45   *Genesis* IV 1-16.
46   Virgil, *Æneid* VII 71-80.

Blonde light and smoke rising through roofs and through buildings,

Vulcanus, wild fire, all over the entire great palace !

They held this vision a dire and miraculous thing ;

Because - they were singing - she herself would be unforgotten

Through God's word and the memory of men, but she meant

A mighty and disastrous conflict to the nation[47].

Notice that both evils have something to do with family relationships : Cain ends up murdering his brother and, here, the omen of evil proceeds from Latinus' own little daughter. It is exacltly the normalcy, the familiarity - in both senses - that the setting implies, that make the vision of fire so startling : and it attacks exactly those elements - the daughter and the house - that had helped to form a "familiar" scene. And I don't have to elaborate on the horrible perversion of family relationships in the Biblical story : "Am I my brother's keeper ?" In the case of the Æneid, it is abundantly clear that whatever was wrong with Latinus' sacrifice was a direct foretaste of the war which was to open with Turnus' burning ; and, while Abel's murder seems distant from the story of the Flood, in fact only forty-six verses separate them[48] and at least one of God's basic laws, pronounced at the moment of Noah's sacrifice, seems a direct comment on Cain's behaviour :

And surely your blood of your lives will I require ; at the hand of every beast will I require it, and at the hand of man ; *at the hand of every man's brother*[49] *will I require the life of man*[50].

It is no very daring inference to suppose that the troubled state of mankind before the Flood goes straight back to Cain's failed ritual and its murderous consequences[51] ; Noah, the survivor of the Flood, was not of the line of Cain, but of that of Seth, whom Adam and Eve begot as a substitute of murdered Abel. Cain's race, then, is wiped out from the Earth ; the race of righteous Seth, whose son Enos had first instituted the worship of the Lord[52],

---

47   Virgil, *Æneid* VII 73-80 : *Praeterea, castis adolet dum altaria taedis*
                                    Et iuxta genitorem adstat Lauinia uirgo,
                                    Visa - nefas ! - longis comprendere crinibus ignem
                                    Atque omnem ornatum flamma crepitare cremari
                                    Regalisque accensa comam, accensa coronam
                                    Insignem gemmis ; tum fumida lumine fuluo
                                    Inuolui ac totis Volcanum spargere tectis
                                    Id uero horrendum ac uisu mirabile ferri
                                    Namque fore inlustrem famam fatisque canebant
                                    Ipsam, sed populo magnum portendere bellum.

48   From *Genesis* IV 17 to VI 4.

49   As I know no Hebrew, I quote this under correction. Of two modern translations I consulted, one weakens the expression ("and from each man, too, I will demand an accounting for the life of his fellow-man"), but another strengthens it and lays emphasis on the word "brother" : "at the hand of man, even at the hand of every man's brother, will I require the life of man". I would welcome clarification from experts.

50   *Genesis* IX 5.

51   There was an early and widespread post-exilic tradition that the sin of Cain had in fact caused the Flood : see J.L. KUGEL, *The Bible as It Was*, Harvard, 1997, p.88, 91, 99-100.

52   *Genesis* IV 26 : "And to Seth, to him also there was born a son, and he called his name Enos ; then began men to call the name of Lord".

survives through Noah ; and Noah gives a new sacrifice, which God accepts. All the story is woven through with questions of righteous and unrighteous sacrifices[53]. Our working hypothesis, then, leads us to suppose that a similar crisis of sacrificial unrighteousness existed among the Latins in the Æneid legend, and among the Irish in the *Lebor Gabála.*

The story of Latinus' ill-omened sacrifice proves that this was the case in the Latium. As for Ireland, the cause of the war for which Lug came to the country was that tribute was being unjustly given to the Fomoire, the demons ; the gods, lords of the island by right[54], were forced to surrender their own labour and their goods. As late as 1513 AD, a Scottish Gaelic bard remembered this as the meaning of Lug's arrival to Ireland and his battle against the Fomoire and Balar : an unrighteous tribute, which he compares to that laid upon Scotland by the English[55]. What, then, belongs to the gods, if not sacrifice ? What is it that cannot justly be taken from them, if not that whose very name means "the thing that are made (*facio*) holy (*sacer)"* ? Lug, the supreme god, came to the island to give the gods what was theirs by right[56].

The working hypothesis seems proved. Clearly, this complex of ideas about sacrifice was a common property of Indo-European and Middle Eastern cultures, however different they might otherwise have been[57] ; and it is legitimate, in this case at least, to use the Semitic flood legends as a counterpart of the Italo-Celtic fire legends, and of any similar stories that may be found in any other Indo-European culture.

Æneas, then, comes to Latium as the gods come on Earth : on the smoke of vessels that burn on the shores of the Great Sea, amidst trailing clouds of smoke very much like thunderclouds. He has come because something is rotten in the state of Latium, something that makes its sacrifices ineffectual and positively dangerous, and that turns such a close family relationship as that of father and daughter into something of incredible danger ; some ritual fault that is going to turn Latinus' pretty, innocent child into a blazing flame that threatens to engulf his whole house and realm.

---

[53]   The story of Gilgamesh is less clear : mankind is guaranteed a future because it will henceforth serve the gods with sacrifices, whereas before the flood thay had just raged around the world, disturbing the peace of the gods. The connection seems to be that, because the gods are now being sacrificed to, they will put up with the rabid chaos of mankind. Behind this - which, as with the rest of of Gilgamesh's moral world, is rather vulgar - there seems to lie a conception that only those who sacrifice well are properly orderly : the opposition is between sacrifice and cosmic chaos preluding to the flood.

[54]   Right of conquest : they had won it in battle from its previous rulers, the Fir Bolg. But the ascendancy the Fomoire enjoyed over the gods was the result of the treachery of the half-bred usurper Bres, not any fair fight.

[55]   K.H. JACKSON, *A Celtic Miscellany,* Harmondsworth, 1971, p.240.

[56]   It is a commonplace in Hindu legend to show the gods being overwhelmed by some new device of the demons (Asura) and taking refuge in the supreme god, either Viṣṇu or Siva, who, with some device of his own or by brute force, reverses the situation. What gods and demons always contend about is the sacrifice : see for instance W. DONIGER O'FLAHERTY, *Hindu Myths,* Harmondsworth, 1975, N°25-26, 37, 41, 43, 46, 48, 62.

[57]   One important fact, even in this complex of ideas, reminds us that we are in fact dealing with noticeably different cultures : the rainbow, which is a positive element in the Jewish legend (God's seal on His own "covenant" with mankind), is negative in the Latin epic (Juno's attendant, whose vision drives the Trojan women mad and pushes Turnus to war).

V.6   The fire of Lavinium

It is in their account of the second burning that historian and poet diverge radically. Dionysios' burning is quite as supernatural as Virgil's. A fire, he says, broke out by itself in the forest close to the future sacred town of Lavinium ; an eagle and a wolf fanned the flames. A fox tried in vain to put them out, and had to withdraw defeated. Æneas read this to mean (says Dionysios with no more explanation) that the new town would become glorious, but should have to fight many - victorious - wars against its neighbours.

The story is at least partly trifunctional : the eagle and the wolf pertain to Jupiter and Mars[58], although it is not easy to place the enemy fox. I know of no legend in which he plays any third-function role[59]. It might perhaps represent, not the third function, but a sort of inferior second function, as the fox is a sort of smaller and weaker version of the wolf. The prophecy speaks of glory and victory, but has nothing to say about any third-function idea, and, in this version, Lavinia herself, the "love interest", is much less of a bone of contention than in the Æneid. Turnus' hopeless passion for her is only mentioned after she is safely married to the greater hero[60]. Indeed, our historian gives a version in which the eponymous heroine of the sacred town was not Latinus' daughter at all, but a Greek prophetess, daughter of Anios, who had thrown in her lot with the Trojans and died there.

If we identify the fox (the "lesser wolf") of this version with Turnus, then I think we may say that this story exactly reverses the Virgilian episode. There Turnus had started the fire, not tried to smother it. But he was frustrated as the fox : the ships were turned to Sea-Nymphs. Turnus himself is a fire-bringer ; he repeatedly burns things - ships, wooden towers - and is often described with fiery aspects. His helmet has a magic image of the Chimæra, a fire-breathing monster, that spat out real flames and grew in heat and fury as the battle did[61]. In IX 731-734, his eyes blaze, his helmet pours out flame[62] and his shield shoots lightning ; in IX 813-814 his sweat is a river of pitch, a most flammable as well as a disgusting element. And let us remember what we found out about Virgil : he dislikes fabulous accounts and tries to avoid them as much as he can. If he gave Turnus these fiery aspects, it is quite likely that his sources were even more fantastic in their descriptions[63].

---

[58]   Of course, if I were to abide strictly Dumézil's principles of interpretation as set out in *Mariages indo-européens* (Paris, 1979), I could not make such a statement : he says very firmly that a trifunctional system must be whole and exclusive, it must exist as a unit and have no other terms except the three in question. My point is rather that the wolf and the eagle are beyond question, the animals of Mars and Jupiter, the upper two of the Roman trifunctional triad, and that Dumézil himself uses them in this sense in his great *Religion romaine archaïque* (cit.). Their functional qualities are established beyond doubt, and I do not need to find a trifunctional context for them to argue from them ; they are a given of the discussion, like the tri-functional principle itself.

[59]   In modern Italy, of course, the fox is the epitome of craftiness and immoral cunning : *furberia*, a beautiful and untranslatable Italian word.

[60]   Dionysios of Halicarnassus, I 64 2.

[61]   Virgil, *Æneid* VII 785-788.

[62]   Just to remind us that the description of of the fire-breathing Chimæra was no joke.

[63]   These fiery characteristics of Turnus as enemy of Æneas provide another Celtic parallel. Fionn mac Cumhaill had several enemies connected with fire, and Fionn, as leader of the Fianna, is particularly comparable to Æneas as the head of his band of young men : T.F. O'RAHILLY, *Early Irish History and Mythology*, Dublin, 1946, p.278 ; E. MacNÉILL - G. MURPHY, *Duanaire Finn*, Dublin, 1904-1954, III p.lxiiiff ; A.D. REES - B. REES, *op.cit.*, p.66.

Yet the force Turnus represents is powerless before a fire made by no human hands, fanned by the sacred beasts of the two higher gods of the Roman pantheon : the fox, their enemy, is unable to restrain it.

We may therefore envisage the mystic significance of this episode as being the doomed attempt of a lesser sort of fire to smother or hinder a greater one[64]. The enigmatic oath of the Mother of Gods when Turnus assaults the ships made from "her" sacred wood are directly relevant :

> *... maria ante exurere Turno*
> *Quam sacra dabitur pinus...*

> ... Sooner shall Turnus by burned by the oceans,
> Than be given holy pines...[65]

The fire-bringing Rutulian cannot burn them : though seemingly made of combustible wood and pitch, they are in effect spirits of water. But the sea can burn him ; and the man from the sea will, in fact, perform that service for him, raising a worse fire. Then Turnus shall have to feed himself to his fury, to keep the whole monarchy of Italy, whose tower he had raised himself, from going down in flames[66].

That Dionysios' fire broke out spontaneously, while the two functional animals only helped it along, indicates that it is self-created and that its nature is greater than that of the three functions[67]. The fire, greater-then-the-three, is to be identified with the Trojans, who are therefore something other than mortal heroes. Seen as flames and, I repeat, as greater than the three functions, they have to be gods, and what we see is a play of gods.

In this light, it is certainly relevant to find that the omen of the "eaten tables", which convinces Æneas and his company to stay in Latium, is parallel with a famous Eddic legend in which it is attributed to a disguised spirit of fire[68]. Both Dionysios and Virgil tell the story of the omen in practically the same terms, except that Virgil endows it with justified solemnity, involving Jupiter both at the beginning and at the end. When the Trojans had landed in Latium, they prepared[69] a meal od which we are told nothing except that the food was spread over flat, round flour cakes[70]. Ascanius, as a sort of joke, says : "Look, we have eaten the very tables", meaning, the cakes on which the other food was laid. Æneas then bursts out in a song of praise and gratitude, remembering a prophecy that, where their

---

[64]   In A. HILTEBEITEL, *The Ritual of Battle, cit.* , there is a rather similar interpretation of the destruction of the Pāṇḍava camp by the incarnation of Śiva, Aśvatthaman, although it works the other way : the fire of destruction (Śiva/Aśvatthaman) being stronger than that of ordered ritual (the Pāṇḍava army's commander-in-chief Dhṛstadyumna, embodiment of the fire-god Agni).

[65]   Virgil, *Æneid* IX 115-116.

[66]   Virgil, *Æneid* XII 554-592.

[67]   Whether the fox be a representative of the third function or not does not matter ; if the fire is greater than the first and second functions together, it is *a fortiori* greater than the third.

[68]   Snorri Sturluson, *Gylfaginning* 46.

[69]   According to Virgil, Jupiter drove them to perform this prophetic act, even forced them perhaps : Virgil, *Æneid* VII 110 : *Sic Iupiter ipse monebat* "Jupiter Himself *warned* or *ordered* (them) thus", with *ipse* to reinforce the great god's name.

[70]   Which sound a lot like pizza : another amusing link between prehistoric and modern Italy.

98

hunger drove them to eat the tables, there they would found that long-sought Italy[71]. Virgil concludes with a most solemn ratification of the omen by Jupiter : he thunders three times, and shakes "with his own hands" a beautiful cloud of golden light.

Now Eddic legend tells that the wandering god of thunder Thorr, together with his attendant Thjalfi and the trickster half-god Loki, is a guest in the house of the giant Utgard-Loki : their host challenges them to show off their feats, and Loki offers to eat faster than anyone there. One, Logi, however, proceeds to eat the food placed before him as fast as Loki, but he also eats the table ! It turns out that Logi is wild fire[72].

The Trojans first manifest themselves on Latin land by raising two altars (sacred places of fire) and consuming a meal in which they eat the tables. The legends are different, but the riddling is the same : what is it that eats even the tables ? Fire. Lay a sacrificial victim on a "table" of wood, and fire will eat both it and the table. The first thing that the Trojans build on landing is not a stockade or a shelter, but altars ; not only because they are pious people, but because altars are the sort of places where the fire first manifests itself, especially sacred fire, fire as part of sacrifice, fire that opens the way between men and gods. Even more clearly, Æneas himself does not actually meet any inhabitant of the land until, after a further boat ride - or should we say, a further sacrifice smoke-ride ? - he alights by the shore of the Tiber just at the very moment that holy old Evander is setting the greatest sacrifice of his calendar into motion. It is very, very much as though the "young man", as young Pallas first calls him, has come down with the fires of the great sacrifice.

Let us tie this up with the identity of the Ships-Nymphs : if the latter are clouds of smoke, then what we have is a picture of the passage of fiery beings from Heaven to Earth, trailing smoke in their wake, as we would say, or borne by their smoke, as the ancient would say. Celts and Latins, of course, have never seen a rocket rise in a trail of smoke ; but they had seen lightning come down and set forests on fire, they have seen meteors burning through the atmosphere ; and, in case of the Latins[73], they had seen fire, smoke and melted rock blasted through the sky by a live volcano. The connection of fire, swift motion and smoke was by no means far from their imaginative possibilities ; only, it would seem, the smoke was seen not at the detritus, but as the vehicle of fire. The smoke of the sacrifice is the ship that bears the gods to Earth.

The Trojans - so to call them ! - are so many divine fires. What is more, they are both self-created and inextinguishable ; two omens, the omen of the eaten tables and the omen of the forest fire, prove it. They are fires whose essence was above and beyond that of the three functions, the normal powers of our world ; like the eagle and wolf in Dionysios, the latter can either help or hinder the rise of this greater fire, but have nothing to do with its being. It

[71]   The origin of the prophecy was doubtful. Each of our fonts attributed it to two different authors : Virgil to Anchises and the hunger-spirit Celæno, Dionysios to the sanctuary of Dodona and one of the several Sybils of Greece. We should notice however that both authors attribute it to 1° supernatural winged beings (Celæno, the doves of Dodona), and 2° the action of a winged Sybil : Æneas reaching Anchises through the mediation of the Sybil, or receiving his revelation from the Sybil of Erythræ.
[72]   Snorri Sturluson, *Gylfaginning* 44-47.
[73]   Campania, with Vesuvius in all its terrors, was part of Latinus' kingdom.

came into being by itself. It becomes manifest to men during sacrifice : the Trojans' great king Æneas first appeared to men in Latium during the great sacrifice to Hercules on Rome's so-called Greatest Altar, *Ara Maxima* [74]. Indeed, his three hundred Trojans, three hundred flames fom heaven, take even physically the image of the greatest sacrifice known to Latium. They appear as a *uer sacrum,* neither more nor less than a mass human sacrifice. Therefore they are sacrifice, both in shape (they appear as a *uer sacrum*) and in substance (being fire).

This would be familiar to students of Indian religion : from the *Vedas* onwards, the supreme god, Viṣṇu or Prajapati, is identified with *yajña,* sacrifice as a category ; and sacrifices, or classes of sacrifices, such as the great *asvamedha* horse-sacrifice whose mystical explanation open the *Bṛhādaraṇyaka Upaniṣad,* are identified with the universe. One of the most important myths of this theology) the story of Viṣṇu as a dwarf - has a parallel in Ireland, as the indispensable brothers Rees pointed out [75] : we are not therefore surprised to find the exact same idea of sacrifice in Latium. Jupiter becomes manifest in this world as the greatest of all sacrifices.

The offerings and the wood given up to fire during the ritual of sacrifice are, from the mundane point of view, a dead loss : Turnus sees wooden ships are mere objects of destruction, and fire is his agent. But what is, from the point of view of an unlightened boor like him, simply wasteful burning, is in fact the trail that joins Heaven and Earth ; and by this it becomes divine itself. Instead of being ashes and smoke to be blown away by the wind, the vehicles of the gods are themselves made into goddesses ; for we should not forget that the ships were not Sea-Nymphs until Jupiter and his mother decided that they should become so. The story is quite unequivocal. The act of what is apparently the most pure waste and loss is in fact the act which gives birth to something divine, that will never be lost, something immortal.

The Trojans, these extraordinary beings, came to Latium to found Lavinium, its holy city. We must not be misled by the unimportance of Lavinium in historical times, when Rome has undergone the political and religious mutation from Latin royal seat to world power : Lavinium declined at the same time as Rome was turning from capital of Latium Vetus to all-Italian and Mediterranean power, a historical change that brought good fortune to most other Latin sanctuaries [76]. Its significance was too narrowly Latin to fit well into the new international Roman world. But in archaic Latium it was indubitably a great deal more important than later developments show.

One of the most notable monuments excavated at the site of Lavinium is a set of, not twelve, but thirteen altars. The number twelve is the canonical number of the great gods in

---

[74]   The reason why this was Rome's "greatest altar" may well be less metaphysical than economic. Apart from the untypical instance of man, cattle was the highest kind of sacrificial matter ; and the Ara Maxima stood in the Forum Boarium, where, from Prehistoric times and certainly before the foundation of Rome itself as a city, cattle has been taken and traded. There were probably more cattle to be sacrificed there than anywhere else. It is not improbable that Rome may have been founded to control and police this important meeting place of cattle tracks.

[75]   A.D. REES - B. REES, *op. cit.,* p.76-79.

[76]   E. COARELLI, *op. cit., passim.*

various cultures, including Indo-European provinces : Germans, Greeks, etc. It is almost certainly so among the Latins, whose god-lists[77] are always in twelves. We have no reason not to believe that this imposing group of thirteen altars belonged to any other order of facts but this. The proper understanding of it must therefore be *twelve plus one*, indicating a complete system of twelve gods plus one that in some way integrates or completes them.

The twelve gods of the twelve great altars must be the geatest twelve objects of cult in the Latin culture, taking their seats in the greatest sanctuary : nothing less is believable. This can only correspond to the story of the foundation of the holy city itself ; with the functional beasts helping or hindering the rise of a fire greater than themselves, the fire that is the cult of Lavinium as such ; for we have seen that that fire was beyond the gods of the three functions, the powers of this world. This is the thirteenth fire, the fire beyond the reckoning of systematizations : the fire above the system.

---

[77]   Like the *indigamenta,* lesser gods, reported by Varro and St. Augustine.

tune to most other Latin sanctuaries[76]. Its significance was too narrowly Latin to fit well into the new international Roman world. But in archaic Latium it was indubitably a great deal more important than later developments show.

One of the most notable monuments excavated at the site of Lavinium is a set of, not twelve, but thirteen altars. The number twelve is the canonical number of the great gods in various cultures, including Indo-European provinces : Germans, Greeks, etc. It is almost certainly so among the Latins, whose god-lists[77] are always in twelves. We have no reason not to believe that this imposing group of thirteen altars belonged to any other order of facts but this. The proper understanding of it must therefore be *twelve plus one*, indicating a complete system of twelve gods plus one that in some way integrates or completes them.

The twelve gods of the twelve great altars must be the geatest twelve objects of cult in the Latin culture, taking their seats in the greatest sanctuary : nothing less is believable. This can only correspond to the story of the foundation of the holy city itself ; with the functional beasts helping or hindering the rise of a fire greater than themselves, the fire that is the cult of Lavinium as such ; for we have seen that that fire was beyond the gods of the three functions, the powers of this world. This is the thirteenth fire, the fire beyond the reckoning of systematizations : the fire above the system.

---

[76]   E. COARELLI, *op.cit., passim.*
[77]   Like the *indigamenta,* lesser gods, reported by Varro and St. Augustine.

CHAPTER VI : THE MADNESS OF MEN
AND THE SANITY OF THINGS

VI.1 Theophany and madness

A recurring theme in the epic is that of the manifestation of gods to mortals, and its effects. Virgil's account of the first ship-burning in Sicily is different from that of Dionysios in that the epic poet gives a religious explanation. The goddess of the rainbow; Iris, sent by Juno[1], takes advantage of the weariness of the weaker part of the Trojan expedition - the women - and rouses in them a rage against the ships. She achieves this by suddenly shedding a mortal disguise and appearing in her own divine form (a *theophany*), blinding them with light ; the sight destroys the women's reason.

This is not the only time something of this kind happens. Time and again, a divine personage, especially a goddess, has only to appear in her own undisguised aspect to break a mortal's reason. The effect is immediate and overwhelming : Allecto, the Dira, drives both Turnus and Amata/Amita to sudden rage ; then, in his final duel with Æneas, an evil spirit sent by Jupiter; also called a Dira, breaks Turnus' strength and resolve, turning him into a whimpering coward.

This is not Hellenic. The Greek gods can fill a man's soul with rage or terror, but they hardly do it by theophanies. They practically never appear in their own form. When they interact with mortals, they are always in disguise, and the mortals never know it until they are gone ; this is not only a matter of the cunning of the gods, but something in the nature of a precaution. While Greek myth agrees that the view of an undisguised god could be an overwhelming experience, it has a different view of its effect on a man : stories as Semele's and Actæon's suggest that if one of the Greek gods ever appeared to a mortal in his or her form, that mortal would simply die.

What is more, the fall of Turnus under the crow-shaped Dira's gaze matches in detail un indubitably Roman legend of the Valerii clan[2], whose excuse is the supposed change of their *cognomen* (hereditary nickname) from Publicola "Mindful of the Public Good" to Corvus or Corvinus "Raven" or "of the Raven".

One of the many succeeding Publicolæ, with the approval of his commander, accepted a challenge to single combat by a Gaulish warrior. These challenges, part of normal warrior ethics among Celts and Germans, were regarded by the orderly Romans as act of *outrecuidance* by unruly Barbarians[3] ; the issuer of one was regarded as a vain boaster to be punished. So, we are not surprised when we see a raven (*coruus*), perched on Valerius'

---

[1] In the *Æneid*, Iris is always at her service.
[2] Livy, VIII 26 3-6.
[3] I am not saying that what we have here is anything but a legend ; but it is a legend that reflects actual Roman military thinking. The fabulously distant episode of the Horatii and Curatii, coming as it does straight from immemorial Indo-European past, does not count, and it was carried out under the auspices of Tullus Hostilius, a king whose moral status is very doubtful, and of the scoundrelly Mettius Fufetius. Cf. G. DUMEZIL, *Heur et malheur, passim*.

helmet, inflict on the Gaul the very same horrors inflicted on Turnus by the bird-shaped Dira. Just as the Gaul, in Livy's account, is "terrified by such a miracle, shaken both in his sight *and in his mind...*", so too, in the *Æneid,*

> His limbs dissolve in a never-known torpor,
>
> His hairs rise in horror, his speaking voice quivers
>
>> *Illi membra nouos soluit formidine torpor*
>>
>> *Arrectaeque horrore comas et uox faucibus haesit*[4],

and when he tries to lift a rock which, we should understand, would ordinarily be easy enough for him not only to raise but to throw, he finds himself changed :

> He knows himself not, not in running, in walking ;
>
> Not hands, as he is heaving the stone's dire burden,
>
> Knees buckle, moans stiffen his red blood with cold...
>
>> *Sed neque currentes se nec cognoscit euntem,*
>>
>> *Tollentemque manu saxumue immanem mouentem ;*
>>
>> *Genua labant, gemitu concreuit frigore sanguinis...*[5]

and then

> And as when nightly quiet presses our eyelids with sleep
>
> And we think we are running, and - where ? Oh, to where ?
>
> We know not, and are ill for the strain of our straining -
>
> Nor our tongue, nor the body we thought we had known
>
> But fail us, and words and our thoughts do not follow ;
>
> So too Turnus tries every way, and finds
>
> The Dira in the midst of them all. Awhirl
>
> His heart is collapsing with thoughts - and the town,
>
> And his Rutuli in sight ; and he fears
>
> To be in the spear's shadow, and trembles, and sees
>
> No tearing himself from the foe, no strength
>
> To tear into him, no chariot or charioteer sister.
>
>> *Ac uelut in somnis oculos ubi languida pressit*
>>
>> *Nocte quies, nequiquam auidos extendere cursos*
>>
>> *Velle uidemur, et in mediis conatibus aegri*
>>
>> *Succidimus, non lingua ualet, non corpore notae*
>>
>> *Sufficiunt uires, nec uox aut uerba secuntur*
>>
>> *Sic Turno, quacumque uiam uirtute petiuit*
>>
>> *Successum dea Dira negat. Tum pectore sensus*
>>
>> *Vertuntur uarii : Rutulos aspectat et urbem*
>>
>> *Cunctaturque metu tellumque instare tremescit*
>>
>> *Nec quo se eripiat nec qua ui tendat in hostem*

---

4   Virgil, *Æneid* XII 867-868.

5   Virgil, *Æneid* XII 903-905.

Nec currus usquam uidet aurigamue sororem[6].

I haven't footnoted the Latin text because I do not want even readers with no Latin to suffer my clumsy intermissions in place of the glorious original. Here, to an extent scarcely seen anywhere else, the content of the poetry really is one with the sound. To deprive any reader of the Latin music at least - even if they fail to hear anything but music - would be a crime against them ; to offer my lead for Virgil's gold, doubtly so. Above all, the reader who does not hear the experience of Turnus in this passage is really deprived of a part of the story ; as well try telling *Aida* or *Fidelio* without the music ! Indeed, we wouldn't be wasting our time if we stopped our whole study to admire these verses, with the terrible weight and gasping stresses of *tollentemque manu saxumue immanem mouentem,* the soft clinching strength of *uelut in somnis oculos ubi languida pressit / Nocte quies* heaving itself up into the broken efforts of *succidimus, non lingua ualet, non corpore notae / Sufficiunt uires, nec uox aut uerba secuntur* ; and that final *Tum pectore sensus / Vertuntur uarii ; Rutulos aspectat et urbem / Cunctaturque metu telumque instare tremescit,* with its trembling, shattering death rattle of dark u's and hard consonants ! *Onorate l'altissimo poeta* "give honour to the greatest of all poets", says the only poet, perhaps, who might be said to be greater[7].

Yet I hold the material to be traditional : apart from Celtic parallels[8], the annalistic legend in Livy shows the same details, down to the bird wheeling and shrieking at the doomed warrior. Livy, always concerned to reduce miracles to human proportions, adds the detail that the bird pecked at the man's eyes, not, as I suppose, in the hope of materializing the legend, but to distract the reader's attention from its fundamental unlikelihood. An animal screaming and biting at a strong warrior in the middle of a battle will irritate, distract and perhamps hamper him ; it may even infuriate him ; but it would be quite unlikely to produce the melting depression shown here. Indeed, if the warrior is worked up enough, he may well ignore it. Here as in the passage on Horatius Cocles[9], Livy has slyly and deliberately written in such a way as to prevent us noticing that a supernatural power, rather than the motions of the enemy's own private souls, are striking them with horror.

In Virgil there is a clear symmetry between the apparition of Allecto, that drives Turnus insane, and that of the Dira, which breaks him. And both these stages in his ruin are exactly paralleled by the behaviour of the Trojan women. Both Turnus and the women are at first in control of themselves, though tempted by unpleasant circumstances which they lack the self-discipline to endure. The Trojan women

> Cried for their lost Anchises, and the deep

6   Virgil, *Æneid* XII 908-918.

7   Dante, *Divine Comedy* I 4 80.

8   Such as the death of King Muirchertach mac Erca, where a goddess of revenge wears a spell of horror and dreams around him (**R C**, XXIII, 1902, p.396ss).

9   Livy, II 10 8. cf. G. DUMEZIL, *La religion, cit.* The legend said that Horatius Cocles was an one-eyed Roman soldier who held a whole Etruscan army at bay on a bridge by glaring at them terribly with his one eye. Live is hideously embarrassed by this, and promptly proceeds to use an ambiguous *oculos,* a plural which might mean either "glances" or "eyes" : to convey, without saying so in so many words, that the hero really had more than one eye !

They all stared at, and cried : "Aïe, aïe, so much weary crossing

And such a great sea still to cross ; aïe, aïe", with one voice all of them

Pray for a city, exhausted by all the sea's labours[10].

But when the disguised Iris first invites them to do something about it, wise old Pyrgo sees through her, and the mothers stand in doubt :

... with little love, yet still in two minds ;

In their eyes the sea-craft, in heart a wretched

Lust for this earth, and the promised land that was calling...[11]

Their senses still haven't deserted them, though they are sorely tempted. It is when the goddess appears (so to speak) in her true colours that, after no more than two lines of flying rainbow,

Indeed then, monster astonished, shaken by rage[12],

they start the burning.

Likewise Turnus, before Allecto shows her actual form, wears the proper self-control of a responsible young ruling prince. True, there are many chinks in his self-possessed armour ; Virgil's narrative and psychological genius lets us see clearly enough that Turnus' majestic quiet is a façade. Nowhere does he say that he would take it equanimously if Latinus, in pious obedience to oracles, were to deny him the bride he longs for : when the monster, disguised as old Calybe, priestess of Juno (!), tells him that the Trojans are coming, the Trojans are coming, and they're gonna steal your woman away, all he says is that he has heard well enough that a fleet has come up the Tiber[13], that he is not worried because Queen Juno will no doubt look after him and - in token of respect for Queen Juno, no doubt ! - will the aged priestess of Juno please leave war and peace to us men, who know about such things[14], and mind her own business, since age has addled her wits[15] ?

The rude dismissal and affected nonchalance prove that the young man finds mention of the coming fleet very unwelcome. In him, therefore, as in the weariness and fears of the women at Acesta, the messenger of Juno finds easy material. The Dira, it seems, has no hold except on souls already shaken by unrighteous passions. Amata's jealousy, Turnus' greed, the women's rebellious impatience. The righteous King Latinus, who had wholeheartedly accepted the decrees of his father, sleeps untroubled by any infernal apparition (unless his whining wife counts as one !).

---

10   Virgil, *Æneid* V 614-617 : *Amissum Anchisem flebant, cunctaeque profundum*
                                    Pontum aspectabant ; Heu tot uada fessis
                                    Et tantum superesse mari, uox omnibus una.
                                    Vrbem orant, taedet pelagi perferre laborem.

11   Virgil, *Æneid* V 654-656 :   *... ancipites oculisque malignis*
                                    Ambiguae spectare rates, miserum inter amorem
                                    Praesentis terrae fatisque uocantia regna.

12   *Attonitae monstris* : a rather grim way to describe the beauty of a rainbow !

13   Virgil, *Æneid* VII 436-437.

14   Virgil, *Æneid* VII 438-439.

15   Virgil, *Æneid* VII 440-442.

When Turnus' unnatural rage vanishes before another Dira, it leaves him feeble, stupefied and terrified. Likewise, there is one specific moment in which the possessed Amata and the obsessed Trojan women realize with blinding clarity what they have done. We should notice how they are roused from their seizure : in both cases, a character appears at whose sight they suddenly wake up to the enormity of their behaviour. Amata is blinded by the realization of the disaster she wrought :

> ... grief bursts in an instant, it shatters her thoughts ;
>
> She screams she's the cause ; and, crime and head of all evils,
>
> Babbling many things in the rage of her anguish[16],

she hangs herself. Likewise, the Trojan women, having suddenly awoken to their behaviour

> But they, through the shores, through the woods,
>
> All over they flee, they seek any rock
>
> With hollows to hide them ; they hate
>
> Their deed and the light ; they're changed, they can tell their people
>
> And Juno is hammered away from their hearts[17].

It will be clear now that the three stories of Turnus, Amata and the Trojan women form a triad. Therefore, by comparison with all the three epiphanies that open the three episodes of madness - Iris, Allecto and Allecto again - and also with the evident and declared epiphany that closes the madness of Turnus - Jupiter's own Dira - we have to conclude that the manifestations of Ascanius and Æneas in the other two are epiphanic. Do notice the violence of that last verb : Juno is not simply exorcized or driven away, she is *excussa*, chased as if with blows or weapons, hammered away. The very sound is vicious. And what is it that has so "smashed" the great goddess ? Amata has seen Æneas, at the head of his army, bringing fire to the city[18] ; the Trojan women, on the contrary, have seen Ascanius *removing* his war gear before them[19]. Both Amata and the Trojan women are shattered and wish to die - the women "hate the light" (*piget lucis*) - ; but the former, having seen her enemy coming in arms, in the terror of his glory, and bringing fire, kills herself ; the latter see the child, weaponless and friendly, and *only then* see Æneas and the host ; and they are forgiven.

Both the madness of Turnus and that of Amata are broken either by a manifestation of Jupiter (Æneas) or by his messenger (the Dira). They are more powerful than her. A Dira thrives Turnus to rage, and another breaks him ; the one is sent by Juno, the other by Jupiter. It seems that Jupiter's power is manifested in three forms, a triad : the Child, the

---

16   Virgil, *Æneid* XII 599-601 :   *... subito mentem turbata dolore*
                                                Se causam clamat climenque caputque malorum
                                                Multaque per maestum demens effata furorem.

17   Virgil, *Æneid* V 678-681 : *Ast illae diuersa metu per litora passim*
                                              Diffugiunt siluasque et sicubi concaua furtim
                                              Saxa petunt. Piget incepti lucisque suosque
                                              Mutatae adgnoscunt excussaque pectore Iuno est.

18   Virgil, *Æneid* XII 596-597.

19   Virgil, *Æneid* V 667-674.

Warrior and the Deathbird[20]. For the sight of Ascanius - it is important to realize this - is no less powerful than those of Æneas and the Dira. The Trojan women see no sinister bird or terrible warrior carrying fire ; all they see is their own Ascanius, a child, removing his helmet. And that glimpse of his face is enough to drive them in desperate flight to any rock that will hide them. And one detail is suggestive : they 'hate the light". They see Ascanius' face, and flee the light. Can we read a connexion ? Is Ascanius' face luminous ? The suspicion is strengthened when we realize that his father has an equal and opposite relationship with another element of the sky : he comes on the scene, the sky darkens and Jupiter's miraculous rain puts out the flames.

In one of the most solemn apparitions of Jupiter in his own person in the whole epic, the will of the god of gods is made manifest through both sunlinght and thunder ; he responded to the omen of the eaten tables with both thunder and light : thundering three times and shaking "with his own hand" a cloud of golden light[21]. It seems more than likely that both of these, and not thunder alonde, were his prerogatives ; exclusive concentration on thunder is one of the ill-effects of his identification with the Greek thunderer of the skies. And if that is the case, then there is nothing odd about investing the mild Child with the gentler and more bountiful manifestation, and the terrible Warrior with the more fierce and devastating one ; both of them would be Jupiter, but in different aspects or persons. The categories of Christian theology are very useful here : the "father" and "son" of Latin epic myth may best be interpreted as two persons with one hypostasis or substance.

But here is a fundamental difference between the two other manifestations of Jupiter and that of Ascanius : the women survive the experience. Amata and Turnus are indeed cured of their madness but, though the operation is a success, the patient dies. The sight of Ascanius, however, is not followed either by a suicide or by execution at Æneas'hands ; the older hero simply forgives the women and allows them to stay and have their "abiding city" in Sicily. And yet there is no special difference between their crimes and those of, in particular, Amata : they had also been guilty of violent rebellion against a divine edict. Really, the only visible difference was that Iulus and Æneas were fonder of the Trojan women, people of their own race and blood, than neither of them was of a stranger like Amata. Iulus, it seems, is Jupiter's benevolent face, shining on those he favours, and only on them[22].

---

[20]   Cf. Odhinn's ravens and death-gathering Valkyries. Even the fact that Jupiter's bird is the eagle, who feeds on battlefield carrion, might be germane.

[21]   Virgil, *Æneid* VII 141-144 :   *Hic pater omnipotens ter clarus ab alto*
                               Intonuit radiisque ardentem lucis et auro
                               Ipse manu quatiens ostendit ab aethere nubem

            The father almighty thrice from above then
            Loud thunder ; and, golden and radiant with light,
            He showed a cloud, and with his own hand he shook it.

[22]   It is worth remembering that the story of the fall of Turnus and that of the duel between the Valerius and the Gaul are also parallel in that in both cases the Dira manifest herself to ruin an enemy of Rome or her ancestors. It seems that Latin religion did not know of any equality of different nations before God ; the God of G.B. Shaw's time may or may not have been an Englishman, but the god of early Latin epic certainly was a Roman.

VI.2 Æneas the alien

Whatever nationalist overtones it may have acquired in Latium, however, the dichotomy of Alien and Kinsman, Outsider and Insider is fundamental to the myths we have been exploring. Lug in his entire nature, both Father and Son, both Avenger and Healer, is a Stranger, even an Enemy, in every legend we have. As we saw, some accounts in the *Lebor Gabála Érenn* put him in conflict with the gods ; and the Welsh group of the Children of Dôn, usually understood as parallel to the Tuatha Dé Danann, does not include him at all. Lancelot is both the Stranger and the Enemy ; as the Stranger he comes from over the sea and keeps his name hidden[23] ; as the Enemy, he is the lord who takes Arthur's bride, and the war against him will usher in the end of Logres. Llevelys, that is Lug as the brother and adviser of Lludd (= Nudd, Nuada, Nodons, the ancestor god of Celtic royalty), is king of a country across the sea, and when Lludd has to communicate with him, he must use a sort of trumpet and cross the sea. Another Lug was almost sinister : Llovan Llawdyfro "Exiled Hand" killed the glorious King Urien at Aber Lleu "the River-Mouth of Lug"[24].

Now, nothing is more central to Æneas' story than the fact that he is a stranger, an alien. Æneas and Evander got their Greek names from their role as designated outsiders, aliens, within the story : names that anyone with the slightest acquaintance with Greek could have made up. The modern world offers easy parallels : think, for instance, of an Italian writer of spaghetti-western comics, with little knowledge of the United States and less English language, making a story with two American characters, and giving one a famous from American legend - Wild Bill Hitchcok, Ulysses Grant whatever - and rummaging through a pocket English-Italian dictionary to find the words for Good and Man to make a "Good-man". This is the situation : Æneas was one of the most famous Homeric characters, and Evander means nothing more than "Good Man" (*eu + anēr*). Greeks had been in contact with Latium since before Hesiod[25] ; but to the Latins, on the far edge of Greek trading routes, the seamen from the South must have been the most distant and semi-fabulous of known peoples.

And the whole story hinges on their alienness. It is because Æneas is the stranger that Latinus is bid to give him his daughter and the Etruscans to take him as a king ; it is because

[23]   In Chrétien's *Knight of the Cart*, our earliest account of him, this thirst for secrecy reaches paranoid proportions.
[24]   R. BROMWICH, *Trioedd Ynys Prydein*[2], Cardiff, 1979, p.424. We should not, it seems, understand Llovan as thoroughly evil : he was involved in some sort of feud and had some kind of right to feel that Urien owed him something. War was an important attribute of Lug, and it general of the Celtic gods, one of whose recognized functions was to stir contention among mortals. This strange idea of the gods was also found among their Germanic neighbours, where much of Odhinn's activity lies in fomenting strife among men, and only the dead in battle go to his paradise ; and may be suspected among the Homeric gods, who sometimes seem to have little more to do than drive men to fight each other.
[25]   Hesiod, *Theogony* 1012-106 ; cf. supra. The fact that Hesiod has a definite knowledge of the home and ethnic name of the Latins means that by the time the poem was compiled there had been enough regular contact between Greece and that surprisingly distant land for quite a long time. Some scholars believe this goes back as far as Mycenæan times.

of his alienness that the Latins and Turnus rebel against him, driving the old king to shelter into his palace and making the Tiber to foam with much blood[26].

Once we understand that, everything falls into place. The Trojan company is the Fire Greater-than-the Three, the Thirteeenth, completing fire of holy Lavinium. It has to come from Outside ; the Twelve make a complete set already, the Thirteenth is naturally outside them. And there is more. Latin theologians must have seen fire as a border element, a transforming element. The stories make it the catalyst of transformation and transmigration from one region of the world to another ; it turns wood (that belongs to earth) to smoke (that belongs in the air) and water into steam ; it thunders down from the sky when the rain (the return of water from the clouds of the sky down to earth and sea) is most savage, most intense, most itself ; when water is most forcefully crossing from one region of the world to another, then the fire of heaven - lightning - appears among clouds and raindrops.

Fire is inherently at the edge, outside the actual realities of any realm, the very image of danger ; because the transformations it brings about are death itself to solid objects such as the bodies of men. Existence continues in an altered form, but individual existence comes to an end. Nothing could possibly be as dangerous ; if it gets out of hand - if the fire of sacrifices is not treated with the proper precautions, that surely parallel the courtesy and respect shown to Æneas when he comes to visit Evander at the height of the great sacrifice - then it becomes, quite simply, the destroyer. A baulked and wounded Æneas is a threat so terrible that, unless what is due to him - Turnus - is finally given up to him, the whole Latin kingdom will founder in fire. Mishandled, the Power to which Latin epic gave the name Æneas is capable of dissolving every ordered relationship between objects, and make fire - the substance that provokes changes of state, that breaks down the borders between land, sea and sky - engulf them all.

But as the power we are speaking about resides in the connection between objects, it is, when properly treated, the guarantee of a stable and fortunate state of existence, bringing together in proper order what would otherwise be no more than the scattered pieces of a heap of unordered and unorderable creatures in constant conflict. Sacrifice is in fact the only possible act of union, whose only alternative is Turnus' ruinous rebellion. In terms of the legend, the alien Æneas comes to a society already formed, with its king and its sacrifices, its warriors and its wars, its lovers and its rich men, its courts and palaces and fields. Latinus is a righteous king, Evander a culture-hero who teaches all crafts. The alien seems to have little to offer in tangible terms : yet he is the one linch-pin without whom nothing may be done right. The culture hero may have invented every craft but, without the alien to make peace between him and the king, he, himself an alien, would expend the rest of his life,

---

[26] An amusing consideration. A modern politician has criminally stirred up racism in Britain with a quotation from Virgil, about the river Tiber foaming with blood, because, he said, Britain was admitting too many foreign immigrants.Anybody with a classical education should have answered that educated demagogue - a demagogue with fluent Latin is no less a demagogue than a demagogue with no fluent Latin - that the crime which the Latins expiated with blood was to resist the aliens who had come among them, and try to drive them back where they came from : an omen for today's Turni and Mezentii out of mouth of their own ideologue.

short enough in any case, in everlasting and mutually ruinous hostility with king and king-dom, as if skills and trades were to be brought to human society from outside and only properly grafted to the vast body of the kingdom of men by another supernatural mediation. Wise Evander is immensely old, near death ; a sad reflexion on matters in Latium ! Think of the long and sterile quarrel of this other alien, come like Æneas from the fabulous Outside of Greece, with the world of Latin normalcy ; think of the good that he might have done, had he been allowed to.

But then, he cannot, not on his own. In some mystical sense, he is sterile : his (grand)son is prevented by his half-Latin blood from leading the Etruscan army to victory against Mezentius, and also (though this is never mentioned) from being himself the bride-groom of Lavinia, destined to make the line of kings fertile. These are the two royal titles of the story, and Pallas is excluded from both. The blood-line of future kings cannot exist without the blood of righteous King Latinus, but it cannot exist without the Alien either, for nobody else is allowed to marry the king's one daughter, his only means of continuation of the blood. Lavinia is a blazing torch bound to burn his house. No doubt, without Æneas, she would have caused war between pretenders, but such war was bound to have no winner or end, because its proper appointed end, Æneas, was not there.

Without Jupiter Indiges, Evander avails nothing ; without Jupiter Indiges, Lavinia can bring only deflagration and ruin. Æneas is fire, sacrifice and language, in their purest and highest forms, and while sacrifices offered without him before his coming, turn to chaos and violence, sacrifices offered in his presence - Evander's sacrifice to Hercules and Latinus' sacrifice of peace before the duel - are acts in which the world gains or recovers its unity, its proper order.

What he has to offer is being the god, not of any one object or area of activity, but rather of the complex of relationships between objects in time and space, their proper order ; in temrs of the language with which he is also associated, we might say that he is their gram-mar. When Lug came to Tara of the Kings, the doorkeeper asked him what new skill he could bring to the court of King Nuada, to be allowed to enter[27]. Lug rattled off an incre-dible amount of skills and accomplishments. The doorkeeper gave each time the name of one of King Nuada's subjects who had it ; Lug then delivered the *coup de grâce* : "Ask the king whether he has one man who possesses all these arts, and if he has not, I shall enter Tara". Without any further argument, the doorkeeper announces him to the assembly as the *Sam-ildanach*, the Lord of Every Skill.

Lug immediately proceeded to prepare the war against the Fomoire and their unrighteous tribute, bringing justice to Ireland and to the gods at last. The *Lebor Gabála Érenn* notices that he had come clothed in the trappings of a king, though the only king in Tara was Nuada Silver-Arm ; likewise in Latium there is no king but Latinus, and yet Æneas comes to Latium

[27] Arthurian and other parallels suggest that royal capitals or ritual sites could not be entered, at least at certain specific times, unless the traveller brought a special skill or knowledge that nobody already there knew : cf. A.D. REES - B. REES, *op.cit.*, p.34 and n.16.

112

as a king and sends ambassadors to Laurentum as one monarch to another : he is a king before he ever acquires a royal title, a king by nature.

In Vedic religion, five gods are most frequently called kings. For two of them the reason is easy to understand : Varuṇa is the creator and ruler of the universe and Indra is the leader of the heavenly hosts, the conqueror, the god who wins rule but over whom nobody can win rule, because he is made to be invincible. Varuṇa rules by right, Indra by strength. The third, Yama, rules over the dead, and that is title enough. But the other two are Agni (the fire) and Soma (the sacred intoxicating liquor), which are neither more nor less than elements of sacred ritual ; and their title of king is explained by the same token as Æneas' : that it is around them as elements of rite that any true order is formed ; for ritual and world-order are one and the same. Therefore sacrifice is, in the proper sense, a feature of monarchy ; if, as Dumézil pointed out long ago, the *flamen Dialis* is a twin of the king, then the king is himself the greatest of sacrificer priests.

We have seen that Æneas is the activity of sacrifice ; as we should expect, since as he bears within himself the relationships of created objects with each other, then that sacred activity in which (as we said) men, gods and cosmic realities are assigned their proper places, must pertain to him in the highest degree. So we are not surprised, as we would have been before this research began, to find that ruling Latium as Latinus' successor is by no means the most important aspect of what he is or does. He has come to Latium to found Lavinium, the holy city. He is priestly[28]. This is shown in *Æneid* XII 189-194 : if Æneas wins the duel with Turnus,

> Not I do either wish for the Trojans to govern your nation,
>
> Nor yet to be king ; both nations, invincible, equal
>
> In law, shall be allied for all time.
>
> *Religion and gods shall I give* ; let Latinus,
>
> Father-in-law, *solemnly rule* and keep *weapons*. The Trojans
>
> Shall build me walls, and Lavinia shall name the new city[29].

The religious rather than political nature nature of Æneas' mission could not possibly have been made clearer[30] : kingship remains vested in Latinus (meaning, no doubt, his

---

[28]   One of the most wonderful things in the world is to see the late Georges Dumézil and H.J. Rose agreeing on anything, but they did agree on this : *mirate coeli !* See G. DUMEZIL, *Mythe et épopée*, I p.384-393 ; H.J. ROSE,*Vergilian Essays II*, London, 1948. This agreement makes Mandelbaum's wilful misreading, castigated in n.30 below, harder to understand, since Dumézil's book, with the Rose reference, is found in Mandelbaum's reading list.

[29]   *Non ego nec Teucris Italos parere iubebo*
Nec mihi regna peto : paribus se legibus ambae
Inuictae gentes aeterna in foedera mittant.
Sacra deosque dabo ; socer arma Latinus habeto,
Imperium sollemne socer. Mihi moenia Teucri
Constituent, urbique dabit Lauinia nomen.

[30]   And therefore, of course, some moderns muddy it in order to attribute to the hero their own little theories of what was really taking place : see for instance Allen Mandelbaum's fanciful rendition of the same lines in his own version of the poem (XII 255-263).

descendants) ; Æneas' business is to give the kingdom of his father-in-law holy things and gods, *sacra* and *deos*.

With no knowledge of our material, the brothers Rees made virtually the same statement about the relationship between the gods of Ireland and the mortal kings they fought. The third *gabál* or invasion of Ireland in the vast *Lebor Gabála Érenn* cycle, that of the military Fir Bolg or Men of Lightning, gave Ireland the institute of monarchy. Then came the gods, the Tuatha Dé Danann, and, says *Celtic Heritage,*

> Unlike all their predecessors Fir Bolg and Tuatha Dé Danann were ruled by kings, and the two peoples seem to be complementary. We have already seen that the Tuatha seem to be divine wizards or druids. It was the Fir Bolg, on the contrary, who instituted the political divisions of Ireland into five provinces, established the kingship, and first administered justice... In the First Battle of Mag Tuired, Fir Bolg and Tuatha Dé Dannan oppose each other. Nevertheless they are kinsmen who speak the same language ; they approach each other with mutual respect, and they agree to forge weapons for one another. One of the Tuatha voices a eulogy of the Fir Bolg javelins, *but the Fir Bolg sorcerers, on the other hand, play only a minor and negative role in the battle in comparison with Badb, Macha, the Mórrígan and the wizards of the Tuatha Dé Danann...*[31]

Though not perfect[32], the correspondence is close, significant[33] and positively beyond the reach of coincidence.

VI.3 Permanence and power : priestly seats at Lavinium, Armagh and Kildare

Ultimately, Æneas has come to Latium to do three things : defeat Turnus, marry Lavinia and found Lavinium, the kingdom's holy city, seat of six hundred priests. In the legends, Lavinium is a firm point, the religious counterpart to no less than three different seats of royal power. We should note that the sequence of Royal seats in Latin pseudo-history - Laurentum, Alba Longa, Rome - is quite legendary ; Latium has been turned over like a glove, and archæologists inform us that no city of any importance ever stood in the sites legend indicates for Laurentum and Alba Longa[34]. There is no particular reason to propose that any other locality but Rome ever was the royal seat of the Latin high-kingship[35]

---

[31]   A.D. REES - B. REES, *op.cit.,* p.108-109.

[32]   This is the grouping of the gods before Lug's coming, whereas in Latium similar ideological contents are given to Æneas.

[33]   In my view, the difference is dictated by the divergent Irish and Latin interpretations of the role of the two burnings in the gods' journey to Ireland or Latium, where the first stage of development in the Latin legend never takes place in Latium at all. Consequently, the ideas that depend on the clash of men and gods become, in Latium, centred upon Æneas alone ; whereas in Ireland they were attributed to the divine tribe without reference to the second, completing arrival - that of Lug - which was an affair of the gods alone, with no mortal Fir Bolg involved.

[34]   Some scholars hold Laurentum to be a corruption of Lavinium. I oppose this view on account of their very separate significances in the myth, but the two names may well have a common root.

[35]   Early Greek documents quoted by Dionysios of Halikarnassus hint at a different set-up, in which Rome was one of two or three important centres, the others being Capua and perhaps Antium. All I am saying here is that, whatever the earliest royal centres of Ausonia/Latium may have been, they certainly were not the mythical Alba or Laurentum.

(though the latter certainly did exist[36]) ; therefore the whole account of how the sacred city remained the same while the royal city moved three times is entirely a legend, constructed around the Latin idea of the relation of temporal power to the sacred.

As such, it tells us a lot more about the beliefs of the people who created it than any merely historical event. Stories are built around beliefs and points of view ; the beliefs and opinions of Virgil, Dante, Thomas Mann or Barbara Cartland shape the stories they tell. It is not so much that the story is built to prove a point, as much as that it shows *what the teller sees*.

And what the ancient Latins saw was that royal power as such is hopelessly floating, based on no certain base. There is no stability, no firm base in Latium except for Lavinium : from vanished Lista[37] to Alba Longa yet to come, and through all the vanished and declined towns of legend and fact - Antemnæ, Crustumerium, Gabii, Ardea itself, whose *fortuna fuit*[38] - power and fame shift, and only memory is left. That many of the cities of Latin tradition never existed only strengthens my point : the legend predisposed men to regard everything in their country except holy Lavinium as transitory. It must be understood as a priestly twin to whichever Latin city was royal capital at the time ; the legends of Laurentum and Alba Longa[39] predisposed it to join any town that held political power. In fact, it related to Rome or any capital of Latium in the same way as the *Flamen Dialis* did to the king. Dumézil pointed out that Livy states plainly that the *Flamen Dialis,* the priest of Jupiter, covers the sacred part of the king's functions, which the king cannot, as a matter of practicality, perform himself[40]. He is no mere sacred secretary filling in for the king, but the king's other self, sitting on the curule chair - the royal throne - and wearing a special dress, to mark his royal rank. His office forbade him to leave the city of Rome[41] or ride a horse[42]. These two prohibitions would considerably hamper a working king ; if they were part of the royal function as such, then the royal function needed to be physically exercised by two different people. And the fact is surely significant that, without Æneas, Latinus may have no descent. In this sense, as well as in a geographical one, without Æneas the kingship of Latium will not be stabilized. Without the presence of the holy things Æneas brings, royalty is not even capable of being itself, an institution whose being is in its own succession, in the presence of regularly appointed figures on the throne ; because there shall be no successor.

In Irish legend, Fir Bolg kings, before the coming of the Tuatha Dé Danann, regularly come to power by killing their predecessor. MacAlister, still under Fraser's spell, calls this

---

[36]   The existence of a vast body of legends dealing with such an institution proves that it existed. Until Tolkien came along, nobody thought of bothering to write vast bodies of origin myths for institutions that did not exist.

[37]   Dionysios of Halikarnassus, I 14 6.

[38]   Virgil, *Æneid* VII 413.

[39]   The reason why a mythical ancient capital was placed on this side is probably that it was sacred to the cult of Jupiter Latiaris.

[40]   Livy, I 20 2.

[41]   This reflects the permanence of Lavinium as compared to the wandering royal seat.

[42]   We remember that the Trojans had no horses, and that it was the king who sent them three hundreds ; the king is *the owner of horses*.

"the *Golden Bough* norm"[43] ; but it is, in fact, not at all the norm in Irish writing, where the killing of a king appears as a peculiarly odious crime. The fated slayers of the great king Conaire in the saga *The Destruction of Da Derga's Hostel* are described in wildly hateful colours, and the historical slayer of King Diarmait mac Cearbhaill, Aed Dub mac Suibni, is condemned in Adamnán's biography of Columcille with such rage that F.J. Byrne is startled[44]. The regular king-slayings before the Tuatha Dé Danann came are the exception, not the rule ; evidently the descent of the Tuatha Dé Danann is understood as having stabilized Irish monarchy. A breath of a similar idea may perhaps be found in *Æneid* VIII 326-330, associating the kings of pre-Æneas age with violence and greed.

To the Latins, the seat of political power[45] might change : would change, one supposes ; as the holder himself of that power can be changed, by the unregulated and merely earthly force that makes him. Roman royal legend shows well enough that the Latins understood royalty, however sacred, as bound to luck and easily taken. But Lavinium cannot change. There the gods insisted they be taken. From there, by another miracle[46], they refuse to be moved. Taken from Lavinium to Alba Longa, the statues of the Penates, the home-gods of the Latium homeland, are on the following day found returned to their previous places in the holy city. Therefore Ascanius, who is king at the time, decrees that they and their rites should remain there, and appoints a company of six hundred people to look after the sacred things. It is significant that it should be neither swift and blazing Æneas nor King Silvius who finally consacrate Lavinium, but Ascanius Iulus, whose characteristics of duration and peace we have already discovered ; God's friendly face, in Latin as in Irish legend, is the face connected with eternal realities.

Lavinium was built by the Trojans alone and all together, as if profane Latins could not be allowed to have anything to do with it. It is significant that the vile, Quisling-souled Drances had all but offered the Latins as slave labour to Æneas for the task of building a new town's walls[47], which only proves the dullness of his sense. Clearly, to remain holy, Lavinium must be the work of that holy company that shares Æneas' nature of divine fire, those whom Latinus himself called the kin of gods[48]. It is to be firmly established ; therefore it cannot be the work of men whose works, in and of themselves, have as little stability as Lista, Laurentum, Ardea...

Dionysios tells us that the descendants of Ascanius, the Æneids of the full blood, surrendered royalty to Silvius Lavinia's son, and received in exchange a sacred dignity that was held to have higher status than kingship[49]. Dionysios uses extraordinary language : this

[43] R.A.S. MacALISTER, *op.cit.,* IV p.1.
[44] F.J. BYRNE, *Irish Kings and High Kings,* London, 1973, p.96.
[45] In so far as the modern category of politics can fit a set of ideas which was essentially religious. What I am referring to here is the temporal, military and economic power vested in the king ; whose definition was however largely by relation to cosmological realities and priestly concepts, rather than to any autonomous political sphere.
[46] Dionysios of Halikarnassus, I 67 1-2.
[47] Virgil, *Æneid* XI 130-131.
[48] Virgil, *Æneid* XI 305.
[49] Dionysios of Halikarnassus, I 70 4.

1 1 6

sacred office is to be preferred to monarchy (*proukhousa tēs monarkhias*) not only because of its honour (*timē*, standard Greek for "dignity"), which makes sense, but also because of the totally undignified and dishonourable reason of its geater *rhastonē kai akindunos tou biou* "its greater ease and dangerlessness of life" ! This only makes sense if connected with what separates Lavinium from the royal seats : permanence ; otherwise, it would be a positively insulting offer to make to anyone who honourably and legitimately sought the royal office. It is doubly atrocious when you realize he was speaking of the ancestors of the Julian imperial family. The fact is that the stability of Lavinium puts it above royal dignity, as wandering and unstable as its seats. Dionysios used the language of cowardice and ease of life, inadequate beyond belief yet superficially close, to mean a dignity that is above war and the danger and decay of merely human nature ; Plutarch or Plato would have found more suitable words.

It is not because they shun *kindunos* "danger" that the sons of Ascanius become priests ; it is because, being entirely of the divine blood of Æneas and with no admixture of the merely royal blood of Latinus, they are to that extent beyond danger and mutation. We have seen that the *sacra* of Lavinium, once established, cannot be altered ; the holy objects remove themselves miraculously from the royal halls of Alba Longa, to be found again in the place of Æneas : Lavinium.

It might be thought that this concept of sacred and royal seats would distance Rome from the Celtic world, where in Ireland at least the centre of the kings is sacrally amd immovably Tara. This is in fact not at all the case : throughout Irish history the glory of Tara has always lain in the past[50]. Indeed the very existence of an all-Irish monarchy at Tara is put, perhaps with excessive caution, into doubt :

> The farther back we go in the study of recorded history in Ireland, the less evidence we find of a centralised monarchy. Yet by the ninth century, when we encounter the first attempts to realize such a concept, Tara had long lain abandoned[51].

The holy men of the two great Christian centres of Ireland, Armagh and the converted fire-temple of Kildare, rejoiced in the fall of the Kings' Tara and the eternity of their own holy places in words that the Laviniates might not have scorned to use about Alba Longa :

> The powerful fortress of Temair
> Has died with the death of her strong men ;
> With choirs of the wise singing wisdom
> Great Armagh endureth through time.
>
>> Quenched is the pride of Loegaire bold ;
>> He found an obstacle too great ;
>> The name for all ages of Patrick

---

50 F.J. BYRNE, *op.cit.*, p.53.
51 The story of Tara's abandonment, by the way, has a few points in common with the legend of the first Aboriginal capital of Latium, Lista. When Lista had to be abandoned, it was consecrated to the gods so that no enemy should take up living there : Dionysios of Halikarnassus, I 14 6. Tara was cursed by the saints of Ireland.

Has glory whose growth does not fade.

Our faith has increased, and we live,

Shall live here, till earth and sea end ;

The Pagans have passed in their sins,

In their raths no living man dwells !

(Oengus the Servant of God, written about 800 AD).

When I stand on Liffey banks, and gaze

Upon the lovely Curragh, and remember

What lot befell on every past great monarch,

I am awed... ! Oh, Brigit ruler

Of the land thet have ruled, yet your fame

Has outshone them whose names were called the King ;

You remain set above each one of them,

The cemetery of those dead in your grace,

That's yours alone, that they shall never claim.

Granddaughter of Bresal the son of Dian,

Brigit triumphant, be unchallenged on your throne !

(from *Hail Brigit*, possibly by Bishop Ortanach úa Coillama of Kildare, first half of the ninth century)[52].

The ideological oppositions these documents describe are not a million miles removed from the opposition of Lavinium and the royal capitals. They express pride in a power that is beyond the fading strength of mere arms[53] and pride in the crowds of wise saints that decorate Armagh. This may fit a Christian view of the world : I say nothing more than that there is something like a little hairline crack running especially through the first poem, the pride in wisdom, something which does not quite fit a religion whose Founder thanked His Father for having hidden truth from the wise and shown it to the simple, but that is rather more in keeping with the great exaltation of wise men characteristic of every Indo-European tradition and certainly of druidic Celts.

VI.4 The fiery face of truth

Who is this then who comes out of the wilderness like pillars of smoke, fair as the Moon, clear as the Sun, terrible as an army with banners ? What have we learned about this hero of ancient Latium : who has left such a trace on our culture through the work of the greatest of ancient poets, and whom nevertheless we only know by a title and a foreign name ?

He is a god. He comes to Latium as a god comes to his sacrifice ; his vessel is holy steam and smoke ; and the holy steam is itself divine, a cloud of female water-spirits

---

52   Versified from prose translations in F.J. BYRNE, *op.cit.*, p.53, 156.
53   It is the *bravery* and *strength* of Loegaire that have been humbled.

manifesting their godhead by fire-light. He and his three hundred followers are compounded of self-existent, inextinguishable fire, from beyond the limits of the world ; inded, from beyond the remit of other gods, who may help or hinder him, but not alter his being.

What happens in the Æneid is therefore his sacrifice, which he has come to attend as the gods of Indo-European and Mediterranean traditions came down along the trail of the sacrifice's odorous smoke to the ceremonies set for them ; and he is himself the Sacrifice, not in the sense of the sacrificial matter (that is Turnus) but of the total sacred act with its effect. He has at least two aspects, warrior and child, the one relating to punishment, the other to benevolence and protection[54].

The sight of his face is epiphanic, dispelling the madness that had been wrought in the souls of the weaker characters by the epiphanies of other gods. The appearance of the latter awakened the repressed instincts of destruction and hate that the greatest Latin poet clearly shows were already present in their victims ; but the manifestations of Æneas or Ascanius awakens them to the larger reality of what they had, in context, being doing. This is an experience of overwhelming force, such as to make a person wish to die ; even so great a power as Juno is not simply confounded by the sight of the milder - milder ! - face of the god, she is *smashed* off.

Iris and Allecto had fired those desires which had slept within the breasts of Turnus and the women, desires restrained not by a real vision of duty and truth, but rather by motives even less honourable : timidity, social convention. In Turnus' case, it is clear that he has no great sense of law to restrain him ; the only reason why his devouring doubts and fears are not boiling over is that he is trying to appear according to his (inadequate) idea of what a majestically calm prince should look like. In the case of the Trojan women, though Virgil is less clear, the only things he says keep them from action are doubt and fear : features, we infer, typical of female nature according to the homosexual misogynist Virgil.

As for Amata, there is hardly need for the goddess to set fire to her ; she is so wrought with hysterical loathing of something she has never seen, that the goddess is almost an excuse to do what she wanted to do anyway. In the end, that is what Iris and Allecto do to all their victims : they wake them up to the subjective reality of their own souls, to what they really would have liked to do, not thinking of the conequences, if they had the courage.

But Æneas and Ascanius are the consequences. Their appearance is the manifestation, not of the subjective reality of the victims' buried needs, but of the objective reality of what those needs have done. This aspect of the poem is quite incredibly contemporary, presenting with devasting accuracy problems and issues that still agitate the twenty-eighth century *ab*

---

54   Even though the child is also known to fight, especially with arrows. But perhaps fighting is the wrong way to describe the activity of Iulus. He is seen shooting twice : once during the unfortunate hunt that will become one of the three causes of war (Virgil, *Æneid* VII 496-499), and once when he punishes the blasphemer Remulus (IX 622-637). This second episode, in particular, has notably religious overtones. I believe that Iulus' archery is related to that of sacerdotal figures such as Apollo and the Indian Brhaspati. The execution of Remulus is closely related, in particular, to Apollo's habit of shooting down blasphemers. In both the Greek and the Indian cases the idea of archery has profound mystical connotations, bound up with the sacral character of the god ; and I feel confident that Iulus bears a similar character.

Vrbe condita : subjective freedom versus objective obligation, the conflict between the need to break the shackles of habit and the dismal realization of what lies behind this apparent freedom. And it is not one-sided. The epiphanies of the goddesses are real religious experiences ; the goddesses themselves are real sacred personages ; in that they do in fact show at least the truth of their immediate souls, beyond shabby masks and pretence born of timidity, they are a step beyond the rather low form of life that the characters had accepted, denying every single level of truth, right up to that moment.

The epic knows worse things than Turnus ; Drances seems to be there exactly to make this point. Even to rebel against truth is better than to make a falsehood of truth by living in a spirit of falsehood, taking it not for its own sake, but because it is the side of power, of advantage, of revenge against one's enemies. At least to rise to the level of your instincts may raise you, like Turnus, to the level of a consecrated victim of the god[55].

The rebellion against this sort of pseudo-goodness is therefore not false ; the truth that the goddesses reveal to their victims is not false merely by being the truth of the subject alone. But Æneas and Ascanius are a higher truth ; to look at them is to see what really is happening, outside "the small circle of pain within the skull"[56]. The first self-revelation of a subject whose self-image had until that moment been entirely conventional and habit-ridden is an experience of such intensity that the perception of what is happening outside the subject is largely lost. Yet there is a world outside the subject, where real things really happen ; and it is in facing Æneas and Ascanius that the perception of this world is suddenly, epiphanically regained. The world manifests itself through them ; and as we have already seen that they are gods, they cannot be known as anything else than the lords of things that they are : the lords of reality, not only in its essence but in the million dismensions and connexions that objects have.

Æneas and Ascanius do not merely embody the brute fact of existence. The women and Turnus have already experienced a certain degree of reality, the reality of their own previously denied drives and lusts, of their own selves. The face of Æneas and Ascanius, however, brings home to them the reality of action and reaction, of the way in which objects coexist and interact in the real world, the way that an action, however true to itself, has a reality that goes beyond itself to all things it affects. Æneas manifests the way in which the things that exist within this existence ; he is the god of natutal laws and inevitable consequences, of reality and destiny.

---

[55] Isn't this rhetoric of the consecrated victim, or, to quote a writer (J. SAVAGE, *England's Dreaming : Sex Pistols and Punck Rock,* London, 1991), the "in-built drive to failure", the core of pop music's romantic worship of suicidal or self-ruined artists like Jim Morrison, Sid Vicious and Nancy, Nico, Janis Joplin, or for that matter Marilyn Monroe ? And is pop music not the central vehicle in our culture for, exactly, romantic rebellion ? And what about the popularity of Sylvia Plath or Pierpaolo Pasolini ? (By this I do not mean to question the value of Plath's or Pasolini's work, only the reason why they are far better known than artists of equal or geater talent).
[56] T.S. ELIOT, *Murder in the Cathedral.* His description of the everlasting self-caged trudging of a hypocrite's thoughts around the weary circle of his excuses.

We come to this conclusion, not only by the effect the sight of him or of his "son" has on the self-deluded, but from at least two other strands of evidence. One is their role as figures of the sacrifice as order, cosmic order, as that action by which things are put in their proper place. The other is the connexion, or even identification, of Fortuna's almighty son (or foster son) with the *sortes* that are the image of events in this world as they come about in the interplay of created things[57].

All these different reasons, based on different data of the material - the deluding and undeluding of Turnus, Amata and the women ; the eventual result of Æneas' coming in making peace between Evander and Latinus ; the cult of Præneste - form a clear, constent, significant picture of a supreme being substantially different from our God, yet deserving, in the religious perspective of those who believed in him, to be called god.

It is no bad thing to call this total revelation of reality Jupiter. The effects of his presence overcome the effects of Iris, Allecto and Juno herself, therefore his nature is greater than theirs : he is necessarily a great god. He is identified with Jupiter by the author, Livy, who of all people is the least likely to welcome outlandish supernatural occurrences. Virgil's slip of the pen in *Æneid* X 83 shows that the original legend identified Æneas' mother Venus with Jupiter's own : he attributes the miracle of the ships to Æneas' mother, Venus, whereas elsewhere he describes it as a miracle of Jupiter's mother, the Great Mother. Certainly no character in the epic may be said to be his match ; and, what is more, he is the only person with the power and the right to marry Lavinia.

The other name of this god - confirmed, this, not just by Livy but by every authority - is *Indiges*. The word is certainly hard to understand, and ancient attempts to explain it... well, the reader will remember my opinion of one of them ; but I have found in a great linguist of our times, Giacomo Devoto, an explanation that fits marvelously with my theory. I note it with some pleasure because it came to my attention after most of this book was written[58]. He gives it as an agent noun resulting from the archaic prefix *ind-* in the enlarged form, and *-ages, -itis,* from the root **ag-* of the Latin verb *aio* "to state, to affirm" : thus "he who indicates" .i. "he who indicates the truth"[59]. Jupiter Indiges, that is to say, is God the Describer of Truth, and is this not exactly what we have found Æneas to be and to do ? Is this not what the *sortes* do in Præneste ?

In Dumézilian terms, the understanding of the inner structure of reality may be the most precise difinition of the first function yet found ; it covers both the prophetic Varunian insight and the oredered statement of law proper of the Mitraic dimension. The prophet is the witness, in an instant of vision, of the internal significance of things, and is therefore able to spreak the True Word, the word which is in agreement with the inner logic of things. But a

---

57   And if the statement that "the world is the totality of events, not of things" turns out to be the intellectual property of a well-known modern philosopher such as Wittgenstein, well this only goes to show what I have been trying to prove in thos whole study, that is that Latins were able to think, and not so badly, even before they became hellenized.

58   And because I myself am a terrible linguist !

59   G. DEVOTO, *Dizionario etimologico*, p.216.

perfect law is a description of the best order, so that a truly wise lawgiver is also a divine prophet delivering truthful words, words that stand. When God appears on Earth - as Æneas, as Lleu - he is different in degree, but not in kind, from the mortals he talks with or fights against ; likewise, he has a wisdom which is equal in kind, but endlessly higher in degree, than that of mortal wise men. The man who has the vision of the structure of things, whether as intuitive seer or as logical and consequential thinker, is a wise man ; but the highest example of the wise man is indubitably that god who bears in himself the order, the wisdom, the sanity of things[60].

---

[60]   I do not need to underline the real difference between the notion of God and Man as kin and the Christian idea of Man as the creature, and no more that the adopted son of God.

APPENDIX I : CIRCE AND LATIUM

One Latin legend does include a woman whose name is given as Circe. The story goes that Picus, hunting, horse-rearing son of the god Saturnus, and faithful husband of the Nymph Venilia[1], was lusted after by "Circe". When he turned her down, she transformed him into a woodpecker. Virgil alludes to it, and Ovid, a few years later, gives a full account ; both give the name of the vaillainess as Circe. We may therefore be sure that by the Augustan age, whatever Italic figure may have been originally featured in this legend had been identified with the Greek goddess. But we may also be certain, from the characteristics of the story, that this was not Circe, nor in any way related to the Sun.

Both in the *Argonautica* and in the *Odyssey*, Circe lives on an island and may only be reached by a sea voyage ; in Ovid, she haunts the forests of Latium, has nothing to do with the sea, and first sees Picus when he is out hunting. In Greek epic, her home is at the end of the world, only reached by the greatest heroes after the most desperate voyages ; in the story of Picus, "Circe" may be stumbled on by a young man during a day's recreational hunting near his own city walls, with his hunting friends with him and his young bride not far away.

And her character ! The Odyssey's goddess is an innocent mixture of beauty and horror : who can forget our first glimpses of her, when Eurylochos' trembling party is surrounded by gambolling and fawning beasts of prey that act like domestic dogs, and over those strange horrors rises the beautiful sound of her songs ? She breaks men into animals because it is her nature to break anything less strong than her ; she is, after all, of the terrible house-hold of the Sun. But she loves Odysseus, without guile or jealousy, for his strength ; and there is a clear hint that she has kept herself for him, the one male she could not break, the man of destiny promised by Hermes, whom she praises in ringing words for his invincible spirit, and we are reminded that she is a marvelous singer. Once she gives Odysseus her word, she keeps it loyally, holding nothing back ; indeed, the men she returns to him are younger and stronger than before. In the *Argonautica,* she knows the rules of Greek law, purifies suppliants at her hearth, but refuses to have anything else to do with her fratricidal niece Medea, guessing at her unconfessed crime : her conduct, in short, may fairly be described as just but merciful. With one of the most notable lovers of Greek legend, Jason, before her in her own house, she pays him no more attention than if he was made of stone. Jealousy, deception and sexual greed are entirely alien to her ; compare her with another of the Odyssey's divine lovers, Calypso, who would have done anything to keep the hero with her against his wish, had not an order from God Himself, by no means unmixed with threats, forced her to let him go !

Is this the same person whom Ovid, not only in the episode of Picus, but also in that of Glaucus and Scylla, presents as a murderous power-mad nymphomaniac witch ? Is this the same person who, begged by the sea-god Glaucus for a love potion to win the heart of the

---

1   Also known as Canens "the Singer" for her beautiful voice.

recalcitrant Scylla, not only goes baldheaded for him herself in complete defiance of honour and of his wishes, but also treacherously transforms the recalcitrant Scylla, guilty of nothing else than being loved by Glaucus, into a most revolting monster ? Is this the same person who has absolutely no respect for Venilia's conjugal rights : Circe, who let Odysseus go as soon as he asked her, altough she knew he was going to Penelope[2] ? The idea is preposterous. Whoever enchanted Picus, it was not the goddes of Homeric legend[3].

And if that is not enough, consider this : Circe enchants and disenchants Odysseus' companions without any further implications for them. When they return to human shape, they may be a bit younger and fitter than they were when they blundered into her pigsty ; but they are essentially the same people, the same human beings with the same destiny of individual death in front of them. But the effect of Lady Whoever-she-is against Picus is not only final ; it is not only dehumanizing ; it is something more. Against, one supposes, her own desires - which were, as the story makes clear, entirely negative - she has made Picus into what he will be for ever after in Latium : the immortal prophetic bird-god, of the line of Saturnus, Faunus and Latinus, an object of worship. Scylla, likewise, is transformed into one of the great immortal monsters of Greek legend[4]. No, : this is not the same character, she does not feature in the same kind of stories, she does not perform the same kind of miracles, she does not move in the same kind of landscape, she does not produce the same results, and she does not belong to the same mythology.

But if the epic Circe has no connexion with the Latin Lady Whoever-she-is, then there is no reason to connect the Latin character with the Sun at all ; and in fact, as I pointed out, she shows no sign of any connexion with the Sun or with the sea in Latin mythology. If any firm conclusion could be drawn from the single legend of Picus, it would be that Lady Whoever-she-is is a figure of the wild : wild forests where men go hunting and meet strange inhuman things ; wild lusts that know nothing of marriage vows or fidelity ; and wild transformations that seem to have no rhyme or reason (why a woodpecker ? we aren't told). And yet these wild and terrible things, things that are unmixedly dangerous, are found, not in the remote distances to which heroes like Jason or Odysseus travel, but practically inside our own known and familiar landscape.

What, in all this, has to do with the Sun ? Nothing. Lady Whoever-she-is is not Circe and has nothing to do with the star of day, whose light is eclipsed by her magic in Ovid's

---

[2] Plutarch underlines this point in the opening sallies of his dialogue of Odysseus and Gryllus ("Grunter", a talking pig), where Circe herself points out with a little annoyance that she is immortally young and beautiful, while Penelope is, by now, getting on in years.

[3] It is worth noticing that Circe kept her humane and attractive features in a Greek writer like Plutarch, who wrote more than a century after Virgil and Ovid. It is only when she crosses the linguistic and cultural border between Greece and Latium that Circe becomes what she has remained ever since in European imagination : the ruthless, sensuous, immoral enchantress. The only western artist I know who caught the spirit of the Homeric Circe is Jack Kirby, the great American cartoonist, who featured her in his *The Eternals* as Sersi, capricious, powerful, uncontrollable, but fundamentally kind-hearted and loyal to those she loves ; a triumph of intuitive genius (for Kirby was not an educated man) matched, in the same series, by his Thena, wise, aggressive, pugnacious, but sensitive and, in the end, a peace-maker : an Athena out of Æschylus.

[4] In this episode we must assume a great deal of Hellenization, though the fundamentals are still Italic.

story of Picus. She cannot be brought up as a proof of the existence of a hypothetical Latin Sun-god for which no evidence exists.

APPENDIX II : THE WELL OF St. ELIAN
AT LLANELIAN YN RHOS

A curious item from the enormous and still insufficiently studied source of information that is Welsh folklore shows a partial but unmistakable parallel with the cult of Fortuna Primigenia at Præneste.

The Well of St. Elian in the tiny hamlet of Llanelian yn Rhos, a mile or two from Colwyn Bay, was known till this century for its cursing powers. People who wanted to curse anyone wrote their enemy's name on a piece of paper, placed the paper inside a piece of lead and tied it to a slate on which were written the initials of the man who made the curse. This package was thrown into the well as the curse was recited according to a particular formula. The person who had been cursed was then informed and promptly rushed around to the well-keeper, paying him over the odds to have the curse package removed and the curse lifted. The well-keeper read two psalms to the curse victims, made them walk around the well three times while reading Scripture, and then removed the leaden piece with its curse from the well and gave it to them. This custom was in full flower for much of the nineteenth century, and a well-keeper who died in the mid-eighteenth hundreds, John Evans, was famous across Wales and was reputed to have profited considerably from his office[1].

Some authors record a belief that the well was originally a wishing well, until the greater potential of the activity of cursing impressed itself on its owners. This is almost certainly an unhistorical legend invented to bring the unusual feature of a cursing well closer to the more familiar idea of a wishing one : the well had been devoted to its unusual function for a century or more, and peasant memory cannot be held to stretch further. What is more, the use of writing curses on metal[2] and then throwing them in water is well documented throughout the Celtic world, including Britain[3].

The points of resemblance between Llanelian and Præneste are readily apparent. They were both unique places in their countries ; people came from all over Wales to curse or be un-cursed at Llanelian, people came from all over Latium to Præneste, because the service they offered were unique. I know of no other cursing well in Wales, and of no other fortune-telling temple in Latium. They were religious sites[4] but with an intensely practical purpose. In both places, the heart of the ritual was in the placing and removing of written words, placed in a "box" made of a very definite material, into a well : even in Præneste, the original placing of the *sortes* in the well was a major part of the foundation legend ; and the *sortes,* after all, must have been replaced in the well after use. And both Llanelian, in its

---

1   F. JONES, *The Holy Wells of Wales,* Cardiff, p.119-122.

2   The use of paper in Wales was probably a matter of practicality : poor Welsh farmers were unlikely to be able to afford carvings on metal.

3   Which suggests in turn that the sites where cursing tablets were found might represent cultic places of this unusual and distinctive type.

4   The Welsh well belonged to a saint and the well-keeper ritually used Scripture in the un-cursing ritual.

own small way, and Præneste in its grandiose one, had dedicated personnel skilled in its par-ticular ritual, and who made a good profit out of it. For that matter, it may not be entirely coincidental that our records of both of them come from educated urban gentlemen (Cicero, W.W. Wynn) who treat them with more or less amused contempt.

The major difference between Llanelian and Præneste is obviously that in Præneste you took words *out* of the well, in Llanelian you put them *in*. The movement is exactly opposite : in Præneste, the child enters the well and takes the box upwards into the light, where it is opened and its content exposed and used ; it is then closed, its content (surely) back inside, and put back down in the well. In Llanelian, the "box" is closed, with its contents sealed inside, and thrown down into the well, from which it is taken up again at the expected end of the affair (when the cursed person pays to have the curse lifted). Hence, also, the difference in materials. The Welsh could certainly have used wood of various sorts (if not olive wood) to make the implements for the curse ; wood is not lacking in the principality. Instead, apart from the practicality of paper, we have lead and slate. I think a materialistic interpretation is useful : quite simply, lead is the heaviest common metal : it sinks, whereas wood floats to the surface.

Instead of passively asking what the future had in store[5], the audacious Welshman took it upon himself to literally put words in the mouth of fate. And it is clearly for this reason that the Welsh ritual includes a third basic element unknown to the Latin : the piece of slate with the initials of the curser. While the words of the Latin well came from an undifferen-ciated, primal single voice of destiny, those of the Welsh well were stictly identified with an individuality. The Welsh curser wants his curse to sink down, down, into the depths of the holy well, to embed itself into the sacred spring and the power it represented. But by the same token, since it is an individual voice, one that does not, like that of Fortuna Primigenia, bind the whole universe, it remains individual and may be worked upon, hence un-cursed.

That being the case, however, the extent to which the two cult-places depended on the same ideas, the same conception of time and fate, the same cosmology, is remarkable. Without the Italian parallel, practically every aspect of the Welsh ritual simply could not been explained. Why write the curse instead of, as is more natural, shout it to the winds ? Why place it in a "box" ? Why put the "box" in a well, instead of, as is more natural, expose it to public view ? All these things, compared with the Prænestine cult, reveal themselves as practical and understandable. The Prænestine cult represents the primary thought ; the Welsh ritual is the result of a sort of commentary on it, mortal men replicating in their normal life the primæval actions of the first gods. But the theology at the back of them both is almost identical[6] ; and so unique that it cannot be imagined anywhere else. It certifies, once again, the peculiar closeness of Latin and Celtic thoughts.

---

5   Fortune-telling has remained an obsession with Italians to this day.
6   Though I suspect the Prænestine priests would balk at the idea of mortals writing their own *sortes*.

APPENDIX III : THE DEATH OF KING TEUDIRIC

A legend preserved in the Book of Llandaff places the semi-legendary king Tewdrig in a light that should be strikingly familiar to us. This is Helen Waddell's translation :

> King Teudiric... began to live a hermit life in the cliffs of Tintern. But while he was in that life, the Saxons began to invade his land against Mouric his son, and beyond himself there was none to help, that his son might not be driven from his inheritance by strangers. Of Teudiric it was said in the days when he held his kingdom that never had he be vanquished by the enemy but ever was the victor, and that once his face was seen in the battle-line, straightaway the enemy were driven to flight. And the night before, the angel of the Lord said to him : "Tomorrow go to the help of the people of God against the enemies of the Church of Christ, and the foe shall turn his face in flight as far as Brockwere, and do thou stand armed in the battle-line, and when thy face as in times past is seen and known, they shall take to flight. And hereafter for thirty years they shall not dare to come against thy country in thy son's time, and the men of thy land and their sons that come after them shall be in quiet peace ; and thou thyself shall die in peace".
>
> So in the morning he rose as the army of Mouric his son came by, and he mounted his horse and rode with them joyous of the bidding of the angel. And he stood in armour in the battle-line above the bank of the Wye near Tintern ford. And at the sight of his face (the enemy) turned their backs and fled, yet one of them hurled a lance, and the lance wounded him even as he has been told, and he rejoiced over it as a man rejoices over the rout of his foe and the taking of the spoil[1]. Then Mouric his son, returning victorious with the captured spoil, would have his father come with him. And he said : "I will not go from this place until my Lord Jesus Christ shall bear me hence to the place of my desire, to the island of Echni where I have willed to lie after my death".
>
> And in the morning at dawn there were two stags yoked and ready with his bier before his lodging. And the man of God, knowing that they were sent on God's behalf, ascended the bier ; and wherever they rested, there springs welled up, until they came to a place beside a meadow towards the Severn Sea. And after they had come to that place, a spring of clearest water welled up and swept the bier asunder, and straightaway he commended his soul to God and bade the stags depart ; and there he remained alone, and after a while gave up the ghost[2].

So far as I can see, this legend has the following basic elements in common with the mythology we have been exploring :

---

[1]   This shows that his fatal wound was a pre-condition of "the rout of his foe and the taking of the spoil".

[2]   H. WADDELL, *Beasts and Saints,* Grand Rapids, 1996, translating from J. RHYS - J.G. EVANS, *The Text of the Book of Llandaff,* Oxford, 1893, p.141.

1° the hero's face simply cannot be borne ; the enemy scatter at the very approach of him ;

2° the hero is slain by a single spear-thrust, like Lleu by Gronw Pebyr ;

3° it is predicted that he will die by the spear, and indeed he cannot die by any other means[3] ;

4° the hero's son has a long and peaceful reign - fifty years for Ascanius, thirty for Mourig - which counts as the foundation of a new kingdom and political order ;

5° the hero's death is associated not only with the flight of his enemy before his face but with the welling up of an indeterminate number of water springs[4] ;

6° the hero is "placed" in the place where he dies, which is near a river and becomes a holy place, like Æneas being *situs* in his sanctuary near the Numicius ; this sanctuary is part of the sacred territories of a great holy place of national significance, Lavinium, Llandaff, and the whole legend is part of the justification for the great abbey/cathedral of Llandaff to own the lands about Mathern without paying any yax to any secular ruler ;

7° Teudiric's wanderings in search of his place of death may have something in common with Æneas' wanderings is search of the place where he is (among other things) to die and be *situs* ; in a much smaller compass, he does wander over land and water, and consecrate the spot where he finally dies ; also, his death does not take place at the spot or time where he won the great battle, as Æneas ruled for three years after defeating and killing Turnus, and Teudiric lived for three days - another coincidence - after routing the Saxons.

The most interesting thing aboutit, however, is the thin ray of light that it sheds about a Roman ritual mentioned earlier, the *deuotio*. The Roman general who performed this extreme (and probably legendary) rite consecrated himself and the enemy army, by a most solemn ritual, to the *Di Indigetes* and *Di Nouensiles* as human sacrifices. When the ritual had been performed, he became a sacred and terrible hero, possessed by superhuman strength, completely irresistible. The enemy army was inevitably destroyed ; but so was he. Now, Teudiric is certainly consecrated ; he is ending his life as a monk, given over to God. And the effect of the story is that the Saxon army is destroyed[5] and so he is, but that no ther Welshman is harmed : "the commander and enemy are devoted to destruction". The highest sacred realities are certainly involved : it is "the angel of the Lord" who orders Teudiric to his destiny, in the full knowledge of what was going to happen to him. He dies a sacrificial death to preserve his people and the crown of his son (not a candidate but an already crowned king, on whose royal prerogatives Teudiric, even when dying, refuses to trespass).

The most famous victims of the ritual in Roman legend were the two Decii Mures, and there is some echo in the Welsh legend and of the Lug the father/Lug the son duality in that

---

3   Since his very face scatters his enemies to the four winds, like Gronw's faithless army : ("there was born in Adwy nobody who attacked me | except Goronwy from Doleu Edrywy") and therefore nobody is able to strike at him, except for this fated blow.

4   Remember Iuturna fleeing before Æneas and/or the Dira and hiding in the many Latin springs whose goddess she was ?

5   It must be, since they are not to come back for thirty years.

they are a couple of father and son and perform the same ritual, saving Rome by their own self-immolation, several decades apart from each other : this has a certain similarity with the fact that Teudiric leaves behind a royal son who will enjoy three decades of respite from the enemy. In Rome, of course, the royal crown was execrated ; the fact that both Decius the father and Decius the son were consuls, heads of the Roman state and entitled to sit on the royale curule chair, is the closest that it can get ; but the two decii preserve the State and win their family immortal glory. Again like Teudiric, both of them already had a long and triumphant career behind them when they consecrated themselves to death for the nation ; one wonders whether this, too, was a necessary part of the story.

The *deuotio* is still to a very large extent a mysterious ritual, but the story of Teudiric helps us understand it. For a start, the *Di Indigetes* of the ritual must certainly include Jupiter Indiges (= Æneas), and may perhaps be reduced to Æneas and Ascanius, possibly to be seen as two *Indigetes* aspects of Jupiter, possibly with Anchises for a third. It seems clear that the self-consecrated victim of the story is taking on the role of Lug the Avenger or Jupiter Indiges, putting armies to rout by the mere sight of his irreversible, Sun-like countenance, but dying as a result. He thus takes on the avenging face of the supreme god, and as we have seen that the avenging face is mortal, so that man dies : the sacrificer's own death is a necessary condition of the *deuotio*.

While Lleu is certainly Lleu, and Æneas is Jupiter Indiges or Sol Indiges, there is no indication whatever that Teudiric or the Decii Mures are so closely identified with the supreme god : theirs are stories of mortal men giving their own lives in battle, that is made very clear. Therefore we must see them not, as with Taliesin and Æneas, as avatars of the god but rather as individual human heroes taking in some fashion the role, or even the essence, of the supreme god as avenger and military saviour. They are men who are given divine power in the course of an extreme ritual, but die as a result.

The ritual is directly connected with the preservation of the sacred space of the tribe from an irresistible but irreligious enemy. God preserves Mouric's kingdom because the Saxons are pagans, but Roman accounts also stress the religious difference and savagery (*ferocia*) of the Decii Mures' enemies, the Samnites. Incredibly, Livy makes them freshly-arrived invaders previously unknown to the Romans[6]. He also insists that the Samnites military successes were recent, while Rome's were a matter of four hundred years of glorious victories ; that is, the Samnites were something new in Italian politics. This is completely unhistorical in the Italian picture but it compares closely to the Saxob element in the legend of Teudiric : a new, barbarous, overwhelmingly powerful enemy.

The *deuotio* therefore is in some sense an attempt to redress the political balance when something completely new and overwhelming has intruded on it, by calling down the very power of Lug/Jupiter Himself as avenger and restorer of right order into the person of the national leader. He himself will die but he has a son to succeed him and, at least in the Welsh

6   Livy, VII 33 6 : *utrisque tamen nouus hostis curam addebat* "having a new enemy (that is, a previously unknown one) added to the nervousness of both sides".

legend, to reign peacefully for decades to come ; in this, too, we see the concern that right order and national existence should continue. Other elements of the legend remain mysterious[7] but its connection with Lug/Jupiter cannot be doubted. It is as God of Things as They Are that he is called upon to provide his power to reddress a situation which may not only be a disaster on a political level but an insult against his settlement of the country's political order, which is seen, of course, as ultimate and permanent.

---

[7]   For instance, we may never find out who and what the *Di Nouensiles* were.

INDEX

140

MÉMOIRES DE LA SOCIÉTÉ BELGE D'ETUDES CELTIQUES
(NOUVEAUX PRIX 2014)

1. **Malgorzata ANDRALOJC. "The Phenomenon of Dog Burials in the Prehistoric Times in the Area of Middle Europe."**
1993, 127 p., 8 cartes/kaarten/maps, ISBN 2-87285-029-5,   15 €

2. **Nathalie STALMANS. "Les affrontements des calendes d'été dans les légendes celtiques."**
1995, 105 p., ISBN 2-87285-037-6,   14 €

4. **Claude STERCKX. "Les dieux protéens des Celtes et des Indo-Européens."**
1994, 201 p., ISBN 2-87285-048-1,   20 €

5. **Jacques-Henri MICHEL - Claude STERCKX (eds). "César, l'homme et l'oeuvre. Mythe et réalité. Mélanges présentés à Michel Nuyens."**
1997, 64 p., ISBN 2-87285-057-0,   12 €.

6. **Claude STERCKX. "Dieux d'eau: Apollons celtes et gaulois."**
1996, 186 p., ISBN 2-87285-050-3,   19 €.

8. **Claude STERCKX. "Sangliers Père & Fils. Dieux, rites et mythes celtes du porc et du sanglier."**
1998, 196 p., ISBN 0-87285-059-7,   20 €.

9 - 10 - 20. **Jean DEGAVRE. "Lexique gaulois. Recueil de mots attestés, transmis ou restitués et de leurs interprétations".**
262 + 259 + 41 p., ISBN 2-87285-061-9/-099-6. (cf. N°20)   43 €

11. **Fabio P. BARBIERI. "Gods of the West: I. Indiges."**
1999, 143 p., 2-87285-070-8,   16 €

12. **Claude STERCKX. "Des dieux et des oiseaux. Réflexions sur l'ornithomorphisme de quelques dieux celtes."**
2000, 128 p., ISBN 2-87285-071-6,   15 €

13. **Lauran TOORIANS. "Keltisch en Germaans in de Nederlanden: taal in Nederland en in België gedurende de Late IJzertijd en de Romeinse periode."**
2000, 156 p., ISBN 2-87285-075-9,   17 €

15. **Claude STERCKX. "Le fils parfait et ses frères animaux. Lugus, Pan et les Draupadeya"**
2002, 60 p., ISBN 2-87285-087-2,   12 €

17. **Marco V. GARCIA QUINTELA (+ Felipe CRIADO BOADO, Francisco J. GONZALEZ GARCIA, César PARCERO OUBINA, Manuel SANTOS ESTEVEZ). "Souveraineté et sanctuaires dans l'Espagne celtique."**
2003, 102 p., 13 fig., ISBN 2-87285-092-9,   14 €

18. **Gaël HILY. "L'autre monde celte ou la source de vie."**
2003, 102 p., ISBN 2-87285-093-7,   16 €

19. **Frédéric BLAIVE. "Recherches sur la Rome archaïque." 2004. (Épuisé. Cf n° 30).**

20. **Jean DEGAVRE. "Lexique gaulois. Recueil de mots attestés, transmis ou restitués et de leurs interprétations. Tome III: supplément."**
2004, 48 p., (voir Mémoire 9)

21. **Marco V. GARCIA QUINTELA. "El reyezuelo, el cuervo y el dios celtico Lug."**
2005, 86 p., 13 pl., ISBN 2-87285-105-4,   13 €

22 - 24. **Claude STERCKX. "Taranis, Sucellos et quelques autres."**
2006, 680 p., ISBN 2-87285-104-6,   50 €

25. **Daniel GRICOURT + Dominique Hollard. "Les saints jumeaux héritiers des Dioscures celtes."**
2006, 126 p., ISBN 2-87285-107-0,   15 €

26. **Bernard ROBREAU. "Les divinités des Celtes. Définition et position."**
2006, 100 p., ISBN 2-87285-111-9,   16 €

27. **Ashwin E. GOHIL. "Ancient Celtic and Non-Celtic Place-Names of Northern Continental Europe."**
2006, 300 p., ISBN 2-87285-112-7,   26 €

28. **Greta ANTHOONS & Herman CLERINX (eds). "The Grand 'Celtic' Story? Proceedings of the conference held in Brussels on 19 November 2005. With contributions by Simon James, Raimund Karl, Lauran Toorians, Claude Sterckx, Nico Roymans."**

2007, 92 p., ISBN 2-87285-117-8,   13 €

29. Michel DAVOUST. "Chronologies mythiques d'Irlande et de Galles."
2008, 110 p., ISBN 2-87285-119-4,   15 €

30. Frédéric BLAIVE, "Recherches sur la Rome archaïque."
(2ᵉ édition revue et augmentée), 2009, 204 p., ISBN2-87285-124-0,   20 €

31. Erwan LE PIPEC, "Approche de la variation dans le breton de Malguénac."
2010, 32 p., ISBN 2-87285-130-5,   11 €

32. Jacques LACROIX, "Le celtique *dēvo*- et les eaux sacrées."
2011, 112 p., ISBN 2-87285-133-X,   14 €

33. Claude STERCKX. "Histoire, langues et cultures des Celtes."
2011, 164 p., ISBN 2-87285-134-8,   17 €

34. Thomas JACQUEMIN. "Étude critique des premières origines prêtées aux tribus celto-belges."
2011, 104 p., ISBN 2-87285-138-0,   14 €

35. Léo SCARAVELLA. "L'arbre et le serpent. Symboles et mythes dans l'art et la religion celtiques."
2013, 242 p., ISBN 2-87285-151-8   21 €

36. Claude STERCKX. "Histoire brève de la musique celte. Des origines au vingtième siècle".
2013, 112 p., ISBN 2-87285-113-5, (Vente on-line sur lulu.com 16€ + 5 € de frais de port)   15 €

Hors série / Buiten reeks :

Claude STERCKX. "Essai de dictionnaire des dieux, héros, mythes et légendes celtes".

fasc. 1 (1998) 158 p. ISBN 2-87285-06   17 €

fasc. 2 (2000) 116 p. ISBN 2-87285-077-5   14 €

fasc. 3 (2005) 122 p. ISBN 2-87285-102-X   15 €

Les mémoires sont disponibles à la vente en ligne sur Internet aux adresses suivantes :

- <u>www.sbec.be</u>
- **www.lulu.com**

Courriel : secretaire.edition@sbec.be

Les Mémoires, correspondent à des études scientifiques originales que leur longueur ou les spécificités de leur mise en page signale pour une édition séparée, peuvent être commandés de la même façon et aux mêmes conditions qu' Ollodagos.On peut obtenir des exemplaires par virement au compte de la SBEC Une réduction de 20% est accordée aux membres de la SBEC.

Paiements au compte de la S.B.E.C. 068-2231909-63
IBAN : BE40-0682-2319-0963- Bic (code Swift) GKCCBEBB Frais de port en sus : Belgique 10% ; étranger 20%.

Als u een boek wil bestellen, schrijft u het bedrag over op rekening 068-2231909-63 van het BGKS, Pierre-Curielaan 21, 1050 Brussel. IBAN-code voor het buitenland: BE40-0682-2319-0963 (Bic-code Swift: GKCCBEBB). De prijs wordt verhoogd met 10 % verzendingskosten voor België, en 20 % voor het buitenland. Leden van het BGKS krijgen 20 % korting op de boekenprijs.

To order a book please transfer the amount to bank account no 068-2231909-63 of the SBEC, 21 Avenue Pierre-Curie, 1050 Brussels. IBAN-code: BE40-0682-2319-0963 (Bic-code Swift: GKCCBEBB). For shipping within Belgium: add 10 % of the total amount. For shipping outside Belgium: add 20 % of the total amount. Members of the Society receive a discount of 20 % on the list price.

www.ingramcontent.com/pod-product-compliance
Lightning Source LLC
Chambersburg PA
CBHW081507290326

41931CB00041B/3230